Imagining the American West through Film and Tourism

The American West is one of the strongest and most enduring place images in the world and its myth is firmly rooted in popular culture – whether novels, film, television, music, clothing and even video games. The West combines myth and history, Indigenous peoples and cultures, rugged natural scenery and wide open spaces, popular culture and promises of transformation. These imagined places draw in tourists, attracted by a cultural heritage that is part fictional and mediatised. In turn, tourism operators and destination marketing organisations refashion what they present to fit these imagined images.

This groundbreaking book explores the mythic West to offer new insights into how the imagination of the West and popular culture has influenced the construction of tourism. In doing so, it examines the series of paradoxes that underlie the basic appeal of the West: including the fact that it is a boundary zone between civilisation and wilderness and between order and lawlessness. It draws on a range of films and literature as well as varying places from festivals to national parks to showcase different aspects of the nexus between travel, film and frontiers in this fascinating region. Interdisciplinary in character, it includes perspectives from cultural studies, American studies, tourism and film studies.

Written by leading academics, this title will be valuable reading for students, researchers and academics in the fields of cultural studies, tourism, history, film studies and media studies and all those interested in film tourism.

Warwick Frost is an Associate Professor in the Department of Management and Marketing at La Trobe University, Melbourne, Australia.

Jennifer Laing is a Senior Lecturer in the Department of Management and Marketing at La Trobe University, Melbourne, Australia.

Contemporary geographies of leisure, tourism and mobility

Series Editor: C. Michael Hall

Professor at the Department of Management, College of Business and Economics, University of Canterbury, Christchurch, New Zealand

The aim of this series is to explore and communicate the intersections and relationships between leisure, tourism and human mobility within the social sciences.

It will incorporate both traditional and new perspectives on leisure and tourism from contemporary geography, e.g. notions of identity, representation and culture, while also providing for perspectives from cognate areas such as anthropology, cultural studies, gastronomy and food studies, marketing, policy studies and political economy, regional and urban planning, and sociology, within the development of an integrated field of leisure and tourism studies.

Also, increasingly, tourism and leisure are regarded as steps in a continuum of human mobility. Inclusion of mobility in the series offers the prospect to examine the relationship between tourism and migration, the sojourner, educational travel, and second home and retirement travel phenomena.

The series comprises two strands:

Contemporary Geographies of Leisure, Tourism and Mobility aims to address the needs of students and academics, and the titles will be published in hardback and paperback. Titles include:

1 **The Moralisation of Tourism**
Sun, sand ... and saving the world?
Jim Butcher

2 **The Ethics of Tourism Development**
Mick Smith and Rosaleen Duffy

3 **Tourism in the Caribbean**
Trends, development, prospects
Edited by David Timothy Duval

4 **Qualitative Research in Tourism**
Ontologies, epistemologies and methodologies
Edited by Jenny Phillimore and Lisa Goodson

5 **The Media and the Tourist Imagination**
Converging cultures
Edited by David Crouch, Rhona Jackson and Felix Thompson

6 **Tourism and Global Environmental Change**
Ecological, social, economic and political interrelationships
Edited by Stefan Gössling and C. Michael Hall

7 **Cultural Heritage of Tourism in the Developing World**
Edited by Dallen J. Timothy and Gyan Nyaupane

8 **Understanding and Managing Tourism Impacts**
An integrated approach
C. Michael Hall and Alan Lew

9 **An Introduction to Visual Research Methods in Tourism**
Edited by Tijana Rakic and Donna Chambers

10 **Tourism and Climate Change**
Impacts, adaptation and mitigation
C. Michael Hall, Stefan Gössling and Daniel Scott

11 **Tourism and Citizenship**
Raoul V. Bianchi and Marcus L. Stephenson

Routledge Studies in Contemporary Geographies of Leisure, Tourism and Mobility is a forum for innovative new research intended for research students and academics, and the titles will be available in hardback only. Titles include:

1 **Living with Tourism**
Negotiating identities in a Turkish village
Hazel Tucker

2 **Tourism, Diasporas and Space**
Edited by Tim Coles and Dallen J. Timothy

3 **Tourism and Postcolonialism**
Contested discourses, identities and representations
Edited by C. Michael Hall and Hazel Tucker

4 **Tourism, Religion and Spiritual Journeys**
Edited by Dallen J. Timothy and Daniel H. Olsen

5 **China's Outbound Tourism**
Wolfgang Georg Arlt

6 **Tourism, Power and Space**
Edited by Andrew Church and Tim Coles

7 **Tourism, Ethnic Diversity and the City**
Edited by Jan Rath

8 **Ecotourism, NGOs and Development**
A critical analysis
Jim Butcher

9 **Tourism and the Consumption of Wildlife**
Hunting, shooting and sport fishing
Edited by Brent Lovelock

10 **Tourism, Creativity and Development**
Edited by Greg Richards and Julie Wilson

11 **Tourism at the Grassroots**
Villagers and visitors in the Asia-Pacific
Edited by John Connell and Barbara Rugendyke

12 **Tourism and Innovation**
Michael Hall and Allan Williams

13 **World Tourism Cities**
Developing tourism off the beaten track
Edited by Robert Maitland and Peter Newman

Imagining the American West through Film and Tourism

Warwick Frost and
Jennifer Laing

LONDON AND NEW YORK

First published 2015 by Routledge

2 Park Square, Milton Park, Abingdon, Oxon OX14 4RN
711 Third Avenue, New York, NY 10017, USA

Routledge is an imprint of the Taylor & Francis Group, an informa business

First issued in paperback 2017

British Library Cataloguing in Publication Data
A catalogue record for this book is available from the British Library

Library of Congress Cataloging in Publication Data
A catalog record for this book has been requested

ISBN: 978-1-138-78523-6 (hbk)
ISBN: 978-1-138-08394-3 (pbk)

Typeset in Times New Roman
by Wearset Ltd, Boldon, Tyne and Wear

Contents

x   *Contents*

Figures

1 Go West

Prologue

Picture a DVD store. It can be big or small, rental or for sale. The extensive stock is arranged in categories (or genres), making it easier for customers to browse. Typical categories/genres include Drama, Action, Thrillers, Romance, Comedy, Musicals. And then there are Westerns. Unlike all the others, Western films are defined geographically. No other place in the world has that distinction. A whole genre named and defined by its location and based on a real place.

How does that affect tourism? How does it influence visitors – their expectations and the images they hold? In turn, how does the imaginary world created by cinema and its fans influence the real place?

Stagecoach (1939)

Stagecoach is the place to begin. Often described as the first A Western, it heralded a Golden Age of cinema Westerns lasting for the next 30 years. In its settings, themes, archetypes and use of landscape it was highly influential of later films and it started the process by which movies created an *imaginary West* that still shapes how tourists see that region today.

Western movies were out of fashion throughout the 1930s. This was despite an increasing interest amongst tourists; fuelled by a sense that these pioneers and the Old West were quickly disappearing and facilitated by increased use of automobiles (DeLyser 2003; Frost and Laing 2015). The paucity of good quality Westerns resulted from the introduction of talkies:

> Westerns looked stiff and artificial on studio soundstages, but authentic audio was hard to record in the great outdoors. In any event, location shooting was costly and complicated ... Westerns were exiled to the land of the B movie, where they grew undernourished on thin plots.... For a while singing cowboys were the rage.... Children may have squealed with delight, but few adults bothered to watch. The Western became a minor, cut rate genre.
>
> (Frankel 2013: 223)

However, by the late 1930s, technical problems had been overcome and audiences were lapping up action blockbusters. Many of these drew on British history for their storylines or background – a peculiar genre that Slotkin (1992) labelled as *Empire films*. This trend was driven by concerns about the rise of Nazism in Europe and the increasing prospect of global armed conflict. Empire films appealed due to their combination of escapism and reassurance, emphasising cultural and political links between Britain and the United States and more generally the importance of freedom and resistance to tyranny and injustice. Hugely popular historical epics included *A Tale of Two Cities* (1935), *The Charge of the Light Brigade* (1936), *The Adventures of Robin Hood* (1938), *Gunga Din* (1939), *Beau Geste* (1939) and *The Four Feathers* (1939). This emphasis on British history and imperialism resulted in many English actors being drawn to Hollywood. These included David Niven, Ronald Coleman, Cary Grant, Claude Rains, Ray Milland and C. Aubrey Smith (a former English cricket captain), as well as the South African Basil Rathbone and Australian Errol Flynn. Also notable were Jewish émigré film-makers, such as the Hungarians Alexander Korda and Michael Curtiz. Developing their craft in the Empire genre were later Western actors in Gary Cooper and Errol Flynn and directors in Henry Hathaway and Michael Curtiz (Lawrence 2005).

Not surprisingly, the public's appetite for escapist historical tales of derring-do and heroism led some American film-makers to reconsider their own history and its potential appeal. 1939 and 1940 saw a massive swing to Americana in cinema. Popular films that romanticised American history included *Gone with the Wind* (the Civil War), *The Wizard of Oz* (early twentieth-century Kansas), *Young Mr Lincoln* (early nineteenth century), *Drums Along the Mohawk* (War of Independence) and *North-West Passage* (Seven Years War). It was not long before a similar rationale was applied to relaunching the Western. However, instead of B graders with singing cowboys and stagey sets, the logic was to apply the big production values of the successful modern epics. The result was the 1939 releases of John Ford's *Stagecoach*, Henry King's *Jesse James*, George Marshall's *Destry Rides Again*, Cecil B. DeMille's *Union Pacific* and Warner

Brothers' *Dodge City*. The Western returned to popularity with a vengeance; whereas A Westerns had been very rare during most of the 1930s, between 1939 and 1941 Hollywood produced 31 A Westerns (Coyne 1997).

Dodge City is worth considering briefly, even though it is nowadays largely forgotten. Jack Warner reasoned that since *The Adventures of Robin Hood* was a bit like a Western – honest Robin forced to become an outlaw to defeat the corrupt sheriff – then stars Errol Flynn, Olivia De Havilland and Alan Hale and Director Michael Curtiz could reprise their roles in nineteenth-century Kansas. The resulting film was highly successful in its day, albeit a straightforward horse opera with a simple plot of good guy Errol versus evil villains. It was distinguished by its lavish set pieces of an immense bar-room brawl and a final shootout on a flaming railway train. Furthermore, it launched Flynn as a Western hero – one of the first of the modern era. As film historian Jeanine Basinger noted:

> As odd as that may now seem. After all, he has a British accent, slight though it is. And he's elegant, graceful, and not an authentically American face like a John Wayne or Randolph Scott ... it seems an odd choice, but it worked just fine. It's a credit to Flynn's strong screen personality that he could appear in American westerns and seem right at home on the range.
>
> (2007: 241)

The reinvention of Westerns required a new approach. They couldn't look like B graders, so there had to be some experiments in casting. Flynn, an established star in Empire films, made four successful Westerns in the three-year period 1939–1941, the last of which had him convincingly cast as George Custer at the Battle of Little Bighorn. Nor was this an isolated experiment. *Destry Rides Again* had Jimmy Stewart and Marlene Dietrich in their first Western roles. *The Oklahoma Kid* (1939) starred Jimmy Cagney as the hero and Humphrey Bogart as the embarrassed villain. Bogart also looked unconvincing as the heavy in *Virginia City* (1940) and would only escape Westerns with his breakout role in *The Maltese Falcon* (1941).

Amongst this burst of Western films, it is *Stagecoach* that stands out, setting new expectations of what a Western could be. Its driving force was director John Ford. In the silent era, he had made around 50 Westerns, but tellingly, none in the previous ten years (Cowie 2004). In the mid 1930s he had forged a partnership with Merian C. Cooper, an Anglophile adventurer most noted for making *King Kong* (1933). With his assistance, Ford rebuilt his career, culminating in the Oscar for *The Informer* (1935). Buoyed by this success, Ford and Cooper yearned to return to the West and seized the chance to make a large-scale Western that would rekindle public interest. The result, 'not only revitalized westerns, but actually revolutionized the genre' (Bogdanovich 1975: 156). Furthermore, as *Stagecoach* was made by a *serious* director noted for his artistic vision, it appealed to critics and demonstrated that cinematic Westerns were a valid art form.

In considering *Stagecoach*, we identify its three main influences on the future direction of Western films and how people would imagine the West.

1 The use of landscape

What most distinguishes *Stagecoach* – and still ensures its popularity over 70 years later – was Ford's audacious use of spectacular natural scenery in the film. *Dodge City*, while impressive, was filmed on the Warner Brothers backlot and at the Sierra Railroad at Jamestown in California's Central Valley. It is what became known as a *Town Western*, focussing on the shifting balance of power within a town and where the action is confined to a few pivotal locations, such as saloons or sheriff's offices (Calder 1974). Such an approach is found in many of these early Westerns, it was cheap to westernise backlot sets and rural California could generically look like anywhere. John Ford took a completely different direction. Not wanting *Stagecoach* to look like other contemporary productions, he headed out of California and filmed at the remote Navajo Reservation in Monument Valley on the Arizona/Utah border.

The spectacular outcrops and desert landscape of Monument Valley dominate *Stagecoach* from its opening credits. Filmed intentionally in artistically stark black and white, it creates a compelling vision of the West as a mythical wilderness. As Slotkin argued:

> Ford is *inventing* the Valley as a cinematic (and American) icon. The Valley is in fact as unique a landscape as can be imagined. The 'monuments' are huge red monoliths of volcanic stone [actually sandstone] shooting up out of rubble piles, shaped like open hands or towered skylines or phallic spires, surrounded by the flat plane of a barren rocky desert. In *Stagecoach* it is the landscape's visual oddity that gives it authenticity – this is not a landscape anyone could invent or build in the San Fernando Valley [near Hollywood].
> (1992: 305)

Similarly, Kitses notes the rhythmic alternation of the interaction between the passengers within the stagecoach – intentionally a *stage* for the drama – and external shots of Monument Valley:

> The tiny stage crosses the valley floor far below, dwarfed by the immensity of the terrain and its enormous geological formations. The nuances of this landscape are remarkable: freedom, danger, the eternal, the monumental.... It could be argued that in juxtaposing the imposing landscape and the discord within the stage, Ford stresses the petty concerns of the travellers. In fact, the magnitude of the environment works to ennoble the pioneers. The expansive scale, overwhelming contours and ageless character of this landscape evoke the awesome challenges and tests of the frontier experience.
> (2004: 48)

Ford's bold statement is that his film is set in the *real* West, not Hollywood. From *Stagecoach* onwards, Ford and other film-makers would parallel wilderness backgrounds with plots invoking a varied mix of heroism, courage, despair, bleakness and vengeance.

Importantly, *Stagecoach* highlights the illusory nature of film-making. Ford shot extensive footage of the stagecoach winding through Monument Valley and these scenes punctuate the action. However, the footage with his cast is filmed around Hollywood, particularly at the Iverson Movie Ranch (Frost 2009; Rothel 1991). If one watches carefully, none of the actors are ever shown in actual close up at Monument Valley. It is mainly shown in longshot or in two or three instances unconvincingly as back-projection. The landscape which the film is famous for is an illusion.

2 Revenge and redemption

Matching his epic scenery, Ford crafted a story that went well beyond the simple goodies versus baddies of previous Westerns. Rather than simple entertaining action, he created 'the first "Adult" western ... and brought an almost expressionistic artistry to a form that until then had been likeable but hardly profound' (Bogdanovich 1975: 157). While there would still be juvenile Westerns, the die was now cast that the genre could be as adult as any, exploring darkness, greed, racism and obsession.

The plot is simple. A lone stagecoach journeys from Tonto in Arizona to Lordsburg in New Mexico. Danger comes from the Apaches; Geronimo has broken out from the reservation and is on the warpath. Thrown together in this desperate situation are seven passengers, plus Marshall Curly riding shotgun and the driver. Ford essentially took a B-grade plot and characters, but gave them greater complexity. Knowing that the audience was familiar with these tropes – and the actors – Ford gave them each a twist. Thus, the Southern Gentleman is a card sharp, Doc Boone a drunk, the Cavalry wife is pregnant and the Banker is an embezzler on the run (Pippin 2010; Slotkin 1992). Classic archetypes, their journey is akin to that of mythical heroes (Campbell 1949). Though it is not their intention, they find that 'suffering their test in the wilderness, most of the characters in their various ways achieve redemption and transformation' (Kitses 2004: 45).

The hero is the Ringo Kid, a stock character of earlier Westerns. Young and headstrong, he has broken out of jail to kill the Plummer Brothers who have murdered his father and brother. In casting John Wayne as the Kid, Ford took a major risk. Wayne was a well-known B-grade actor, making approximately 80 cheap hour-long Westerns during the 1930s. He had even served time as a singing cowboy. The Ford logic was to take a familiar actor and surprise the audience by putting him in such a prestigious production. Hedging his bets, he also went for an ensemble approach, so that each character is given similar screen time. Even though *Stagecoach* made Wayne a star, it is not a star vehicle.

On the coach, Ringo meets Dallas (Claire Trevor) and they fall in love. She tries to convince him not to go to Lordsburg, she fears the Plummers will kill him. Again, that was a standard plot – the girl influencing the hero to abandon revenge. Except in this case Dallas is a prostitute who has been forced to leave Tonto. For Ford and Cooper this was the key element of the film, as they argued to David O. Selznick, 'the picture would have the most appealing love story in the world, the growing love between a good bad man and a good bad girl' (quoted in Eyman 1999: 192). In focussing on how Dallas is redeemed – transformed from prostitute to rancher's wife – Ford deliberately crafted a melodramatic Western that would appeal to adult audiences and most importantly draw in female viewers (Kitses 2004).

Whereas most other Westerns of the time were paeans to Manifest Destiny and progress, Ford provided an *Elegiac* vision – an approach that would be copied in many later films. His West is fast disappearing. Progress is not to be celebrated, rather it is to bring to an end this purer, more authentic era, to be replaced by the ordinariness of modernity. The stagecoach is symbolic. A primitive and uncomfortable form of transport, it belongs to a transitional stage of development; only operating for a short period before being replaced by the railroad (Fradkin 2002). The Southern Pacific Railroad pushed through to Lordsburg in 1881, placing the action of *Stagecoach* somewhat earlier than that.

Tonto is represented as a town that has changed. Even though it is on the frontier, it has quickly become a law-abiding and self-righteously respectable place (Pippin 2010). The Law and Order League holds sway, convincing the authorities to force Dallas and Doc Boone to leave town by the next stage. That Dallas is a prostitute is only implied, it was specifically stated in the original script but the censors forced it to be cut. Leaving the town – a dull Hollywood set – the stagecoach plunges into the spectacular scenery of Monument Valley. Here in the wilderness, the dynamics of the group begin to change and Ringo, Dallas and Doc Boone move towards redemption. Ford's message is clear. It is only in the wide open spaces that transformation is possible.

Lordsburg, in contrast, is a rollicking western frontier town. Shot at night, it has an extensive red light district (the censors must have been asleep). Alas, modern-day Lordsburg is disappointingly nothing like its cinematic representation. Ringo kills the Plummers, suggesting that Lordsburg's wild days are now coming to an end as well. Marshall Curly and Doc Boone conspire to let Ringo and Dallas escape over the border into Mexico. Doc Boone closes the film by proudly pronouncing, 'we have saved them from the blessings of civilisation'.

3 *Native Americans as the savage other*

For all its positives, *Stagecoach* was disturbing in its representation of Native Americans. They are the *savage Other* – dangerous, malevolent and brutal. It was a portrayal that would be repeated again and again in Westerns.

The film starts with the news that the Apaches under Geronimo have broken out of the reservation. For most of the journey they are an unseen threat. Here Ford borrowed from his earlier *Lost Patrol* (1935), where British soldiers in Iraq were picked off one by one, but their Arab enemies were never shown. It is only in the last part of the journey, when the travellers think that they are finally safe, that the Apache attack.

No attempt is made to fill in the back-story for the Apaches. Why are they on the reservation? What has led them to break free? Their history of poor rations and ill-treatment is ignored. There is no sense that this is their land and that it is the travellers in the stagecoach who are the intruders. Emphasising the marginalisation of the Apache, they are literally given no voice. They have no lines and there is no rationale given for their actions. A force of nature, they appear, attack and are beaten off. Reinforcing the displacement of the Apache; their parts are played by Navajo extras and White stuntmen and the action shot in California and Monument Valley rather than Apache ancestral lands.

Stagecoach sets the pattern of misappropriating the Native American narrative. Portrayals of Native Americans were minimalist, often with little dialogue or a few words of broken English. Little attempt was made for nuanced character development. If any complexity was required, White actors were used. The most famous example of this occurred in *The Searchers* (1956), widely regarded as John Ford's masterpiece. Ethan (John Wayne) engages in an obsessive six-year search for his niece, who has been kidnapped by the Comanche war chief Scar. Fuelled by hatred and racism, Ethan does not want to rescue Debbie, but rather to kill her. Matching Ethan in his hatred and obsession is Scar. His sons have been killed by the Whites and he too wants revenge. Ethan and Scar are the same, they are doppelgangers. The challenge for Ford was to find an actor to play Scar who could match John Wayne for presence and menace. His choice was Henry Brandon. Tall, muscular and blue-eyed, he successfully matched Wayne scene for scene. Apart from his physical attributes, Ford chose Brandon because he was an outsider. Born in Germany, his real name was Heinrich Kleinbach. The Navajo extras nicknamed him the 'Kraut Comanche' and Ford kept him in costume for most of the shoot to maintain an emotional distance from the American actors (McBride 2001: 565). For *Two Rode Together* (1961), Ford used Brandon and Black American Woody Strode to play the two main Comanche warriors. Even though he was strikingly Germanic, Brandon became typecast and most of his career was in playing Native Americans on television.

Nor was Brandon an isolated case. Australian Michael Pate played Apache chiefs in *Hondo* (1953) and *Major Dundee* (1965). Like Brandon, his appeal was in already being a foreigner and he too worked extensively in television Westerns. Even more bizarre was the career of Iron Eyes Cody. Born Espera De Corti, he was of Italian descent. Adapting Corti to Cody, he started playing Native Americans as an extra, before graduating to speaking roles. Most filmmakers actually assumed he was Native American. Even in the supposedly more enlightened 1960s, such casting continued. Starlet Raquel Welch played an Indian in *100 Rifles* (1969), as did Julie Newmar in *MacKenna's Gold* (1969). In all these cases, such casting prevented Native Americans from working in Hollywood and portraying their own culture and heritage.

There is a striking contrast to this in Australian films. In 1955, Charles and Elsa Chauvel made *Jedda*, which was highly successful and had certain parallels to *The Searchers*. Its two romantic lead characters were Aborigines. The story was focussed almost entirely on them and they have the majority of the dialogue.

However, rather than using White actors with dark makeup (which did happen in Australia from time to time), the Chauvels used indigenous actors Ngarla Kunoth and Robert Tudawali to carry their film. Despite its success, such casting never happened in Hollywood during the golden years of Westerns.

Film and tourism

Our aim in this book is to explore the linkages between film and tourism in the American West. Through popular culture and media, places such as the West are collectively reimagined, with certain elements and features exaggerated and others ignored. These imagined places draw in tourists, attracted by a cultural heritage that is part fictional and mediatised. In turn, tourism operators and destination marketing organisations refashion what they present to fit these imagined images. The West is an exemplar of this concept, with the imagining through media and popular culture dating back to the nineteenth century and reaching a peak during the 1950s. Furthermore, it is a process which continues unabated today, with new media and tourism productions focussing on a mythical West. Our interest is in places within the American West where culture, image and tourism have all been refashioned to fit these expectations. For us, the prime driver of this process of imagining is cinema, though we do recognise and discuss the influence of other media, including television, art, music and books.

Film-induced tourism has been an area of growing research interest for the last two decades (Beeton 2010; Connell 2012). Initially the focus of researchers was on recently released films triggering bursts of tourism visitation and the development of attractions and tours. Examples included *Dances with Wolves*, *Field of Dreams* and – certainly the most well-known – *Lord of the Rings*. However, recently there have been changes in direction for film tourism research and these strongly inform this work. Three inter-related developments are particularly important.

The first is the growing realisation that individual case studies have been overdone and that often their lessons are difficult to apply to other instances (Beeton 2010; Connell 2012). This has led to a greater interest in the collective impact of groups of films produced over a long period of time featuring the same location or region. Examples of this include studies of cinema and other media representations of the Himalayas (Howard 2012; Mercille 2005) and the Australian Outback (Frost 2010).

A second conceptual shift has been from *film tourism* to *media tourism*. This change recognises that tourists both consume and create a range of media around film (Månsson 2011; Mercille 2005; Reijnders 2011). They not only watch a film, but also read the book it was based on (either before or after viewing). Examples include *The Da Vinci Code*, *Lord of the Rings*, *Twilight* and *Harry Potter*. In addition, they consume organic and induced media coverage of the locations featured in the film and this may motivate travel to these locations. In some cases, tourists will aim to replicate what is represented in media; for example, many tourists are inspired by the exploits of explorers and adventurers, becoming themselves *explorer travellers*, albeit at a less extreme level (Howard 2012; Laing and Frost 2014; Mercille 2005). The rise of social media further encourages tourists to create and post their own commentaries and experiences based on – and even critiquing – the media they have consumed. We can no longer just talk about media production, but rather we need to understand that is another example of consumer *co-creation*.

The third change is a dramatic swing from a supply to a demand focus. Much of the early work on film tourism was industry-based, for example considering how tourism marketing organisations could work with production companies to promote a destination. Now we are seeing a greater emphasis on the tourist and their experience. An exemplar of this approach is the research by Reijnders (2009 and 2011) on what he has termed *places of imagination*. Drawing on examples as diverse as *Dracula*, James Bond films and *Scandinavian noir*, Reijnders argues that fans imagine real places that they have read about or seen in films or on television screens, and are motivated to find and visit them. For Reijnders, these tourists are making 'concrete comparisons between imagination and reality ... driven by an emotional longing for these two worlds to converge'. This leads them on a 'search for physical references to a phenomenon that actually takes place in their mind' (2011: 233, 234).

Examining film tourism from the tourists' perspective raises questions of what they are seeking. There are a range of possibilities. Many studies focus on iconic scenery and landscape. In their quantitative study, Macionis and Sparks identified that the prime motivation for film tourists was 'to see the scenery and landscape in real life' (2009: 97). Similarly, Carl *et al.* (2007) emphasised that tourists wanted to visit the *actual* places where their favourite films were shot. Butler (2011) linked this interest to genre and argued that Westerns in particular were strongly connected to place and scenery. This focus on place led Jewell and McKinnon (2008) to postulate that films were creating a new form of cultural landscape, overlaying history with an imagined cinematic identity.

While film tourism studies often focus on scenery, it is also recognised that the story, characters, settings and atmosphere contribute profoundly to audience engagement. Kim and Richardson posited that 'the level of emphatic involvement with film characters can affect the perceptions viewers have of the place depicted' (2003: 222). Beeton continued on this theme, proposing 'we view movies through ourselves in such a way to gain some personal meaning' and 'we put ourselves in the story, sights, sounds and emotions of the movie' (2005: 229). Frost went further, arguing 'projecting striking visual images is rarely sufficient to carry a successful production ... scenery is just a background'; instead the key appeal 'for the audience of potential tourists is these storylines present a "promise" of what might occur if they were to travel to the locations featured' (2010: 723).

At the deeper levels, this engagement is distinguished by *fandom* and *authenticity*. In analysing interest in Korean television dramas, Kim characterised audience involvement as a *parasocial interaction*: an 'imaginary sense of intimacy

by an individual audience member with a media figure [for example, an actor]'
(Kim 2012: 389). This intimacy may be intensified by fan groups undertaking
tours, their emotions heightened by the shared experience and camaraderie
(Buchmann *et al.* 2010; Reijnders 2011; Roesch 2009).

This raises issues of authenticity and the tourist experience. On the one hand,
it may seem to have little place in tourism that is based on fiction – or in the case
of *Lord of the Rings*, a film representation of a novel heavy with CGI (Butler
2011; Tzanelli 2004). Nonetheless, research suggests a form of *existential
authenticity*, where the tourist sees themselves as central and are more interested
in how the experience makes them feel (Beeton 2005; Buchmann *et al.* 2010;
Tzanelli 2004). More prosaically, authenticity may derive from going *backstage*, understanding special effects and the illusory manipulation of locations
(Beeton 2005; Frost 2008, 2009).

The mediatisation of the West relies heavily on this perception of authenticity. Paradoxically, Westerns are often characterised by high degrees of invention
and historical distortion (Calder 1974). Indeed, rather than striving for authenticity in terms of historical facts, many film-makers focus on a convincing image in
costumes, weapons and other paraphernalia, for 'as long as you get the look
right, you may freely invent characters and incidents and do whatever you want
to the past to make it more interesting' (Rosenstone 1995: 60). Such issues have
been noted for historical theme parks in general (Lowenthal 1998) and Butler
(2011) discusses it for the Western theme park Old Tucson in Arizona. That
enterprise was the venue for an instructive quantitative study of tourists by
Morganstern and Greenberg (1988). They found that perceptions of authenticity
dropped significantly if visitors were told the truth that it was originally established as a set for a movie. Like the movies, the Western experience requires a
suspension of disbelief.

Western cinema and history

The West is one of the strongest and most enduring place images in the world.
The myth of the West is firmly rooted in popular culture – whether novels, film,
television, music, clothing, even video games – and its distinguishing markers
are still instantly recognisable in the modern world. While it is argued that
'Westerns are America's unique contribution to that body of mythic lore familiar
to most of the human race' (Pilkington and Graham 1979: 1), their popularity
has also been attributed to drawing on universal narratives, archetypes and
legends dating back to the Ancient Greeks (Clauss 1999; Coyne 1997; Pippin
2010). The West combines myth and history, rugged natural scenery and wide
open spaces, popular culture and promises of transformation. From the early
nineteenth century it has fascinated people and drawn tourists keen to engage
with this distinctive region.

Underlying the basic appeal of the West is a series of paradoxes. The constructed imagination of the West is full of contradictions, adding to its complexity and drawing power. These paradoxes include:

- It is a frontier, which must be settled and therefore disappear as a frontier.
- It is a harsh and savage environment, which may also be seen as beautiful and sublime.
- It is constructed as an empty wilderness, America's Manifest Destiny to settle, yet is already inhabited by Native Americans.
- It is a lawless zone, where outlaws (such as Billy the Kid, Butch Cassidy and the Sundance Kid) are heroes.
- Taming the frontier requires violent and driven individuals (for example *Shane*). Yet, once the frontier is settled, there is no place for such people in society.
- It is constructed as a male domain, yet women are needed and have a place in its history.
- Freedom and individualism are valued, but there is also fundamentalism and bigotry.
- It is the birthplace of the national parks movement (Yellowstone 1872), but also a byword for extreme environmental damage.
- An environment of extremes, it offers both adventure and danger. It is a place to escape to, to hide in, perhaps to be transformed.

Such paradoxes have resulted in multiple – often conflicting – interpretations of the West. These range from the setting for White expansion (often represented in Cowboys and Indians and the Pioneer Myth) through to the recent shift towards a *new history of the West*. The latter eschews development and heroic narratives for a greater focus on Native Americans, gender, class and the environment (Limerick *et al.* 1991; Reisner 1986; Riley 1999; Tompkins 1992; White 1991). Just as cinema provides multiple interpretations of the West, so too do historians.

The West has long captured the imagination as an evocative frontier, constructed as a boundary zone between civilisation and wilderness, even between order and lawlessness. Since Frederick Jackson Turner (1962 [1893]), it has been viewed as the engine of transformation. Turner saw it as the root of American exceptionalism – and therefore of the triumph of Manifest Destiny – a view still common among some today. Perhaps more importantly, in modern society it is seen as the setting for personal transformation, a place of freedom and individualism (Slotkin 1992). The imagery of the West is constructed through popular culture, particularly popular film (Coyne 1997; Kitses 2004; Pippin 2010; Slotkin 1992; Tompkins 1992). Cinema uses the Western landscape as a wild and untamed setting for mythic stories, encouraging tourists to visit places such as Monument Valley and Tombstone. Furthermore, the storylines, characters and tropes of Western film are widely seen as defining the West as a transformative landscape.

Scope and structure of this book

Researchers (like tourists) are heavily influenced by their cultural backgrounds. Both of us have a strong affection for Western cinema and travelling the American West. These are interests which are deeply embedded. For Warwick:

Westerns were a key part of my childhood. Favourite films on television included *Fort Apache, North-West Passage* and *Go West*. They had to be watched every time they were shown. Western television series, in contrast, didn't grab me. Too slow, too small. During summer holidays, cinemas would always show John Wayne movies. Unlike television, these were in colour. When I was six (and my brother nine) we saw *The Searchers* at a cinema in the resort town cinema. We liked the action, but didn't get there were sub-texts. The idea that Westerns had hidden messages and allegories would not come for years.

For Jennifer:

My West was largely imagined through the saga of *Little House on the Prairie*, particularly the books but later on the television series starring Michael Landon and Melissa Gilbert. During school holidays, I used to write myself stories about covered wagons travelling across America – the length and arduousness of the journey fascinated me, as well as the idea of setting up a home in the wild. The Grand Canyon was high on my list of places I wanted to visit as an adult, after seeing the *Brady Bunch* trek down to the bottom on the back of mules. The other influence was the craze for Holly Hobbie, with a multitude of memorabilia, including birthday cards, porcelain figurines, fabric, lunchboxes and teasets emblazoned with little girls with poke bonnets, button-up boots, patchwork dresses and lace-trimmed pantaloons. My sister dressed in this fashion for a fancy dress party. By contrast, I can't remember ever dressing as a cowgirl or Pocahontas. My West was essentially populated by prim and proper girls and women who never toted a gun or wore a Stetson.

In our academic careers, we have continually felt ourselves drawn to the American West as a setting for research and enquiry (with Warwick even teaching American history for some years). In recent years, our focus on the interplay between tourism, media and the imagination has often touched on the West as an intriguing exemplar. In this volume, we have followed on from themes and issues in our *Books and Travel: Inspiration, Quests and Transformation* (Laing and Frost 2012) and *Explorer Travellers and Adventure Tourism* (Laing and Frost 2014). In the former we examined how novels and travel books encouraged the idea that travel was transformative; and it contained two chapters on the West. One looked at books by and/or about iconic Westerners such as Davy Crockett, Kit Carson, Wild Bill Hickok, Buffalo Bill Cody and George Custer. The second examined the novels *The Searchers*, *True Grit*, *Little Big Man* and the reminiscences of *The Little House on the Prairie* series. In *Explorer Travellers*, we looked at the myth of travelling to the frontier and the application of Joseph Campbell's *Hero's Journey* to adventure travel. With this volume, our aim is to extend these concepts, through a strongly-focussed geographical study.

In the past, works on tourism in the West have tended to be historical with strong emphases on nature-based tourism, such as national parks and ski resorts. These studies are striking in their lack of discussion of popular culture and the cowboy/Wild West aspects of Western tourism. Such an emphasis dates back to the seminal work on Western tourism by the historian Pomeroy (1957) and still dominates the more recent literature as in major studies by Rothman (1998) and Wrobel and Long (2001). Valuable as these studies have been, it is time for a change in direction. While still giving attention to national parks, this work delves more deeply into how the cultural heritage of the West drives tourism today.

This book comprises a series of chapters exploring how Western cinema has constructed an imaginary West dominated by the promises of transformation and existential authenticity for tourists. It also examines how that cinematic version of the West has come to alter and influence reality. Nearly all of these essays are *place-based*, focussing on particular locations (such as Monument Valley, Tombstone, Little Bighorn) that have featured in films and where we have conducted fieldwork. Our choices are subjective. While tempting, it is simply not possible to cover all places in the vast area of the West. Accordingly, instead of an encyclopaedic coverage, we present a selection of places. Three chapters are the exception to our place-based approach. In one we look broadly at Western fashions, in another we compare the Western imagery and persona developed by two iconic actors in John Wayne and Charlton Heston and in a third, we focus on fictional outlaws. Finally, while our primary focus is film, at times we also stray into other media where appropriate – particularly travel books and paintings.

2 Monument Valley

We enjoy Westerns, we like watching them. But we don't like *always* being the bad guys. That makes us sad.

(Navajo guide, Monument Valley)

Introduction

Cinema has made Monument Valley the iconic landscape of the West. Its spectacular rock outcrops are instantly recognisable and familiar to many film-goers (see Figures 2.1 and 2.2). Closely linked with John Ford, it has been the iconic backdrop for some of the great Westerns. However, there is a dissonance between it as a *place of imagination* mediated by cinema and reality. In beginning this chapter, we highlight four key paradoxes.

1   While well-known, recognisable and attractive, Monument Valley is very remote. On the Utah–Arizona border, it is 270 kilometres from the nearest large urban centre in Flagstaff – which is also the closest Interstate Highway. It is about the same distance from the Grand Canyon to Monument Valley. From Santa Fe it is 560 kilometres and from Salt Lake City nearly 600 kilometres. This is not a destination for day-trippers.
2   It is a cultural landscape as well as a natural one. Situated in the Navajo Nation, it is operated as a Tribal Park. Despite its iconic status, it is neither a US national park nor a UNESCO World Heritage site.
3   Despite its cinematic status, not that many feature films have been made here. John Ford, who is intrinsically linked with Monument Valley, made nine films here. Since his last – *Cheyenne Autumn* (1964) – there has been a tendency for the iconic sandstone buttes to be featured only briefly to establish Western authenticity. Examples of such cameos include *Back to the Future III* (1990), *Forrest Gump* (1994) and *The Wild Wild West* (1999). Perhaps even more influentially, Monument Valley has featured in cartoons such as the Road Runner and Coyote (from 1960 onwards), *Cars* (2006), *Toy Story III* (2010) and *The Lego Movie* (2014). These animations have reinforced a sense of Monument Valley as imagined, unreal, even otherworldly. Also contributing to this have been its use in comedies such as

Figure 2.1 Monument Valley (photo W. Frost).

Figure 2.2 The iconic trio of the two Mittens and Merrick's Butte (photo W. Frost).

National Lampoon's Vacation (1983) and science fiction such as the British television series *Doctor Who* (2011).

4   Adding further to this geographical dislocation and dissonance is the consistent use of Monument Valley to represent somewhere else in the West. John Ford started this with *Stagecoach*. Its setting was the trail from Tonto, Arizona to Lordsburg, New Mexico; places over 500 kilometres south. *Fort Apache* (1948) also utilised Monument Valley for southern Arizona. Both films were concerned with Apaches breaking out of their reservations and utilised local Navajos to play these roles. In *The Searchers* (1956), the setting was even further away in Texas and the Navajo were cast as Comanche. For *The Lone Ranger* (2013), Monument Valley was once again placed in Texas.

A First Nation's National Parks

Monument Valley is not a national park and is not managed by the US National Parks Service (NPS). Instead it is formally designated as the Monument Valley Navajo Tribal Park, established in 1958 and operated by the Navajo Nation Parks and Recreation Department. However, for all intents and purposes, this is a national park; there are uniformed rangers, an entrance fee, accommodation facilities, a visitor centre, tours and trails. It is just not an official national park.

These arrangements are in contrast with Canyon De Chelly National Monument, about 100 kilometres to the south. Like Monument Valley, Canyon de Chelly is in the Navajo Nation, has striking rock formations and is a cultural landscape with sacred sites. It has not featured much in films, the main exceptions being *The Big Country* (1958) and *Mackenna's Gold* (1969). However, in 1931 it was established as a national monument. The concept of national monuments was developed by President Theodore Roosevelt in 1906. Establishing national parks required an Act of Congress, but national monuments legislation was passed to allow the president to act quickly in protecting areas by decree. However, Roosevelt used these powers widely, protecting quite large areas without resort to Congress, most notably the Grand Canyon in 1908 (Rothman 1989). At the same time as Canyon De Chelly was protected, there were efforts to include Monument Valley within the NPS, but these came to nothing. Further unsuccessful attempts were made in 1943, 1953 and 1983 (Dilsaver 2003).

Being under different jurisdictions has affected the tourist development of both sites. Since the 1980s, the NPS has been under constant budgetary pressure from both neo-liberal and conservative forces within US politics. At the most extreme, cutbacks and financial instability have led to temporary national park closures, as occurred throughout the United States in 2013. For Canyon De Chelly, this has meant that expenditure and staffing have declined relative to growing visitor numbers. In contrast, Monument Valley has avoided these problems by not being part of the larger system (Sanders 1996). Most notably, a new hotel – owned and operated by the Navajo – has recently opened in Monument Valley.

Monument Valley holds a special place as an indigenous owned and controlled national park. In the national parks and tourism literature there is much discussion of the desirability of increased indigenous control of national parks (see Zeppel 2009 for a good summary). Much of the focus is on *partnerships* between local groups and national parks agencies. Ironically, the governance structure at Monument Valley is missing from this discussion. Seemingly, the notion of complete indigenous control is beyond current consideration; instead, indigenous involvement is usually conceptualised as taking place only under the aegis of national agencies. It is notable that while Canyon De Chelly is described as a good example of such partnerships, Monument Valley is ignored (see for example Zeppel 2009).

John Ford's Monument Valley

John Ford and Monument Valley are forever linked together. The great Western director shot nine movies here: *Stagecoach* (1939), *My Darling Clementine* (1946), *Fort Apache* (1948), *She Wore a Yellow Ribbon* (1949), *Wagon Master* (1950), *Rio Grande* (1950), *The Searchers* (1956), *Sergeant Rutledge* (1960) and *Cheyenne Autumn* (1964). Bogdanovich summed this special relationship up, 'in Hollywood they call it Ford Country; it has become so identified with him that other directors feel it would be plagiarism to make a picture here' (1978: 10). Indeed, apart from Ford's, very few films have been extensively shot here.

Ford 'discovered' Monument Valley, utilising it as backgrounds for *Stagecoach* (which was mainly filmed in southern California). In an interview, Bogdanovich asked Ford, 'How did you find Monument Valley?' Ford's reply was, 'I knew about it. I travelled up here once, driving through Arizona on my way to Santa Fe' (1978: 69–70). An alternative explanation – now widely accepted – was that it was through the efforts of trading post operator Harry Goulding. He had settled there in 1923 and in 1938 taken photographs to Hollywood. These are the stories which appear widely in books on Western cinema. While privileging Ford and Goulding, they tend to downplay other possibilities. Monument Valley featured in the Zane Grey silent film *The Last American* (1925). It was a major hit, reaching a wide audience. Consideration must also be given to the National Parks Service declaring it a national monument in 1938. Did that process influence or inspire Goulding?

Economically, the area was marginal. The expenditure involved in making films gave a welcome boost. Goulding expanded into an accommodation lodge, servicing the cast and crew and later tourists (Figures 2.3 and 2.4). The local Navajo worked as extras and as casual labourers, developing a strong relation-ship with Ford:

> They'd been hit pretty bad by the Depression.... Well, Mr Ford came here to make *Stagecoach*, and gave a score a jobs to the Navajos and a lotta lives were saved. Then, just after he'd finished shootin' *She Wore a Yellow Ribbon* here, we had a blizzard ... planes dropped food in. Thanks to that, an' the two hundred thousand dollars or so he'd left behind, why, another tragedy was prevented.
>
> (Harry Goulding quoted in Bogdanovich 1978: 15)

The Searchers (1956)

In the opening scene, Martha opens the door of her homestead, revealing the full glory of Monument Valley. A figure on horseback approaches from out of the desert. It is Ethan, the man she loves. He has been away for three years and has finally come back. Except, it is quickly apparent that they are not married. Instead, her husband is Ethan's brother Aaron. Since the end of the Civil War, Ethan has been wandering – according to John Ford – most likely down in

Figure 2.3 Goulding's Lodge (photo W. Frost).

Figure 2.4 View from Goulding's Lodge towards Buttes (photo W. Frost).

Mexico fighting for the Emperor Maximilian (Bogdanovich 1978). Now he has come home. Is he there to force a reckoning? To finally claim Martha? Perhaps, but he hesitates. Enjoying the company of the children Ben, Lucy and Debbie (Deborah), he makes no move. The next day, the homestead is attacked by the Comanche led by Scar. Aaron, Martha, Lucy and Ben are killed and Debbie kidnapped. Ethan (John Wayne) begins the long search to rescue her. He is accompanied by Marty (Jeffrey Hunter), an orphan adopted by the Edwards. As their long quest unfolds over the years, Marty realises that Ethan is no longer on a rescue mission. Rather he intends to kill Debbie, who has been adopted into the tribe. Made at the height of the Cold War, the slogan 'Better Dead than Red' has special resonance here.

Nearly all the external scenes were filmed in Monument Valley. For the first 40 minutes in particular, Monument Valley dominates the screen, with hardly any interiors to break its spell. Unlike *Stagecoach*, all the actors and action were in Monument Valley; riding, walking, fighting, interacting with the landscape. It was shot in colour – clear blue skies contrasting with red soil and rock. Ford preferred black and white, particularly with cloud formations; but for this film he bowed to pressure for a modern approach, utilising the colour that television was yet to achieve. *The Searchers* remains the best and longest use of this location in any film. Monument Valley was as much the star as John Wayne.

Standing in for Texas, Monument Valley is constructed as a biblical land-scape. The settlers are self-consciously righteous. It is a wilderness, but they will make it their promised land. This view of wilderness and the mission to tame it had been a major part of the frontier settler experience since the Pilgrim Fathers (Nash 1967). Ethan is the prodigal son returning. Whatever he has been doing for the last three years is of no account and remains an unresolved mystery. Most of the family have biblical names: Ethan, Aaron, Martha, Benjamin and Deborah (the exception is Lucy, whose fate parallels that of the third-century St Lucy). Ethan, as befits his Old Testament name, seeks revenge and destruction. However, in the end, it is Martha – the only character with a New Testament name – who stands for compassion and forgiveness.

Two other pivotal characters are defined by their biblical names. Overseeing the community is the Reverend Samuel Clayton (Ward Bond). He knows about Martha and Ethan, but voices no judgement. A warrior/priest, Samuel presides over funerals and marriages and leads the Texas Rangers against the Comanche. That his communal religious ceremonies are constantly interrupted by danger signify that their nascent society is fragile (Peary 1982). Ethan (representing the savage frontier) and Samuel (civilisation) constantly clash. It is Samuel who overrules Ethan in giving permission to Marty to sneak into the Comanche camp and rescue Debbie. Then there is Mose (Moses), played by perennial character actor Hank Worden. It is Mose, the humblest of the settlers, who finally finds Debbie – leading them to their goal.

Complementing these biblical dimensions, there is an underlying theme of Greek mythology. Influenced by Campbell (1949), Ford and other film-makers incorporated elements of the *Hero's Journey* into their storylines. Ethan's return home is a failure, he is unable to claim the woman he loves and then she is lost entirely. Kitses argues that his coveting of his brother's wife is 'an intolerable, Oedipal sin' and he must bear the guilt for her death 'the outsize punishment of the gods like a hero in a Greek tragedy' (2004: 96). The long quest becomes a *Katabasis*: a common narrative in Greek mythology whereby the hero makes a gruelling descent into hell. In *The Searchers*, the descent is into an infernal fron-tier wasteland of never-ending vendettas and massacres in order to find and rescue Debbie (Clauss 1999; Frost and Laing 2012; Laing and Frost 2012).

Frankel argued that Ford 'used the scenery like some modern directors use special effects – to create drama and stun the audience' (2013: 268). The dra-matic role of Monument Valley in *The Searchers* has been the subject of mul-tiple interpretations. At one extreme is the view that it is full of menace and the settlers are unwelcome outsiders. As Kitses argued, in the opening scene, 'the immensity of the landscape brooding over the lonely homestead speaks volumes about its vulnerability to savage forces'. Out of this rides Ethan, and for the rest of the film, this 'unearthly barren world ... is home to the obsessed Ethan, hospitable to his state of mind' (2004: 97). Such a view was similarly held by Slotkin, who generalised that the 'revenger Western gives us a landscape that mirrors the hero's introvert psychology. Often it is a desert landscape' (1992: 382). Others saw contrasting meanings. Peary (1982: 311) commented on the 'breath-taking physical beauty ... the stunning rock formations are both gorgeous and eerie'. Cowie (2004: 178) theorised that individual formations were symbolic. Mitchell Butte and Gray Whiskers, framing the Edwards homestead, he saw as 'guardians of the valley' – the opposite interpretation to that by Kitses. Cowie also argues that the West Mitten, seen at the burning homestead and later funeral, represented the lost mother and child (Martha and Debbie). Cowie was not correct in some of his identification, the West Mitten was not shown during the funeral, but rather earlier when Ethan realises that Debbie has been kidnapped. Further backing Cowie's theory, the West Mitten was shown again during the final rescue of Debbie. The two Mittens are the most well-known formations in Monument Valley (Figure 2.2) and it is intriguing that Ford carefully framed many scenes to exclude them, so that they only dramatically appeared at a few critical moments.

For the first half of the movie, the Comanche are simply devilish villains. That this is the settlers' land is unquestioned and there is absolutely no contemplation that they have sparked the Comanche attacks by invading their homeland. Manifest Destiny is paramount. Around the middle of the film dissonant notes are added. Whites are met (such as Futterman), who are utterly rapacious and treacherous. The Seventh Cavalry massacres a Comanche village, killing women and children as well as braves. Ford shot a scene where Ethan meets Custer, with the latter portrayed as the more bloodthirsty, but then cut it as it softened Ethan's character (see Chapter 12). When Ethan finally meets Scar, we find that they are equals in stature, presence and hatred. Scar explains that because both of his sons were killed by Whites, he takes many scalps in vengeance – in essence exactly what Ethan is doing. Indeed if scalping is seen as barbarism, it is notable that in the end Ethan scalps Scar.

The longer their search continues, the more *lost* Ethan is. To journey through this hellish realm, Ethan and Marty must become more like the Comanche, learning their ways. They become traders, seeing this as a way to gain intelligence, but they are gradually integrated into Comanche culture and customs. Marty learns some Comanche, though mysteriously Ethan is already fluent. When Scar and Ethan finally meet, they are both surprised that the other can speak their own language. For both, fuelled by the quest for vengeance, there has been the contradictory need to understand their enemies. Over the years, some of the settlers have become disgusted with Ethan and Marty; for they have mixed too closely with the Comanche. There is only a brief glimpse of this in the film, but it is a stronger theme in the Alan LeMay novel (Frost and Laing 2012). Tellingly, in the film's final scene, Marty and Debbie walk into a settler's home, but the door shuts with Ethan still outside – neither able nor fit to rejoin the community.

Once Upon a Time in the West (1968)

Sergio Leone was one of the leading lights of the *Spaghetti Westerns* of the 1960s. Made by Italians, filmed in Spain and usually starring one or two American actors; these were characterised by violence, existential heroes, operatic plots and avant garde musical scores. Initially working in *Peplum* epics, Leone achieved success with his Dollars Trilogy (1964–1966). The last of these – *The Good, the Bad and the Ugly* (1966) became his most well-known work. It starred Americans Clint Eastwood, Lee Van Cleef and Eli Wallach, was set in New Mexico during the Civil War; but was shot entirely in Europe, primarily in Spain's arid Almería region (Cumbow 2008; Frayling 2005; Kitses 2004).

Around 1939, just as the boom in Westerns started, the young Leone started going to the movies in Rome. Like many Italians of his generation, he saw the United States as a magical land of possibilities. At the age of nine or ten, he watched *Stagecoach* and his favourite actors were Gary Cooper and Errol Flynn. In 1941, this influence stopped, as the Fascists banned Hollywood films. After the war, Leone – again like many of his contemporaries – was intoxicated by all things American. He started work in the Italian film industry, which was booming. With post-war currency restrictions that prevented remittance of profits, Hollywood studios and producers were forced to make films in Europe. Leone worked under directors such as Raoul Walsh, William Wyler, Fred Zinnemann and Robert Aldrich. He tried to talk about Westerns with them, but found that they were all disillusioned by the changing film scene. Having worked on about 35 films, Leone scraped together enough money to make his own Westerns (Frayling 2005).

The huge success of his Dollars Trilogy led to a contract with Paramount and a higher budget. Though still primarily filmed in Almería and Rome's Cinecittà Studio, he was able to do some filming in the United States and hire a wider array of American actors. In particular, he was able to cast Henry Fonda as the villain and Charles Bronson as the hero. To emphasise his new status, Leone initially planned to have Bronson gun down Eastwood, Van Cleef and Wallach in the opening credits. Van Cleef and Wallach agreed, but Eastwood, now a major star, refused to take a cameo. The slower pace, style and elegiac message of the resultant film was very different to the Dollars Trilogy and this combined with the absence of Eastwood led to it failing in the United States. Nonetheless, it was a critical success and its reputation as one of the great Westerns has continued to grow.

The film draws heavily on the cinematic mythology of the Western and 'the single spirit that most haunts *Once Upon a Time in the West* is John Ford's' (Cumbow 2008: 67). As with Ford's *Stagecoach*, the plot is familiar from many past productions, but is twisted, played with and taken to a higher level (Cumbow 2008; Frayling 2005). In simple terms, widow Jill McBain (Claudia Cardinale) owns a farm in the desert. The railroad needs it and evil gunman Frank (Henry Fonda) is hired to do the dirty work. The mysterious Harmonica (Charles Bronson) comes to her aid, assisted by the *good* outlaw Cheyenne (Jason Robards). Harmonica's motivation is only slowly revealed and this is that he has sworn to kill Frank, who murdered his brother years earlier.

Simple, B movie material. However, the widow McBain is not only a beautiful young woman, she was also previously a prostitute. Evil Frank is played by perennial all-American hero Fonda. Bronson looks like he should be the villain. Cheyenne's motivations are unclear. These simple Western archetypes are further layered through two recurring motifs. The first is that each has their own musical accompaniment, composed by Ennio Morricone. The second is the association of the characters with elemental forces – Jill with water, the gunfighters with fire.

References to Ford's film and other Westerns abound. The massacre of the McBain family parallels that of the Edwards in *The Searchers*. The interior of the McBain homestead looks like that of the Edwards. Harmonica's long search parallels that of Ethan and they both share lost years that are never explained. That it is women, like Jill, who build and lead the community echoes many of Ford's works and this is one of the few Westerns that has a female actor as first named in the credits. Like Ethan, the violent and obsessed Harmonica cannot find a place in the new and peaceful community. Other Westerns referenced include *Johnny Guitar*, *High Noon*, *3:10 to Yuma* and *Shane* (a detailed list is in Frayling 2005: 59–63).

Importantly, it was through the use of Monument Valley, that Leone so emphatically referenced Ford and provided authenticity for his film. Conscious that his earlier films were criticised for being shot in Spain, the funding from Paramount allowed him to take a crew to this iconic location. Nonetheless, that budget was limited; he could only afford to shoot a small portion in the United States. Accordingly, *Once Upon a Time in the West* is punctuated by two scenes in Monument Valley, each being just two and a half minutes long. The first has Jill arriving at the railhead at Flagstone (Flagstaff?), that set being in Spain. She then takes a buggy ride through Monument Valley to the McBain homestead. Accompanied by a soaring Morricone soundtrack, it symbolises that she has left civilisation (town, railway) behind and entered a timeless and majestic wilderness. And, of course, it echoes the early shots of Ford's *Stagecoach*.

The film only returns to Monument Valley for the final confrontation between Harmonica and Frank. As they face off, Harmonica experiences a flashback. The full story is now told of Frank's killing of his brother. This is the incident that has driven Harmonica for years and explains all the mysteries in the plot. The flashback is set in Monument Valley, again emphasising that this is a mythical and timeless place. And again, it directly echoes and references Ford. *The Searchers* began with a family being wiped out in Monument Valley. Ethan then searches for years for Scar, a long quest for vengeance taking him all over the South-West. That search is only ended when Scar returns to Monument Valley, symbolising the futility of Ethan's journey. In *Once Upon a Time in the West*, Harmonica's family is killed in Monument Valley and his long search for revenge begins and ends there.

While the Westerns of Ford and others were a major influence, Leone's background in Peplum film-making also left its mark. These films drew heavily on stories and characters from European – particularly Greek – mythology. It is a recurring theme that Westerns draw much from the Old World and this fits in with Campbell's views of universal tales of the hero's journey (Frost and Laing 2012; Laing and Frost 2012). Cumbow outlined the common formula for Peplum films, which is not only strongly evidenced in *Once Upon a Time in the West*, but could also be partly applied to *The Searchers*:

The typical peplum story centers on an outsider, a man from another land or country, whose wanderings bring him to a new land, rich, decadent, and oppressed.... The outsider makes it his business to strike a blow for freedom and right, and to rid the country of the oppressor. In doing so, the outsider also gets his revenge on the very forces that destroyed his family or village, and caused him to become a rootless wanderer in the first place ... the typical peplum hero has a private mission and a public mission – to gain revenge for a personal wrong done to him, and to free others from a similar wrong ... the two missions merge when the oppressor turns out to be the same villain.

(2008: 8)

One key difference between the two films, however, is in the role of the railway. In *The Searchers*, the settlers are way out on the frontier, far from any railway or town. As Mrs Jorgensen philosophises, 'a Texican is just a man way out on a limb'. In contrast, in *Once Upon a Time in the West*, a railway is being built through Monument Valley, symbolising that civilisation is coming and the age of the gunfighters will soon be over. Furthermore, the railway is the Peplum oppressor, its weapon in Frank both killed Harmonica's family long ago and kills the McBain family. Defeating Frank provides Harmonica with revenge and saves Jill. This fits the narrative of many Westerns, where the railway represented both progress and capitalistic tyranny – opportunity, but also exploitation (Calder 1974). The placement of a railway in Monument Valley has a certain irony, as it was reputed to be the furthest place in the United States from a railway line (Frankel 2013). Nonetheless, there is spectacular potential in the juxtaposition of two such iconic images of the West. In *The Harvey Girls* (1945), Monument Valley is repeatedly shown back-projected through the windows of the train and recently trains travelling through Monument Valley have been used to great effect in *Toy Story III* (2010) and *The Lone Ranger* (2013).

Monument Valley post-Ford

It is over 50 years since Ford made his last Western in Monument Valley. It is curious that no production has been substantially filmed there since; perhaps Ford's shadow is too intimidating. What has occurred has been the widespread use of Monument Valley for short referencing or establishing shots. These pay homage to Monument Valley's mythical imagery and status. In showing Monument Valley, usually for a short period at the beginning, film-makers are saying to audiences that this is going to be an *authentic* Western, in the style and spirit of the great films of the past.

Two examples illustrate this. In *Back to the Future III* (1990), Marty travels back in time to the 1880s to rescue Doc. Once there, he is in Monument Valley – where he is attacked by Navajo and rescued by the cavalry. It is a beautifully filmed segment, highlighting the rich red colours of the landscape. With hardly any dialogue, it visually establishes that Marty is in the *real* Wild West. The rest of the film can now take place on a set near Jamestown in California. Similarly, *The Lone Ranger* (2013) opens with a wild and exciting chase scene involving a runaway train in Monument Valley.

Perhaps the most compelling and vivid example of the modern use of Monument Valley occurs in the television cartoon *Charlie and Lola* (2006). Lola is six years old (and the target audience is about five to ten years of age). She and her friends are pretending to ride horses in the schoolyard. As her imagination takes hold, for about 20–30 seconds we see them riding real horses through a Western landscape. The background is Monument Valley, with both the Mittens accurately portrayed. Even for modern children who may never have seen a Ford or Leone film, Monument Valley *is* the West.

3 Tragic and vulnerable heroes
Chuck and the Duke

> I felt personally closer to Ethan than any other character I ever played.
> (John Wayne, quoted in McGivern 2000: 265)

It is a surprising admission by John Wayne, given that Ethan in *The Searchers* (1956) is 'unwanted and rejected by society, a hostile, restless and impatient man, doomed to be a wanderer' (McGivern 2000: 265). While the Western hero is often mythologised as independent and self-reliant, there is another darker side. They are also loners unable to fit into society – tragic and vulnerable heroes. This chapter explores this duality through some of the Western films of John Wayne and Charlton Heston and how they have coloured our image of men as part of the Western myth.

Marion Morrison and John Carter: the road to stardom

John Wayne began his life as Marion Morrison in Iowa in 1907. His birthplace is now a museum containing memorabilia of his film career. Named after his grandfather, he spent his childhood dealing with taunts about his girlish name. The family moved around a lot, as Wayne's father tried to make a living, first as a pharmacist and then as a farmer, and they struggled financially. Wayne's mother dominated the household and overtly preferred his younger brother, while his father was kind but ineffectual (Eyman 2014). This perhaps explains his continual search for a father figure, exemplified in his relationship with the director John Ford, but also why he enjoyed playing the role of a paternal protector in many of his films.

His life-long nickname of *Duke* was bestowed upon him at the age of nine, when local fireman started to call him Little Duke, in a playful reference to his Airedale dog, Big Duke. Thereafter, he was always Duke to his friends. Morrison changed his name to John Wayne when he was awarded a contract with Fox in the early 1930s. On paper, a plain and ordinary name, it evoked certain qualities and character traits – stoicism, bravery, unflagging energy, wry humour and an indomitable spirit. This fortitude saw Wayne endure years of B Westerns, before Ford gave him his break, which he looked back on as giving him a solid grounding and a strong work ethic. Wayne never took his success for granted, even after he was regularly listed as one of the top ten actors in the world over a period of 26 years (Luhr 2004).

His image as the personification of masculinity and the 'most prominent embodiment of the frontier myth' (Holtan 1970: 275) was often satirised. In the film *Midnight Cowboy* (1969), when Joe Buck (Jon Voigt) is told that his cowboy outfit appeals to homosexuals, his first reaction is to exclaim 'John Wayne! Are you going to tell me he's a fag?'. Furthermore, clips of Wayne feature in the music video for Joe Jackson's 'Real Men' (1982), a song about the difficulties that gay men have in living up to masculine images. While Wayne never played an overt homosexual role in a Western, his characters often spent the majority of his time with and around other men or ended up alone. The Western therefore largely depicts a *homosocial* society (Leith 2002). The subtle link made between cowboys and homoeroticism in many classic Westerns eventually became manifest in the Oscar-winning film *Brokeback Mountain* (2005).

Wayne was often a man of few words on screen, letting his commanding physique, deliberate movements and those blue watchful eyes express what a Western hero couldn't say. One only has to think of Ethan in *The Searchers* (1956), a coiled-up spring of a man ready to explode with rage at the loss of his sister-in-law Martha, and the abduction of her daughters Lucy and Debbie by the Comanche. Wayne spent his life trying to live up to the frontier myth, embodied in the Western, and mourned the loss of its centrality, not just in the movies but in American life more generally. He often looked back to the past as a golden era, despite the fact that the Western is a 'genre about ceaseless change' (Eyman 2014: 276).

There were more paradoxes about Wayne, perhaps underlining his complexity both as a man and as an actor. He eulogised the military, yet failed to serve in the Second World War, for reasons that still remain unclear. It may be that he did not want to suffer the humiliation of being a private after playing authority figures (Eyman 2014). He was implicated in the blacklists of Hollywood and befriended racists and bigots, yet defended freedom of speech. Wayne gained the respect of many liberals, who enjoyed sparring with him and were won over by his personal charm and professionalism, particularly on set. He let some directors walk all over him (notably John Ford), while battling with others, such as Don Siegel and Budd Boetticher (Davis 1998). Wayne was gregarious, but famously played a loner.

Ford gave him his breakthrough role, as the Ringo Kid in *Stagecoach* (1939). Prassel (1993: 286) observes that this 'transformed the image of the western outlaw' to that of the 'good badman', leading to an assumption by audiences that Wayne's characters are generally lawless for some worthy reason (see Chapter 7 on the 'good' outlaw). Wayne called Ford 'Pappy' and endured Ford's irascible personality both on and off set. Their partnership produced some of the greatest performances of Wayne's career, including *The Searchers*, *She Wore a Yellow Ribbon* (1949) and *The Man Who Shot Liberty Valance* (1962). Their relationship was competitive as well as admiring, like many father–son relationships.

Wayne always maintained that it was he who had introduced Ford to Monument Valley (Figure 3.1), which he discovered accidentally while working as an assistant on a Western, although Ford's version of the story discounts Wayne's involvement (Eyman 2014).

Charlton Heston was born in Chicago rather than small-town America like John Wayne. His childhood was unsettled, living in Ohio, Georgia, Michigan and Wisconsin, after his parents divorced and his mother remarried; rather like Wayne's experience as a young boy. Similar to Wayne, Heston used a name

Figure 3.1 Image of John Wayne at Goulding's Lodge, Monument Valley, Utah (photo W. Frost).

throughout his life that he was not born with. Charlton was the surname of his mother and Heston was his stepfather's surname. He does not reveal his real name in his 1995 autobiography, although it is acknowledged to be John Carter (curiously the same name as the lead character in Edgar Rice Burroughs' novel *A Princess of Mars*, 1917). His friends called him Chuck. Heston appears to have admired his stepfather and certainly he did not seek approbation from the directors he dealt with as a young man, along the lines of Wayne's relationship with John Ford.

Heston's career was not as intrinsically linked with the Western as John Wayne, yet his Western films are acknowledged as some of his finest work. Like Wayne, he had chiselled features and a strong and rugged physique (Figure 3.2), but it was his deep and authoritative voice that allowed him to take on – and succeed in – such a diverse range of roles, from generals to artists and presidents to circus managers. Making a Western had always been an ambition: 'From the day I signed to make movies, I'd been aching to play in one', for he saw the Western as a work of art:

> Along with jazz, the Western is the only totally indigenous American art form. Nobody else can do it, and now some of us have lost the touch. That's too bad. More than any other kind of film, the Western cries out for a camera and uses it most gloriously. Indeed, the Western reaches for its basic images many millennia back before the camera to man's first instinctive creative urges in the cave paintings in Lascaux and the Cretan murals: the running horse, the weaponed confrontation, and the steady eye, unfearful.
>
> (Heston 1995: 118)

Over the years, Heston worked with some of the best-known directors of the genre – William Wyler (*The Big Country*, 1958) and Sam Peckinpah (*Major Dundee*, 1965) – but interestingly not John Ford, although the director had tried to woo him. Heston's response was that Henry Fonda had warned him off the 'mean son of a bitch' (Eyman 2014: 495).

Heston and Wayne made just one movie together, *The Greatest Story Ever Told* (1965), in which Heston played John the Baptist and Wayne had a much pilloried cameo as the Centurion at Jesus' crucifixion, although they were sometimes considered for the same roles as they got older. Heston was a potential co-star of Wayne in *The Comancheros* (1961), but his profile post-*Ben Hur* made Heston unwilling to play second fiddle to the older actor. Heston was also one of a coterie of actors who were earmarked for the role of John Elder in *The Sons of Katie Elder* (1965) and Rooster Cogburn in the 1975 sequel to *True Grit*, both played in the end by Wayne (Eyman 2014). At one time, Wayne and Heston were suggested for a remake of Peckinpah's elegiac *Ride the High Country* (Weddle 1996). Heston appeared in Sam Peckinpah's *Major Dundee* (1965), yet Wayne kept his distance from the director, commenting that the 'realism' of his films was not to his liking: 'Peckinpah got the attention of the public by throwing away what I still think pictures are all about – illusion' (Eyman 2014: 510).

LEVINE COMMUNICATIONS OFFICE, INC.

CHARLTON HESTON

Figure 3.2 Autographed photo of Charlton Heston, acquired at signing of his autobiography (in possession of J. Laing, photo Levine Communications Office).

One of the characteristics that people most associate with Wayne and Heston
is their right-wing political views. The intertwining of the Western and American politics has a long history. Examples include Presidents Theodore Roosevelt
and Ronald Reagan, who 'exploited his connections with Western iconography'
(Horrocks 1995: 19). Wayne was a strong supporter of the Vietnam War, a
stance which was strongly criticised by many young men, such as Ron Kovic,
author of *Born on the Fourth of July* (1976), who felt that Wayne had betrayed
them (Luhr 2004). It has been argued that Wayne's politics 'informed his acting'
(Eyman 2014: 279), in that the characters he liked to play were the personification of self-reliance and anti-authoritarianism. He dreamed for years about

making *The Alamo* (1960) as a paean to dead heroes – 'a call to arms that would revive America's combative strength' (Eyman 2014: 340), even though the film cost him financially and never attracted the plaudits or the level of respect that he hoped for. Heston became famous for his support of the right to bear arms and became President of the National Rifle Association between 1997 and 2003.

The anti-hero

The classic Western narrative features the hero, usually a cowboy or a soldier, who displays virtues such as courage, chivalry, a desire for justice and dogged determination. This was often the character played by John Wayne and the one that he thought his fans most wanted to see. Yet it is his role as Ethan Edwards in *The Searchers* that has received the most acclaim over the years, despite Ethan being complex, neither a 'clear-cut villain' (Walle 2000: 164), nor a hero. The film is often described as a 'misunderstood masterpiece' (p. 165), and is still being dissected to this day. It is contrasted with his other famous anti-heroic film, *Red River*.

The Searchers (1956)

The Searchers opens with a song, containing the lines 'What makes a man to wander, what makes a man to roam, what makes a man to wander, and turn his back on home?'. In the case of Ethan Edwards (John Wayne), we don't know, although we can guess at some of his back-story. He has taken part in the Civil War and is in love with his sister-in-law Martha (Dorothy Jordan), a love that is revealed through small details on both sides, such as the way she carries his coat and the way he looks at her. For an actor who is often criticised for lack of subtlety, Wayne is remarkably restrained in the way he shows us so clearly Ethan's yearning for Martha.

A Comanche raid results in the deaths of Martha and her husband and the abduction of their daughters Debbie and Lucy. Ethan and the adopted son Martin set out to find the pair. The film revolves around *vengeance* (Wright 1974). Lucy's body is quickly found. Debbie (Natalie Wood) has been taken by the Comanche Scar (Henry Brandon), possibly as his squaw. The question of what Ethan will do if and when he finds Debbie dominates the film. Will he kill her, as she has been *tainted* by her life among the Native Americans? Is the shame of letting her live too great?

It was a confronting subject for a film in the 1950s and remains so to this day. Walle (2000: 166) argues that the film 'was not a trend setter because it conflicted too strongly with the mindset of the American people'. To modern audiences, the racism is shocking and the themes highly confronting. Walle (2000: 163) observes that the film 'revolves around anti-heroic themes; it concerns a hate which borders on insanity and a lust for revenge which can best be described as fanatical obsession'. Wayne himself labelled Ethan an anti-hero

(McGivern 2000). While Ethan's actions are not senselessly vicious or violent –
there is a purpose to what he is doing, even if we find it hard to understand and
even more impossible to forgive – the film does not glorify him or his actions
(Luhr 2004). It is a very different role for Wayne and one which he embraced.

Wayne was the perfect choice for playing Ethan, perhaps because he understood the importance of the unyielding quest in the Western narrative – the
man who will not give up in pursuit of a goal, no matter what it cost him. This
became the template of '*the* John Wayne type – a completely competent loner
of utter integrity, the only man capable of accomplishing the necessary task'
(Eyman 2014: 276). There is also the idea in the Western that 'the hero who is
pushed beyond his limits again and again eventually loses his capacity to feel'
(Tompkins 1992: 213–214). He can merely *endure* (Luhr 2004). Ethan
becomes deadened, frozen, much like the landscape around him. John Ford
intentionally gave him little dialogue to work with, relying on Wayne's physical presence and that granite-like face to tell the story: 'We largely dispensed
with language. Ethan was a man of strength and few words' (quoted in
McGivern 2000: 265).

The final scene shows Ethan, framed in a doorway, with the others having
gone inside to celebrate Debbie's return. Ethan cannot join them and his isola-
tion evokes *Shane* (1953) (see Chapter 7). Ethan has seen and done too much to
be able to re-join the community. This is also consistent with the life he appears
to have led before he began his quest to find Debbie. The town or home life
entraps a man; merely another form of death in comparison to the stark dangers
of life in the desert or on the open range. As Tompkins (1992: 87) observes:
'The Western is always bombinating between these alternatives'.

Red River (1948)

This was the first time Wayne played a man meant to be older than himself. Ford
famously said that until he saw this film, he didn't know that Wayne could act
(McBride 2001). Whether Ford was merely being facetious or was serious in his
assessment, *Red River* was a turning point in Wayne's career, when he started to
play characters who were largely unsympathetic, unlikeable and scarred by
something in their past (Freedman 2007; Luhr 2004; McGivern 2000). Wills
(1997: 251) labels this type of character the 'driven avenger', which reaches its
apotheosis in the character of Ethan in *The Searchers*.

Tom Dunson (John Wayne) wants to establish his own cattle ranch and leaves
Fen, the woman he loves behind, arguing that it would be too dangerous for a
woman. He says he will send for her. Tragically, her wagon train is attacked by
Native Americans and she is killed. He remains single thereafter, although he
does adopt an orphaned young boy, Matt Garth (Montgomery Clift). Thus
Dunson can 'maintain the supremely confident and self-sufficient masculinity
that he exemplifies throughout the movie' (Freedman 2007: 22). Of course, his
past also leaves him embittered, brooding and intractable, which will subsequently be his undoing.

Years pass and Dunson decides to take his cattle north to Missouri on the Chisholm Trail, to find a market for them. He is obsessed with the idea that everyone involved in the cattle drive must stick to this goal: 'I don't like quitters, especially when they're not good enough to finish what they start', and makes all the men sign contracts to that effect. Dunson's compulsion to fulfil his quest leads him to questionable moral behaviour. He wants to kill three men who have deserted the cattle drive and pigheadedly wants to continue on the original course that was set, even when it proves to be foolhardy. He is a kind of Captain Ahab, who does not know when to give in (Freedman 2007). Tom and Matt engage in a power struggle; Wayne's stubborn masculine strength juxtaposed with Clift's more 'feminised masculinity' (Leith 2002: 135). There are thus homoerotic undertones, as well as the familiar father–son rivalry.

Matt finally wins the 'Oedipal battle' (Freedman 2007: 22), telling Tom that he is taking over and they will be going to Abilene, rather than Missouri. Tom is furious, promising: 'Every time you turn around, expect to see me, 'cause one time you'll turn around and I'll be there. I'm gonna kill ya, Matt'. Eventually there is a rapprochement between the pair, after a savage brawl, and the branding of the cattle is changed from a D to a DM, reflecting Dunson and Matt. Matt marries a girl he met on his journey, Tess, a saloon girl (Joanne Dru), but Tom remains alone.

The tragic hero

In Greek tragedy, the hero may be doomed, sometimes due to a fatal flaw or because it is the will of the gods to see them fall, due to the hero's excessive pride or because they excite the jealousy of the gods in some way. Occasionally it is simply their fate, which they cannot escape. Both Heston and Wayne have played the tragic hero in a number of films, but this trope is best illustrated by the two films analysed below.

The Alamo (1960)

John Wayne plays the American legend, David Crockett. It was a labour of love for Wayne, as it took him years to raise the capital and he put much of his own fortune into it. He was captivated by the heroism of the men who refused to give in to Santa Anna's troops, and saw them as a symbol of all that was great about America. Wayne wanted to play the small part of Sam Houston, to concentrate on directing the film, but was persuaded to take on the iconic role of Crockett by his backers, who felt that Wayne needed to be the star to attract audiences. Wayne chose to film it in Texas, even though that made it even more expensive, as a gesture to the locals, although it was not filmed in San Antonio, where the ruins of the Alamo are located (Figure 3.3), but on a ranch in Bracketville, where an earlier version of the film was made (Rothel 1991). The set remained after filming finished, and other Westerns were filmed there, but Wayne himself never returned, perhaps jaded by the difficulties of filming *The Alamo* (Wills 1997).

Figure 3.3 The Alamo, San Antonio (photo J. Laing).

Crockett realises all too quickly that the men are doomed, but also that he cannot leave. He soliloquises that 'There's right and there's wrong, you gotta do one or the other. You do the one and you're living, you do the other and you may be walking around but you're as dead as a beaver hat'. This fits with Wayne's worldview – 'Crockett is Wayne philosophizing about his own Wayne-ness' (Wills 1997: 221). The film was generally well patronised but was never acclaimed as the masterpiece that Wayne wanted it to be. The failure to be nominated for an Academy Award for best director rankled and he blamed it in part on 'the left, by all those who were soft on Communism' (Wills 1997: 227).

Major Dundee (1965)

MAJOR DUNDEE: If I ever do get out of here, the war won't last forever.
TERESA SANTIAGO: It will for you, Major.

The Civil War is reaching its climax, but Major Dundee (Charlton Heston) is trapped in a dead-end job of running a prison. His disgrace is due to his obsessive tendencies, though what he did is never disclosed. He abandons his post to lead troops into Mexico to hunt down Apache raiders, and rescue some kidnapped boys, akin to *The Searchers*. Like Ethan Edwards, he is obsessively driven to seek revenge, even when the boys are released. And like Tom Doni-phon in *Red River*, he is 'unable to make the adult commitment to marriage and family – to society building' (Mesce 2001: 111). In a village, Dundee meets Teresa, a female doctor (Senta Berger). They fall in love and there is the pro-spect of a changed life. However, after being wounded, Dundee takes to drink and lives with a prostitute. When Teresa finds out she abandons him. Perhaps this is subconsciously what he desires? The prostitute offers him no strings – nor any moral censure. His 'retreat to the whore' is his 'final, ultimate collapse of character' (Mesce 2001: 112), demonstrating his self-loathing and self-destructive tendencies. While the film went over-time and over-budget, involved a difficult director, and was not a critical success upon release (Crowther 1986), it remained a film that Heston was proud of, another example of his predilection for 'dark, driven men' (Heston 1995: 334).

The trouble with women

Both Wayne and Heston consistently play roles where the hero finds it difficult to understand women or consciously abstains from settling down with a woman. This is a familiar trope of the American West, and one of its paradoxes, in that the cowboy or rancher, the symbol of masculinity, is fated to live alone, or with another man. Freedman (2007: 19) labels Wayne a *post-heterosexual*, in that 'he is a man with a heterosexual past, who has outgrown that phase of existence and so is free to glory in his unalloyed masculinity without being suspected of the least abnormality'. We have already mentioned examples of this trope in *The Searchers*, *Red River* and *Major Dundee*.

In *Will Penny* (1968), Heston made a film that is often unsung amongst West-erns. It is one of his finest characterisations, as he brings the ageing cow-puncher to life. Heston read the novel on which the film was based on a plane and wrote in his journal: 'I read the first forty pages of a damn good Western ... if the rest is up to the beginning, it could really be something' (Heston 1979: 256). Penny is an example of a man who has never had a serious romantic entanglement with a woman, until he meets Catherine. However, he lets happiness slip through his fingers, too scared to take a risk.

Will Penny (1968)

Will Penny is an ageing cowboy (Figure 3.4). Heston reveals the vulnerability of men like Will, who are growing old with nothing to show for it, and his essential decency and kindness, which are not qualities that he has had to display much in his solitary life on the range. Will has always been on the move, and never learned to read, signing his name with an X. He comes to the aid of two of the men he has worked with, Blue (Lee Majors) and Dutchy (Anthony Zerbe), when they are shot at by the Reverend Quint (Donald Pleasance at his most crazed) and his three sons. One of the sons is killed, and Quint vows revenge. Will helps to take Dutchy to a doctor, and on the way, meets Catherine (Joan Hackett) and

Figure 3.4 Charlton Heston as Will Penny (photo Lydia Clarke Heston).

her son Horace or H.G. (Jon Francis) in a roadhouse. The pair are travelling with an escort across to California, so that they can join Catherine's husband and start a new life as farmers.

Reaching the shantytown of Alfred, Will has a prostitute stay the night, but makes her leave at first light, much to her chagrin. This is the kind of interaction with a woman that he has been used to – no strings attached. Leaving Dutchy with the doctor, Will takes on a cowpoke job at the Flatiron ranch for Alex (Ben Johnson) and is sent out to ride the line until spring. Alex tells Will to let him know if they have any 'nesters' in and around the shack. He heads to the shack, to find the chimney smoking. Will discovers Catherine and H.G., who have been abandoned by their escort and must stay here until the winter is over. Will tells them that when he comes back 'you need to be gone'. His decency shows through ('I ain't gonna hurt you none').

Will is attacked on the range by the Quint family. They knife him, steal his gear and then leave him for dead. He staggers back to the shack in the freezing cold, and collapses on the doorstep. Catherine nurses him back to health and Will starts to learn what it is like to have a settled domestic life, with someone to care for him and look after his needs and someone he can take care of in his turn.

He develops an affectionate relationship with H.G., nicknaming him 'Button', and is moved to tears when the boy hugs him. When H.G. asks him about whether he has killed before and how it felt, Will's response is terse – 'Bad'. Like the title character in *Shane*, Will does not glorify violence to impress a young boy.

The growing relationship between Will and Catherine comes to a head when Will tells her that he should sleep elsewhere: 'I've been alone since I was a button like him.... Now here you are, you and him. You ain't even mine!' Catherine kisses him and murmurs 'Stay, Will'. This idyll comes to an abrupt end when the Quint family burst in and take them hostage. Will eventually escapes their clutches and rides off to get help. He encounters his old friends Blue and Dutchy, who have been looking for him and they help him to kill Quint and his sons.

Will now must make a decision. Catherine asks him to go with her and pleads that her husband would 'never notice if we never showed up'. When she asks if he loves her, Will is quick to reply: 'What do I know about love? Love? I guess you could call it that ... and more. I want you and the button for my own but...' He tells Catherine that he is too old to provide her and the boy with a secure home: 'It's too late Cath, too late for me. I ain't a good gamble for you'. He rides off with Blue and Dutchy and takes one last look back at them. Like Shane and Ethan, he is doomed to keep wandering through the West. Unlike them, it is not a violent act or past that he runs from, but his fear that he could never make Catherine and H.G. happy. His *sacrifice* for others is another recurring motif in the Western.

A man of honour

Many of the roles made famous by Wayne and Heston across their careers stress the importance of standing up for one's principles and not abandoning them when situations become challenging. We focus below on the role of John T. Chance played by Wayne in *Rio Bravo* (1959), to illustrate the upright Western hero.

Rio Bravo (1959)

We get the first glimpse of Wayne in this film as the leg of Sheriff John T. Chance, kicking a spittoon away from his former deputy Dude (Dean Martin). Martin is a hopeless drunk and suffers from the shakes. As he enters the saloon, one of the men taunts him by throwing a dollar into the spittoon. As Dude bends to pick it up, Sheriff Chance stops him from this ultimate degradation. We see later the nature of their relationship – Dude feels guilty for letting Chance down, and Chance is trying to get Dude back on the path towards rehabilitation, refusing to let him abandon his self-respect. This is a familiar plotline in many of Wayne's films in the middle to late stage of his career, when he displays a 'fatherly concern' (Freedman 2007: 22) for a younger man or occasionally a young woman like Mattie Ross (Kim Darby) in *True Grit* (1969).

There is a familial banter between Dude and Chance – Dude calls the older man 'Papa' at one stage – and when Wheeler questions Chance about the need to look after Dude, Chance turns the question on its head: 'He's been doing a pretty good job of taking care of me!' Chance is not however afraid to show Dude tough love when he needs it. When Dude says 'A man ought to have sense enough to know when he's no good no more', Chance accepts his resignation. He brings up the spittoon incident from time to time to remind Dude how low he had sunk and to channel that shame into something more positive. Chance is a man who takes his mentoring role seriously. He is not the cardboard tough sheriff, nor is he the Western male who cannot show his feelings. While *Rio Bravo*, like many Westerns of its era, is based on the idea that the 'heroes are now professional fighters, men willing to defend society only as a job they accept for pay', Chance's sheriff does appear to personally uphold 'ideas of law and justice' (Wright 1974: 85) and goes beyond the call of duty to safeguard them.

Dude will redeem himself by mastering his addiction and standing by Chance, when they must guard Joe Burdette (Claude Akins) in the town jail until the marshall arrives. The only other ally they have for most of the film is the elderly Stumpy (Walter Brennan), named for obvious reasons, leading Pat Wheeler (Ward Bond) to quip to his friend Chance 'A game-legged old man and a drunk. That's all you got?' Chance's reply is more optimistic: 'That's what I got'. He believes in his men and that they will be there alongside him in a crisis. Wheeler is killed by Burdette's hired guns while walking through town, as a message that those who try to assist Chance will not survive. The young gunslinger Colorado Ryan (Ricky Nelson) initially refuses to help guard Burdette, but when Wheeler is killed, he changes his mind. Chance rebuffs his offer of help but is quietly admiring of the young man: 'I'd say he's so good he doesn't feel he has to prove it'. This is a strange reaction, given the vulnerable situation in which Chance has found himself, but illustrates that unlike Kane in *High Noon*, the sheriff can fight his own battles (Wayne and director Howard Hawks disliked *High Noon* for what they saw as Kane's lack of self-reliance). Subsequently Colorado comes to Chance's rescue on several occasions and lives up to Chance's assessment of his character, being sworn in as a deputy. Order is restored to the town, after several shoot-outs.

The other character who comes to the aid of Chance is Feathers (Angie Dickinson), an alluring young woman who is wanted along with her ex-partner for being a card-sharp. Chance falls in love with her and when she explains that she was duped about the card games, he chivalrously tells her that he will recall the 'wanted' handbills with her description on it. This is one of the few films where Wayne does get the girl, and she is his equal. Feathers makes Chance articulate his feelings for her, transcending the cliché of the silent Western hero: 'You're going to have to talk. You're going to have to say you want me'. The film ends with Chance throwing her black stockings out the window. We know exactly what he wants and what he's going to get.

Sacrifice

A consistent theme across Westerns involves the lead characters making a sacrifice for the right cause. Sometimes this is atonement for past misdemeanours, which redeems these men in the eyes of society – or often a woman. In other narratives, it is seen as simply the right thing to do. This sacrifice is an integral part of the classical *hero's journey* (Campbell 1949), where the hero suffers hardships and is tested in some way, sometimes changing their lives forever (McGhee 1988). The katabatic narrative also involves a sacrificial victim. We focus here on the last film Ford made with Wayne.

The Man Who Shot Liberty Valance (1962)

Unlike most of Ford's masterpieces, *The Man Who Shot Liberty Valance* was shot largely in the backlots, rather than on location (Wills 1997). The landscape is thus not the feature that it was in other Ford films, notably *Stagecoach* and *The Searchers*. The focus is *psychological*, on the motivations of the lead characters and the decisions they make that have long-lasting consequences. There is a melancholic quality to the film, which symbolises both the closing of the frontier and the demise of the Western, although in hindsight we know that the latter flourished again. While Wayne and James Stewart are too old for their roles, they bring to them the experience of actors at the top of their game, which helps to make this one of the most satisfying films of the Ford canon.

Wayne's character, Tom Doniphon, is likened by Wills (1997) to a Western Cyrano de Bergerac, whose sacrifice goes unnoticed and unappreciated for many years. Eastern lawyer Ransom Stoddard (Jimmy Stewart) has a gunfight with vicious bully Liberty Valance (Lee Marvin). Standing in a side alley, Doniphon shoots Valance, but everybody else thinks Stoddard has done it. Acclaimed a hero, Stoddard is elected senator and wins the heart of Hallie (Vera Miles), Doniphon's girl. Highlighting the subtlety of the film, we have different interpretations of what happens. Jennifer's view is that in Doniphon's eyes, Stoddard is a more appropriate suitor for Hallie, being an idealistic young lawyer with a political career in front of him. Warwick thinks that Doniphon does not forsee that his intervention will lead to the loss of his girl. Either way, 'Ford's last great film once again involves Wayne's character denying himself a relationship with a woman' (Eyman 2014: 359).

Stoddard is not a true Western hero, in the way that Doniphon is, because he is neither *self-reliant* nor *self-sacrificing* (Hocker Rushing 1983). Doniphon is bemused by Stoddard's insistence that he only wants to see Liberty Valance in jail, not killed, and observes: 'Out here a man settles his own problems'. This echoes Wayne's line as Breck Coleman in *The Big Trail* (1930): 'I kill my own rats'. Just by doing nothing, Doniphon would probably have won Hallie but this is not his way. He may have been too proud to be treated as second-best by Hallie or to see Stoddard turned into a martyr, or he may simply have loved her too much to want her to suffer (Freedman 2007). Doniphon's second sacrifice occurs when he lets Stoddard know that he was not the true killer of Valance, so that the latter doesn't have to live with this on his conscience. Doniphon takes the burden upon himself, saying to Stoddard: 'I can live with it'.

A true Western hero is also *taciturn*. Stoddard however talks 'too much' according to Doniphon; an accusation which is more likely to be aimed at a woman in a Western (such as Angie Dickinson's Feathers in *Rio Bravo*, who keeps apologising for being loquacious). Doniphon is the last of his breed; a man whose *actions* speak louder than words. He brings Hallie a cactus rose, rather than articulating his feelings. He represents the past, while Stoddard represents the future; the bringing of civilisation to the wild (McGhee 1988). Stoddard has been freed to become a delegate to a convention to vote on statehood. This leads to the end of the open range and the advent of the railroad, through 'the building of the American nation' (Freedman 2007: 26).

At Doniphon's funeral, Hallie is told the truth about the shooting and what Doniphon did to make her happy. She sees his old ruined house with the room he never finished, the one that was meant for her. Stoddard and Hallie are faced with his coffin, a plain wooden box, and the reality of a pauper's funeral. Stoddard makes a last remorseful attempt at honouring Doniphon's memory: 'Put his boots on, and his gunbelt and his spurs'. He places a comforting hand on Doniphon's ranch-hand, Pompey (Woody Strode), but doesn't touch Hallie. The guilt is too great.

When a newspaper owner tells Stoddard: 'This is the West, sir. When the legend becomes fact, print the legend', the irony is clear. Stoddard's life has been essentially a lie, even if it wasn't his idea to have Doniphon carry out the impersonation. He didn't confess the true situation to Hallie, which might have led to her ending up in Doniphon's arms. When Hallie places a cactus rose on Doniphon's coffin, like the one he once brought her, Stoddard notices it. He has to face the truth – Doniphon was the real love of her life. The film has a kind of 'nihilistic darkness' (Wills 1997: 267), as none of the main characters have a happy ending. Both Stoddard and Hallie ultimately pay for Doniphon's sacrifice and have been disappointed with their lot in life and the choices they made.

Redemption

In the Western myth, men (and women) can always attain redemption by a pure act. Kirby York (John Wayne) in *Fort Apache* does not betray his commanding officer's failures, perhaps because he considers him *redeemed* through his bravery and loyalty to his men. We focus here on two other films that illustrate this.

Angel and the Badman (1947)

This film was made by Wayne's own production company, with his old friend Jimmy Grant as the writer and director. The credit sequence features Monument Valley, in homage to his old mentor John Ford. The plot is simple – Wayne plays a gunslinger called Quirt Evans who is taken in by a Quaker family, the

Worths, after he has been shot by Laredo Stevens (Bruce Cabot) and is slowly nursed back to health. He eventually gives up his old life to marry their daughter Penelope (Gail Russell), although not without some struggles. While not a very believable transformation, even if Gail Russell is strikingly attractive, it does endorse the *good outlaw* myth, which we explore more deeply in Chapter 7. There were rumours that Russell and Wayne were lovers, although Wayne always denied this (Eyman 2014). Sadly, Russell was an alcoholic who died young, yet there are no hints of this on screen.

Evans' reputation is such that he doesn't need to use violence to get his own way in this community. He asks a neighbour of the Worths, living on a property above their own, to take off the first two planks of his dam, in order to let more water flow into the Worth property. The neighbour, Carson, fearful of Evans, is only too ready to oblige. His action, which the Worths interpret as altruistic, leads them to shower him with food and Mrs Worth takes off a boil on his neck that has been troubling him. The lesson here is that being neighbourly *pays*; one absorbed by both Carson and Evans. When Evans tells the family: 'Looks like your prayers straightened everything out', he is told in return that the Lord some-times uses 'strange instruments'.

Evans doesn't become transformed overnight. As he observes to Penelope: 'If I'm going to be holy, I'm going to get some fun out of it'. Marshall McClintock (Harry Carey) drops by, suspicious that Evans has been involved in shady deal-ings, and is using Penelope merely as an alibi. The Quakers by contrast applaud Evans' conversion. They give him a Bible monogrammed with his initials, and Mr Worth states that he has demonstrated that 'All men are good if they're shown the light'. Evans, fearful of being hemmed in, goes back to his old life of saloons, but it is no longer attractive to him.

He returns to Penelope, but his presence puts her life in danger. After she is nearly drowned by the actions of Laredo Stevens and his men and is left unconscious, Evans is out for revenge, even though he is told that Penelope would not want this. He has a showdown in the street with Laredo Stevens, but then Penelope turns up. Evans drops his guns. Two shots ring out and Stevens is killed, but it is the marshall who has stepped in. Evans is thus untainted by the violence and free to marry Penelope. The film ends with Evans' declaration: 'From now on I'm a farmer'. His guns lie on the ground, but they are no longer needed. The marshall makes the point: 'Only a man who carries a gun ever needs one'.

The Big Country (1958)

Heston wasn't top billing (only fourth) but his agent persuaded him that *The Big Country*, directed by William Wyler, was not to be passed up: 'Don't you know actors take parts with Wyler without even reading the damn *script*?' (Heston 1995: 164). It was a move that paid dividends. Heston impressed Wyler enough for him to offer Heston the lead role in *Ben Hur* (1959), which won him an Oscar for best actor.

This is a sprawling film, replete with widescreen vistas of the plains and the memorable and stirring opening theme music composed by Jerome Moross. Yet the story is remarkably intimate, focusing on the importance of self-respect and not bowing to peer pressure. We meet Charlton Heston's character, Steve Leech, the foreman of a ranch, at the start of the movie. Hot-headed and passionate, but unable to articulate what he feels, he is in love with the blonde and spoilt Pat Terrill (Carroll Baker), the daughter of his employer, Major Terrill (Charles Bickford), but she doesn't respond to Steve's clumsy overtures. He tries to hold her hand and she says he is hurting her. There is a scene later in the film where Pat hits Steve with a whip, and he grabs her and kisses her. She then bites his lip. It appears that the more Pat is cruel towards him, the more Steve pursues her. There is a sexual tension in this relationship which is not present in Pat's relationship with Jim McKay (Gregory Peck), a man she has met in the East and who has just arrived in town.

Unlike Steve in his cowboy rig, Jim is buttoned up in a suit and hat. Steve tells him to take the hat off or 'one of these wild cowboys might take it into their head to shoot it off ya'. Steve is jealous of this newcomer and tries to humiliate him, but his efforts come to naught. We learn quickly that Jim is comfortable with who he is and doesn't feel the need to play the tough hero to impress others, even Pat. This riles Steve even more, as he doesn't understand this type of behaviour. In his culture, a man is only a man if *others* think he is so. The Major tells Jim: 'This is the West ... a man is still expected to defend himself. If he allows people to think he won't, he's in trouble. Bad trouble'. Steve realises after a fight that Jim is his equal in terms of muscle and fortitude. He slowly comes to respect Jim, and it changes his mindset about the nature of manliness.

Steve's road to redemption continues when he observes a lynch mob shoot a hole in the water tower belonging to the Hannassey clan. Major Terrill wants to destroy the Hannasseys, headed by Rufus (Burl Ives), over a land dispute involving the water that they both need for their cattle. Steve is shocked at this unprovoked act and asks Major Terrill if that is what he wants. Terrill's reply is 'Let them have their fun!' This is the first hint that Steve has a conscience and doesn't like what he is doing. He is later taunted by Hannassey about 'shining the Major's boots' and this hits home. Steve also listens when one of his men says that he doesn't like chasing cattle away from water. He is starting to see that his hero, the Major, has feet of clay.

Steve proves his worth when the Major rides on the Hannassey property, to rescue Julie (Jean Simmons) who has been kidnapped by the uncouth and violent Buck Hannassey (Chuck Connors). The Major is told not to head into the canyon, that it could be a trap. His men refuse to accompany him. Steve won't let the Major ride off alone and be humiliated in front of his men, even though he knows the Major is making the wrong decision. Once he does this, the rest of the men are shamed into following Steve. Steve is shot while trying to assist the Major in the shoot-out, but not fatally. He has redeemed himself through his sacrifice and his recognition of what it takes to be a *good* man. He also appears to have won the hand of Pat as his reward.

The Wayne/Heston legacy

Both Wayne and Heston were noted for playing macho tough men, roles which matched their conservative politics. However, many of their roles were elegiac, projecting a complex vision of Westerners in a world that is changing around them or in which they cannot fully share or participate. They contributed to the Western myth, by showing that these frontier men could be complex, fragile and flawed, but also magnificent when put to the test and capable of a nobility of spirit and a tender solicitude for others. Wayne himself makes clear that he tried in his films to 'have some human weaknesses and admit those weaknesses' (quoted in McGivern 2000: 262).

The men who Wayne and Heston played are capable of being role models for the troops who they lead or the younger men with whom they work, displaying kindness, courage and honour under pressure. This self-sufficiency may however be channelled into obsessive behaviour. Sometimes they are doomed, but they may equally be transformed or redeemed, when others believe in them or they begin to have faith in themselves. We see this in other genres, but it is the Western hero who most exemplifies this dichotomy.

While this chapter has emphasised the post-heterosexuality of the characters played by Wayne and Heston, it would be wrong to assume that their films eulogise this state of affairs or see it as the natural conclusion of the story for these men. The rare moments when they let their guard down, let a woman in, and display their vulnerability is when they are at their most appealing to audiences. We want Will Penny to find a love he will not run away from, just as we hope that Ethan can find something in this world to assuage his loss. The legacy of these two actors is that they teach us that a hero can be found in many guises, with or without the conventional happy ending. It is why their films never grow stale and why we still look to them to help us understand the complexity of the American West.

4   Route 66

If you ever plan to motor west, travel my way,
Take the highway that's the best
Get your kicks on Route 66!
('Get Your Kicks on Route 66!',
written by Bobby and Cynthia Troup, 1946)

Introduction

The fantasy of driving along one of the interstate American highways, with their spectacular vistas and monumental landscapes, did not last long. The most famous example, Route 66, was established in 1927, but was mostly replaced by multi-lane highways in the 1950s and 1960s (a time period roughly equating with the Golden Age of Western films). The new interstate highways now offer little by way of scenery. The driver is insulated from visceral experience as much by the highway as by their car, and could be anywhere in the world at times. Perhaps because of this, Route 66 retains its mystique as authentic and romantic and is the setting for many films and novels focussing on the *road trip*.

The appeal of the road can be understood as an element of the broader myth of America as 'the second chance, the New Garden of Eden' (Holtan 1970: 273). This concept also encapsulates the idea that the city is corrupt, and in contrast the country is an idyll. Just like the Garden of Eden, there is disillusionment to be found in the frailties of humankind, and the destruction of innocence (Holtan 1970). This duality is important for understanding the Western myth, as 'the frontier eras represented escape and opportunity for many, but they also involved deprivation, untrammelled violence, and the virtual extermination of Native Americans' (Klinger 1997: 191; see also White 1991 and others of the New Western History movement). The death of the myth of agrarianism is vividly depicted in Steinbeck's *The Grapes of Wrath* (1939), where the Joad family realise that they are now essentially working for subsistence wages, with little hope of ever owning their own piece of land again.

There are competing visions of the road in Hollywood films, dependent on whether the protagonists are *on the road* or *on the run* (Slocum 2007). The difference lies in opportunity for self-efficacy. Those on the road may be *transformed* in the sense of 'a translation of the self into something purer and more authentic, more intense, more real' (Tompkins 1992: 4). *It Happened One Night* (1934) is an example of the road as a 'utopian space' (Cohan and Hark 1997), where the heiress (Claudette Colbert) gets to enjoy the company of ordinary people, free of class barriers, and learns what she is made of.

These films may also be seen as *quest movies* (Laderman 2002). There is a search for personal benefits, often a new beginning or a better kind of relationship. Within the context of the Western myth and the American Dream, such a search may be obsessive, unfocussed and ultimately unfulfilled; yet the idea remains appealing. A recent example is *The Guilt Trip* (2012), where Joyce, an over-protective and interfering mother (Barbra Streisand) bonds with her son Andy (Seth Rogen) on a road trip from the East Coast to Las Vegas. Time together on the road in the confined space of the car allows the characters to engage with each other, without external distractions (Laderman 2002). Joyce and Andy are able to deal with long-standing issues and get their frustrations with each other and their lives out in the open. Joyce finds out that her son moved to California to attend the best organic chemistry school in the country, rather than to get as far away from her as he could. Life on the road shows them what they have been missing out on. After Joyce wins a steak-eating contest at The Cattleman's Roundup Steak Ranch, she observes 'Maybe I need a bit more adventure in my life?' Little things have changed for her – she now picks up hitch-hikers – and gets her ears pierced in Las Vegas. Andy notes that the week hadn't gone as he had planned, only to be met with Joyce's rejoinder: 'This was the best week of my life'.

For the traveller *on the run*, 'transformation was not readily possible, if at all, and the prevailing social relations and economic structures were unforgiving' (Slocum 2007: 125). This is true in some but not all cases. In *Thelma & Louise* (1991), two women (Geena Davis and Susan Sarandon) are pursued cross-country by the police and it is only a matter of time before they get caught. Yet even as events make a turn for the worse there is a lot of humour in the film, particularly between the two female characters. This is characteristic of the road movie, crossing over with the *buddy movie*, which 'has always relied on the wit and liberation of its principal couple, whether a heterosexual one like Bonnie and Clyde or a homosocial pairing like Butch and Sundance' (Sturtevant 2007: 43). Despite their seemingly hopeless situation, Thelma and Louise become very different people the further they drive and distance themselves from their humdrum lives. When asked by Louise 'Found your calling?' Thelma replies: 'The call of the wild'. They have reached a state of contentment with who they now are and what they have done. As Thelma says: 'Something's crossed over in me. I can't go back. I mean, I just couldn't live'.

The road can be alienating as well as liberating in the Hollywood road movie. Some journeys are aimless, as depicted in *Two-Lane Blacktop* (1971). *Duel* (1971) is the nightmarish tale of road rage from an unseen and therefore anonymous truck driver against a car, where the logical (senseless) outcome is the death of one or both of them. Perils come from picking up hitch-hikers, such as the femme fatale Vera (Ann Savage) in *Detour* (1945), who recognises the car that Al Roberts (Tom Neal) is driving and blackmails him over the death of the car's owner. It is the fateful – and fatal – decision to give Vera a ride which proves to be Al's undoing, leading to the death of Vera herself and the final scene of Al in a diner: 'Someday a car will come to pick me up that I never bummed'.

In *Sullivan's Travels* (1941), John Sullivan (Joel McCrea) is a film director who wants to make a movie that is 'a commentary on modern conditions … a true canvas of the suffering of humanity'. He dresses as a hobo and takes to the road. After a whimsical series of setbacks, which see him right back in the town where he started ('maybe there's a universal law saying Stay Put!'), he finds himself beaten up, robbed, arrested and part of a chain-gang. The 'greatest expedition of modern times' is no longer a game. He realises all too quickly what real life is like for those travelling without money or connections. There is a happy ending, with Sullivan ending up with The Girl (Veronica Lake with her peeka-boo hair), but he has realised that those living rough don't want to see reality paraded before them on screen. They go to the cinema to escape: 'There's a lot to be said for making people laugh'. This film was referenced by Jack Kerouac in his novel *On the Road* (1957), with a comment about a 'gray, dirty dawn, like the dawn when Joel McCrea met Veronica Lake in a diner' (p. 80).

The automobile, while potentially a source of danger, is also a *cocoon* or *bubble* which shuts the driver and passengers off from the outside world. In contrast, the motorcycles in *Easy Rider* (1969) provide a means of escape – not from home (these people appear to have no home and seemingly no purpose in life) – but from *conventionality*. While the motorcycle is also a machine like a car, the rider is squarely placed in the landscape, free to transgress society's rules and boundaries, although this does not necessarily make them any happier. The mood of this type of film is *existential*, in that life on the road appears to be no more fulfilling than life in suburbia (Ireland 2003; Laderman 2002).

Get your kicks on Route 66!

Common geographical pathways were trodden in the road genre. Mostly the route is East to West following the journey made by the early settlers (Ireland 2003) and this is often the way that Route 66 is travelled in novels and films. Route 66 officially began life in 1927. The number 66 was chosen as it was 'easy to remember' (Henriksson 2014: 4). It is curious that it is pronounced *root* rather than the common American pronunciation of *rout*. As more and more households found themselves with an automobile, motoring across America became a national pastime, particularly post-Second World War. A plethora of motels, gas stations, cafés and diners sprang up along the way to service this growing tourist market (Figure 4.1), in what became a 'celebration of car culture' (Slocum 2007: 126). In some towns, the clustering of small independent motels became known as 'motel row' (Olsen 2011). Examples can still be seen today, such as Amarillo, Texas and Williams, Arizona. They are part of the attraction of travelling Route

Figure 4.1 Frontier Motel sign at Truxton along Route 66 (photo J. Laing).

66 (Caton and Santos 2007); considered by visitors to be highly authentic and a refreshing change from the 'ubiquitous corporate presence' of some of the modern chain hotels and motels (p. 378).

Some of the landmarks which have contributed to the fantasy of Route 66 include the Wigwam Village in Holbrook, Arizona. Opened in 1950, this was a child's dream where guests slept in one of 15 facsimiles of a Native American wigwam or tent, made of steel and concrete rather than the traditional hide (Olsen 2011). These wigwams were depicted on a postcard in the opening credits of *National Lampoon's Vacation* (1983), and have now been listed on the National Register of Historic Places. Another attraction, the Jack Rabbit Trading Post in Joseph City, Arizona, opened in 1949, and offered visitors a cornucopia of Native American souvenirs, including rubber tomahawks, headdresses and bows and arrows (Olsen 2011). Known for the rabbit on its roof, this symbol featured on billboards stretching for miles along Route 66, an advertising gimmick which made it almost impossible not to stop upon reaching the trading post (Olsen 2011). The final sign, 'Here It Is!', is still standing, as is the trading post and its jackrabbit, a favourite photo opportunity for travellers.

Postcards featuring these places were a popular souvenir, symbolising and promoting oneself as a Western tourist to those back home (Brown 1988), while the neon signs advertising their names became a familiar sight on the road. The

Luna Café in Mitchell, Illinois, had a sign featuring a cocktail glass with a maraschino cherry. When the cherry was lit up, 'the ladies [of the night] were waiting and available upstairs' (Olsen 2011: 62). It was also said to have been a pit stop for Al Capone and his gang in the 1920s and regularly hosted illegal gambling (Olsen 2011).

Another element that has helped to make Route 66 so iconic is the link with the media. It is difficult to think about the highway without bringing to mind the famous 1946 song 'Get Your Kicks on Route 66!', which sums up 'the euphoria of road-driving' (Krim 1998: 49) and has been sung by everyone from Nat King Cole to the Rolling Stones. It lists the various towns along the way ('don't forget Winona') and thus becomes a musical road map of the route (Krim 1998). There was also the television show *Route 66* (1960–1964), in which two friends (Martin Milner and George Maharis) wander across America in a Chevrolet convertible, which kept the image alive.

In 2006, Disney/Pixar released the animated movie *Cars*, set on Route 66, where the town of Radiator Springs is put back on the map after the bypassing of the highway, thanks to the efforts of the racecar Lightning McQueen (Owen Wilson). Disney utilised the film (and Route 66) in Cars Land in the Disney California Adventure Park, complete with its own Cozy Cone Motel, a pit stop for snacks and drinks, the Radiator Springs Racers ride and replica Route 66 signs.

Checking in at the roadside motel

Unlike Disney's version, the American highway motel became a symbol of dark desires and hidden secrets in many Hollywood films. These often linked narratives of the pathos of the lonely travelling salesman, the criminal on the run and the clandestine relationship. It gives the central character or character a reason to stop (much like the gas station or roadhouse café or diner) but is somehow more menacing than these other places; a symbol of the nihilistic journey being undertaken. *Detour* (1945), a *film noir* about Al Roberts (Tom Neal), who hitches a fateful ride in a car on Route 66 and tries to cover up the suspicious-looking death of the driver, features a motel stay, as depressing and hopeless as Al's outlook appears to him. This is the road trip of nightmares (Laderman 2002).

In Orson Welles' *Touch of Evil* (1958), Janet Leigh is the only guest at the Mirador motel, and is greeted by a creepy 'night man' who refuses to make up her bed but is ultimately harmless. She does, however, have to endure being drugged by the Grandi boys, who have taken over the motel and pipe loud music into her room day and night. Leigh also appears in perhaps the most famous film about a scary motel, *Psycho* (1960), directed by Alfred Hitchcock, where she encounters another operator (Anthony Perkins) who turns out to be full of menace, stabbing her in the shower. In *Easy Rider* (1969), the two lead characters can't even get a room in a cheap roadside motel, which illustrates the depths of their 'marginalized status' (Bapis 2006: 164). In *No Country for Old Men* (2007), the motel is both the place to hide the loot and where the hero might get trapped by the psychopathic hit man.

Steinbeck and Kerouac: the reality of the open road

Some of America's greatest writers took it upon themselves to tell the less palatable stories of life on the road, which touched a raw nerve in their readers and still resonate to this day. Jack Kerouac's paean to the Beat generation, *On the Road* (1957), features 'thieves, thugs, womanizers and sexual predators with pedophilic tendencies' (Ireland 2003: 477); people on the fringe of society. Some of these people are casualties of the Great Depression, and it has been argued that Kerouac was influenced by his own family struggles in the 1930s, which manifest themselves in disappointment at the 'disturbing anomalies of a capitalist system' (Spangler 2008: 321). Sal sees his friend Dean's 'criminality' in romantic terms, reminiscent of the outlaw: 'it was a wild yea-saying overburst of American joy; it was Western, the west wind, an ode from the Plains, something new, long prophesied, long a-coming (he only stole cars for joy rides)' (p. 13). Frontier references abound, with Dean described as looking like a cowboy, 'a young Gene Autry – trim, thin-hipped, blue-eyed, with a real Oklahoma accent – a side-burned hero of the snowy West' (p. 8). Both men are constantly seeking a new city, a new adventure, yet the experience is never fulfilling and they are soon craving other sensations in other places (Cresswell 1993). Throughout his journey back and forth across America, Sal chases after:

> the mad ones, the ones who are mad to love, mad to talk, mad to be saved, desirous of everything at the same time, the ones who never yawn or say a commonplace thing, but burn, burn, burn like fabulous yellow roman candles exploding like spiders across the stars.
>
> (p. 11)

They are modern heirs to the tradition of the American tramp (Seelye 1963), who must endlessly wander the open road.

In 1960, John Steinbeck took a road trip in a renovated van with his dog Charley. The resulting book, *Travels with Charley in Search of America* (1962), paints a portrait of pre-Kennedy America, starkly describing segregation in the South. Steinbeck's motivation was to test himself, an opportunity he thought that men in Western society have largely lost, thanks to over-protected lives and pressure from loved ones:

> I had seen so many [men] begin to pack their lives in cotton wool, smother their impulses, hood their passions, and gradually retire from their manhood into a kind of spiritual and physical semi-invalidism. In this they are encouraged by wives and relatives, and it's such a sweet trap ... I knew that ten or twelve thousand miles driving a truck, alone and unattended, over every kind of road, would be hard work, but to me it represented the antidote for the poison of the professional sick man. And I am not willing to trade quality for quantity. If this projected journey should prove too much then it was time to go anyway.
>
> (1962: 17–18)

This was not Steinbeck's first encounter with the vagaries of the road. For families faced with poverty and ruin in the Dust Bowl in the 1930s, Route 66 was an escape route towards a chance for a better life in California (Olsen 2011). Their farms had been repossessed by landlords and banks, and there was nothing to do but to head west. Travellers slept in their vehicles, or sometimes in roadside parks. Even when they reached California, the land of oranges and hoped-for work, they were met with prejudice and distrust on the one hand and exploitation as cheap labour on the other. The pathos of this situation both touched and angered Steinbeck, inspiring *The Grapes of Wrath* (1939), which was made into a film barely a year later.

The book is powerful in the way it juxtaposes chapters about the plight of the migrants with the personal story of the Joad family from Oklahoma, and uses their own language, with its unique rhythms and expressions, to bring them to life. Steinbeck had driven the highway and spent time in the camps that dotted the route to California, creating a strong authenticity for his fictional road trip. He paints the way the families dealt with the psychological strain of displacement: 'They settled into a new technique of living; the highway became their home and movement their medium of expression. Little by little they settled into the new life' (pp. 276–277). Their desperate journey is described in inexorable and terrifying detail, which only added to the mythology of Route 66:

> 66 is the path of a people in flight, refugees from dust and shrinking land, from the thunder of tractors and shrinking ownership, from the desert's slow northward invasion, from the twisting winds that howl up out of Texas, from the floods that bring no richness to the land and steal what little richness is there. From all of these the people are in flight, and they come into 66 from the tributary side roads, from the wagon tracks and the rutted country roads. 66 is the mother road, the road of flight.
>
> (1939: 213)

The Grapes of Wrath (1940)

Director John Ford is nowadays better known for his Westerns, yet *The Grapes of Wrath* is one of his masterpieces. Beautifully shot, it focused on an era that, like the opening up of the West, is part of American mythology. He himself labelled it one of his favourites, with the story reminding him of his family's migration from Ireland (Sickels 2006). This is a film of shadows, an element we tend to associate with *film noir*. Torches, candles and headlights illuminate people's faces, showing them as both haunted and hunted. It is an appropriate device for a story where lives will inevitably be shadowed by poverty and death. The interplay between dark and light is most notable in the scene when Tom Joad (Henry Fonda) comes back to his family home, now abandoned, and is silhouetted against the horizon, along with the preacher Jim Casy (John Carradine). The focus is on their eyes, full of bewilderment at what they have found. The men watch the tractors smash down the house, and realise that life here as they knew it is over for them. There is no option open to them but to flee.

The scenes on the overstuffed truck as the family heads west are interspersed with Route 66 signs, advertising for gas stations and signs of welcome and fare-well for various places along the way; the latter an ironic touch, given the harsh treatment given to the 'Okies' by many people throughout their journey and the desire to 'move them on'. One gas attendant says to another in the film 'They aren't human. Human beings wouldn't live like they do'. The trucks are watched by a lone Native American as they pass by. Their crossing of the desert into California can be likened to a type of *katabasis*, literally a descent into hell (Frost and Laing 2012; Holtsmark 2001; Laing and Frost 2012), rather than the bountiful paradise that the family expected. The grandmother dies during this part of the journey, unable to stand the strain and the loss of her husband shortly after they left home. Ford stalwart Ward Bond has a cameo as a Californian policeman who has the decency to express anger at the misleading advertising handbills that had been circulated, which gave families like the Joads the false hope of economic security. The bleakness of their situation when they reach the camps is reflected in the people's faces around them, etched with disbelief at their betrayal.

Henry Fonda is the emotional heart of the film. Joad is an example of the *Fordian hero*, who acknowledges and attempts to mediate the tension between the frontier/agrarian myth and the 'urban industrial reality' (Sickels 2006: 64). At the end, Tom Joad must leave the family to protect them, as he fears being picked up by the police for the death of the Reverend's killers. We again see his small silhouette against the broad sky as he flees, while Ma (Jane Darwell) turns her back on him and weeps. Laderman (2002: 29–30) argues that Joad is 'no longer a captive of the road' and has 'had a revelation ... following a calling to discover the truth and fight for its discovery by others'. This is part of the trans-formative effect of the road (Laderman 2002), and the various katabatic trials that Joad has had to undergo since leaving Oklahoma. Ma is also galvanised after this shock, and the film ends with her speech to Pa (Russell Simpson) and her other son Al (O.Z. Whitehead) as they start again on the road: 'We keep a comin'. We're the people that live'. The film ends on a high note, as the family is not browbeaten. It differs from the more controversial (but still uplifting) con-clusion of the book, where Tom's sister Rosasharn breastfeeds a starving old man, after her baby is stillborn, illustrating the survival of compassion and altru-ism amongst the migrants, despite all their hardships. For Hollywood sensibili-ties at the time, this would have been a bridge too far and possibly would not have made it through the censors.

The modern wanderer

The road movies grew out of several genres, including *film noir* and the Western. Laderman (2002: 23) labels the Western 'the road movie's grandparent', based on the often ubiquitous thematic structure of a journey or *wandering* in the former, as well as the ability of the journey to transform characters or offer redemption in some cases. For others, there is no salvation on the frontier, akin to the bleakness of *film noir* as exemplified by Al Roberts on the run and in the hands of fate in *Detour*. The Old West is marked by a conviction that there are certain shared values that underpin life on the frontier, but the 'ethical certainties of the B-film gave way to a darker understanding of human beings' (Horrocks 1995: 28) and led to the birth of the anti-hero. Examples include Ethan in *The Searchers* and the title character in *Shane*. The Hollywood anti-hero reaches his/ their apotheosis in the outlaw biker films of the late 1960s, such as *The Wild Angels* (1966), *The Glory Stompers* (1967) and *Hells Angels on Wheels* (1967), starring respectively Peter Fonda, Dennis Hopper and Jack Nicholson. All three actors subsequently starred in *Easy Rider*, which remains as provocative today as when it was first released.

Easy Rider (1969)

According to Dennis Hopper in the documentary *Shaking the Cage* (1999), about the making of the film *Easy Rider*, the term *easy rider* refers to a man (not a pimp) who lives off a whore. Many of the people that the two bikers, Wyatt (Peter Fonda) and Billy (Dennis Hopper), encounter on the road see them as spongers or dropouts, a threat to the fabric of society through their drug-taking and anarchic lifestyle, but at the same time the subject of envy (Kohlberg and Gilligan 1971). They are *outlaws* ('shaking the cage' as Fonda puts it, which gave the documentary its name) in an era of protest (Hocker Rushing and Frentz 1978). Their names are a tribute to two of the most famous figures of the American West – Wyatt Earp and Billy the Kid – and they 'encounter the sheriff, town, jail, and the most important element of a Western, the pristine landscapes' (Bapis 2006: 159), while their bikes are essentially 'iron steeds' (Ireland 2003: 475). Billy wears a suede-fringed Buffalo Bill jacket with a necklace of teeth around his neck and a cowboy hat on his head. He has the long hair that we associate with Custer, which ironically would have made the latter a renegade to conservatives in 1960s America. Throughout the film, there are visual and verbal references to Western films (Peary 1989).

Fonda, the son of Henry Fonda, grew up aware of his father's role in many of the classic Westerns. He saw parallels with *Easy Rider*: 'For me it was a Western idiom we were working with. We were riding the motorcycle and wearing spurs ... and we were going across John Ford's America'. One of the scenes in the film shows them riding windswept through Monument Valley, the landscape most intertwined with the oeuvre of Ford. This is a cinematic tribute, an example as in many Westerns of 'nostalgic desires for landscapes of grandeur' (Bapis 2006: 175). It would be wrong however to see Monument Valley as lacking history in its own right, beyond its cinematic connections, as Ireland (2003) argues. There is a Native American history in the region which deserves to be remembered. Wyatt and Billy are told by a hitch-hiker that this site is a memorial and 'belongs to the ones buried right under you'; one of only a few references made to Native Americans in this film (one being a drunken expletive).

Wyatt and Billy are an example of the *male couple* in the Western, who dally with women but ultimately prefer to turn to and rely on each other, exemplified in *Gunfight at the OK Corral* (1957) and *Butch Cassidy and the Sundance Kid* (1969). Horrocks (1995) argues that in many cases there is a love which can only be 'hinted at' and perhaps a sexual tension, but this is not apparent in the relationship between Wyatt and Billy. They are brothers in arms, united by their desire to flee from convention and experience life on the road. There is a nominal destination in front of them – Mardi Gras in New Orleans, which is notable for a chaotic and drug-fuelled scene in an above-ground cemetery, with the two men and the two prostitutes they pick up (Karen Black and Toni Basil of *Mickey* fame) variously hugging statues, stripping naked and screaming out to and about the voices in their heads. However, the heart of the film lies in what happens before and after this event. All the scenes with drugs are in fact authentic – the actors were often stoned while filming, as Hopper confirms ('we were all out of our minds ... half of us were on acid').

The silver bikes are gleaming, with Wyatt's motorcycle featuring a tear-shaped petrol tank emblazoned with the Stars and Stripes, as is his helmet, which he straps to his bike but doesn't wear. Fonda laughs about the bike in the documentary: 'I'm just driving one big phallus down the road'. After a quick drug deal in Mexico and exchange in the back of a Rolls Royce in Los Angeles, the men head cross-country towards Louisiana, travelling along part of Route 66. A cowboy compliments them: 'Sure is a good-looking machine'. Wyatt returns the compliment: 'It's not every man that can live off the land, you know? [You] can do your own thing in your own time. You should be proud'. This is a central theme running through the movie, the desire for an anti-authoritarian life, even though paradoxically the cowboy is tied down to his farm and can neither escape the laws of nature nor economic systems. This is yet another reference to the myth of agrarianism (Bapis 2006), with the farmer as the 'authentic American' (p. 165). The men's ultimately fruitless search is summed up in the slogan for the advertising poster of the film: 'A man went looking for America and couldn't find it anywhere' (Ireland 2003).

The bikes are mostly filmed as the only objects on the highway, the fantasy motorcycle ride, although there are glimpses of people beside the endless stretches of road who gaze and sometimes wave at the pair. Yet the road is not benign. They are arrested for joining a street parade on their bikes and in a diner in Texas, they are taunted by rednecks. Charlie (Jack Nicholson), an alcoholic lawyer they encounter in jail, sums up the fear that their presence brings to many of the people that they meet: 'They're not scared of you. They're scared of what you represent to them'. When Billy replies 'All we represent to them is somebody who needs a haircut', Charlie responds: 'What we represent to them is freedom'. This is more than just the *generation gap*; they must be eliminated to re-establish order (Kohlberg and Gilligan 1971).

The men understand that fear of freedom makes people *dangerous*, but it is moot whether they anticipate what will happen next. There are hints, however, at the commune, when the hitch-hiker they had picked up (Luke Askew) tells them:

'Your time's running out'. Wyatt's response is enigmatic: 'I'm hip about time but I've just gotta go'. Charlie is killed that night by thugs, presumably the same men they met in the diner, while Wyatt and Billy are beaten up but left alive. The attackers aim to see the two motorcyclists charged with Charlie's death; a warning to those who would like to follow in their footsteps, such as the young teenage girls in the diner, who flock admiringly around the bikes.

The soundtrack of the film is the perfect accompaniment, featuring music by 1960s icons such as the Jimi Hendrix Experience and the Byrds that conjure up the Haight-Ashbury years and the 'tune in, turn on, drop out' mantra associated with the drug counter-culture. It was one of the first films, along with *The Graduate* (1967) to use a soundtrack of selected current music, rather than a commissioned score, to create a 'sense of generational identity' (Shumway 1999: 38). The song most associated with this film, 'Born to be Wild' by Steppenwolf, is played as the bikes cross the Colorado River, with its opening lyrics perfectly attuned to the cool hipness of the two bikers:

> *Get your motor runnin'*
> *Head out on the highway*
> *Looking for adventure*
> *In whatever comes our way.*

Even though Wyatt throws his Rolex away, in a symbolic gesture, he knows that their drug-dealing has sullied them. Perhaps Charlie's observations had hit home: 'It's real hard to be free when you've bought and sold in the marketplace'. When Billy tells Wyatt 'We've done it … You go for the big money and then you're free', Wyatt's reply is prescient: 'We blew it'. The next scene, we see the men on the road with other cars for the first time, and a couple of hicks shoot at them from a truck. Billy is shot and lying in a ditch. Wyatt goes to get help and rides past the truck again, seemingly daring them to do the same to him. The final shot of the film is his burning bike, viewed from above, the same apoca-lyptic shot that we glimpsed in New Orleans as Wyatt looked at a plaque about death. All three men are now dead and the background song by Roger McGuinn of the Byrds, which Dylan contributed to, features the haunting lyrics 'All he wanted was to be free. And that's the way it turned out to be'. It echoes the ending of *Thelma & Louise*, another buddy movie where death is depicted as the ultimate escape, preferable to the chains inherent in going home or selling out.

Riding the female road

While many road movies feature the male as the central and active character, with the woman either a passenger or sidekick (Laderman 2002), we think that the role of women in cinematic road trips has been overlooked. In the screwball comedy *It Happened One Night* (1934), the focus is on the journey of Claudette Colbert's sassy socialite, Ellen Andrews, who is running away from her father. She is assisted on the road by an undercover reporter Peter Warne (Clark Gable), and the story traces Ellen's evolution from spoilt and indulged heiress to Peter's acknowledged equal in resourcefulness. We see them on a bus and also hitch-hiking, at which Ellen proves to be adept through flashing her stockinged legs at passers-by. The repartee between the pair is sparkling and transcends their class divide, symbolised by the 'Walls of Jericho', a blanket strung on a rope across the rooms that they share on the way, maintaining Ellen's privacy and chastity. Ellen encounters the reality of poverty and for the first time in her life has to queue for what she wants. She tells Peter: 'I've always been told what to do and how to do it and when and with whom'. This taste of freedom is intoxicating. Finally the lovers reunite after the usual Hollywood plot twists and misunder-standing. This is a couple who may never have met or fallen in love with each other except for being on the road. In the final scene, the Walls of Jericho finally come down.

A more recent example of a female comedic road trip is *My One and Only* (2009), set in the 1950s, where Anne Devereux (Renee Zellweger) drives her two sons, Robbie (Mark Rendall) and George (Logan Lerman), across the country in search of a new father after the breakdown of her marriage to Dan (Kevin Bacon). George is loosely based on the perpetually tanned actor George Hamilton and features the range of wacky characters the family meets as they travel towards Los Angeles and an eventual (schlock) film career for George, including *Love at First Bite* (1979) and *Zorro the Gay Blade* (1981). Their itin-erary includes Route 66 and we are aware of their journey spatially, as George sends his father postcards from everywhere they go, and Robbie embroiders a map of their route in cross-stitch.

The film portrays Anne as a loving if somewhat distracted mother, who doesn't even know which schools her sons go to, yet is fiercely protective of them. The car they buy is a pale blue Cadillac Eldorado, which attracts admiring looks all the way, as does Anne, who is a curvaceous and chic blonde. Anne's story arc is that she discovers self-reliance through her journey, realising that she can overcome adversity without a man by her side, after several failed relation-ships. When Dan asks her to come back, after they have reached LA, she responds: 'I don't know if I love you anymore. I *do* know I don't need you anymore'. Anne is able to look on the bright side, even in the face of theft of her money, being fired from her job as a waitress, a bogus engagement to a serial proposer who is already married, and a spell overnight in jail when a detective sitting in a hotel bar mistakes her flirtatious overtures for solicitation. This deter-mination to remain optimistic rubs off on those around her. George tells his world-weary girlfriend: 'In the end everything works out. It always does'.

We conclude this section with an analysis of *Thelma & Louise*, the most famous road trip heroines in cinematic history.

Thelma & Louise (1991)

The narrative of *Thelma & Louise* is firmly in the tradition of the Western. This road trip is a manifestation of the desire of Thelma (Geena Davis) and Louise

(Susan Sarandon) to escape dreary urban lives and find a transformation. The film begins with a shot of the open road, which becomes twilight, a portent of the transience of the women's journey. In contrast, once they start driving, the black and white images turn to colour, symbolising the richness of the Western landscape, and how life begins once they hit the highway. Thelma is in a suffo-cating marriage and says of her husband Daryl: 'He never lets me do one goddam thing that's fun'. She packs a gun, an omen that this trip will not end happily. The women head off in a 1966 T-bird convertible, with Louise's hair covered in a head-scarf which blows off in the wind, symbolising the shedding of conventional identities. At first, they are playing similar roles to those they had at home, with Louise the more dominant personality and Thelma more vague and needy. It will take some time for these roles to be dropped and even reversed, when Thelma eventually displays a level of ingenuity and cold-bloodedness that amazes her sidekick.

The journey initially starts as a girls' bonding weekend, with a visit to a country-and-western themed bar. Thelma is attacked by a man in the car park and Louise shoots him. From this point on, the women are on borrowed time, as they attempt to outrun the law. The road is now a means of a getaway, as they plan to head to Mexico. Despite this sense of impending doom, there is almost a feeling of euphoria, manifested at times in bouts of hysterical laughter at each other and their situation (Sturtevant 2007). Even if this is a type of 'gallows humour', the tables have turned, and the women have asserted power over their environment.

Even their bodies change, 'presented as a honed muscularity, rather than the traditional feminine frills and curves' (Horrocks 1995: 174). This masculinisa-tion is an example of the 'chaos of the carnivalesque moment [that is travel]', which results in 'inversions of social role' (Sturtevant 2007: 48). Their clothes are also increasingly tight-fitting and sexy, along with their hair, which is worn loose and tousled. Even their identities are mutable, symbolised by Thelma wearing Louise's sunglasses. Louise shows her softer, more vulnerable side more readily, with tears in her eyes as she reunites with her boyfriend Jimmy. Thelma increasingly takes the initiative ('I've got a knack for this shit'), and experiences her first orgasm when she meets a young cowboy J.D., played by a young Brad Pitt, as well as learning from him how to stage a hold-up. J.D. becomes a sex-object to the women in a reversal of the way that women are traditionally viewed by men. But things start to unravel. The attempted rape scene is evidence of that, as is the theft of their money by J.D. As Sturtevant (2007: 49) explains: 'Rather than a simplistic exploration of the road as a site of carnivalesque freedom, [*Thelma & Louise*] offers a lesson in the double binds associated with control and its loss, ambivalence, trauma and pleasure'.

The women drive down the highway as a crop-duster flies overhead, an allu-sion to Hitchcock's *North by Northwest* (1959). There is an aerial shot of the car like an ant in the landscape, a reminder of their vulnerability. Unbeknown to them, a detective, Hal Slocumb (Harvey Keitel) believes in their innocence ('How many times must they be fucked over?') and is trying to track them down.

He has a series of phone conversations with Louise, in which he tries to convince the women to turn themselves in to the authorities. Slocumb and Louise's boyfriend Jimmy are possibly the only sympathetic male characters in the film, with the others portrayed as misogynists, rapists, con-men or buffoons, in contrast to the active and powerful roles played by Davis and Sarandon. *Thelma & Louise* was criticised for this when it was first released, with Sturtevant (2007: 43) theorising that 'in becoming outlaws, Thelma and Louise certainly write themselves into the mythology of the American West, but they simultaneously mock that mythology'. The scene where the women blow up a tanker, in retaliation to the lewd comments of its driver, is clearly phallic and Sarandon told a reporter that the director, Ridley Scott, was determined to include it in the film. A *Time* magazine cover weighed into the debate, posing the question: 'Why *Thelma & Louise* Strikes a Nerve?' Others, however, delighted in the story of female liberation, arguing that the penultimate scene of the pair in flight over the Grand Canyon, their car hovering over the abyss, gave women a moment to applaud.

Monument Valley was used in the promotional poster for the movie and is one of the more haunting backdrops, where the two women realise they will never reach Mexico and freedom. Their conversation is poignant. 'I always wanted to travel. I just never got the opportunity' says Thelma. Louise's response is a weary 'You got it now'. The soundtrack is Marianne Faithfull's 'The Ballad of Lucy Jordan', a song of yearning and 'wasted opportunity' (Gorbman 2007: 75). This is a fatalistic story, and is thus following a tradition of Westerns, albeit with the twist of female leads. As Walle (2000: 154) explains: 'the heroes are incapable of effectively dealing with modern society even though they are superior to it'. Their inability to compromise is their undoing. The road is a means of escape, but only temporarily. Their real freedom ultimately lies not just in death but how they choose to die – holding hands rather than being the passive recipients of capital punishment.

Reshaping the contemporary road

The heyday of Route 66 began to fade with the bypassing of various towns, and staggered on until the 1970s, when the highway was replaced by various interstate highways and the route was officially decommissioned in 1985. Official Route 66 signs can still be seen in some places (Figure 4.2), while others use it as branding (Figure 4.3). There is still a lot of support for keeping it alive. Olsen (2011: 7) notes the existence of volunteer groups who 'continue to fight to save and preserve our icons from destruction', while there are festivals along the route which attract visitors and a multiplicity of Route 66 souvenirs for sale (Henriksson 2014).

Its iconic name still intrigues and there is a proposal to rename the Newell Highway in Australia as Route 66. The towns along the way would 'develop Americana themes, bringing snippets of the original Route 66 experience to Australia' (Bain 2014: 19), despite the fact that there is no discernible link to the

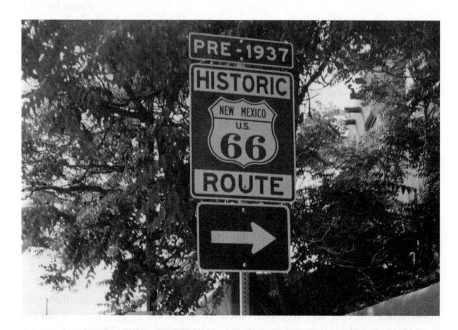

Figure 4.2 Route 66 sign in Santa Fe (photo J. Laing).

Figure 4.3 Route 66 imagery at the Hackberry Gas Station and General Store (photo J. Laing).

former highway. It arguably conjures up a wistfulness for a bygone era, 'the quest for the last good decade of the United States via the 1950s Route 66' (Henriksson 2014: 19–20), although Caton and Santos (2007) argue that nostalgia does not propel tourists to travel Route 66. They found instead that a combination of 'challenge and personal growth' was sought (p. 380):

> While the participants saw themselves as participating in a legacy of travel, they did not seem to confuse the experiences available today with those available in the past or to indicate that they were less valuable than those available in the past. Rather, they saw the corridor as an evolving place that offers a different, and highly valuable, set of experiences for tourists today than it offered in the past.

The town of Williams, Arizona has reinvented itself with themes of 1950s diners, music and cars (Figure 4.4). Souvenir shops abound (Davis and Morais 2004), selling Route 66 memorabilia, as well as stores featuring Western gear, such as Stetsons, belts, boots and shirts. Williams features two one-way streets – one headed east and one headed west – and its eastbound street (Bill Williams Avenue) is lively and studded with motels, cafés and shops. In 1984, it was the last town on Route 66 to be bypassed. That same year, the Downtown Business

Figure 4.4 Williams 1950s memorabilia (photo J. Laing).

District was placed on the National Register of Historic Places and in 1989, Route 66 through Williams was similarly listed (Olsen 2011). Part of the reason that it has survived while other places on the old Route 66 have not is that it is the location for the Grand Canyon Railway Station, which takes passengers to and from the South Rim, as well as its proximity to the turn-off to the Grand Canyon at Parks. The town of Williams does however have its pressures (Davis and Morais 2004), which we highlight in Chapter 10 on the Grand Canyon.

The flourishing of Williams contrasts with the plethora of ghost towns along Route 66 that have simply died with the rerouting of the highway. These ghost towns now provide a romantic foil to the towns that have survived but also add to the authenticity of Route 66, as they illustrate its failures and 'the inevitability of change' (Caton and Santos 2007: 380). One is Hackberry, Arizona (Figure 4.5), which still retains its old gas station and general store, complete with old petrol pumps. A thriving business, it now caters for drive tourists.

The yard is scattered with old wrecks of automobiles and the occasional cow skull, like a living Georgia O'Keeffe painting, along with old Route 66 logos and signs. Inside, a display of Western photos lines the walls, showing early twentieth-century residents of the area, and stickers left by visitors from all over the world, a reminder of the perennial and global interest in this motoring heritage.

Figure 4.5 Hackberry Gas Station and General Store (photo J. Laing).

5   Tombstone

I knew him ... I often think of Wyatt Earp when I play a film character. There's a guy who actually did what I'm trying to do.

(John Wayne, quoted in Tefertiller 1997: 340)

I knew Wyatt Earp. In the very early silent days, a couple of times a year, he would come up to visit his pals, cowboys he knew in Tombstone ... and he told me about the fight at the O.K. Corral. So in *My Darling Clementine*, we did it exactly the way it had been.

(John Ford, quoted in Bogdanovich 1978: 84–85)

Introduction

In 1877, prospector Ed Schieffelin headed out into the wilds of southern Arizona. Some soldiers he knew joshed with him, warning that rather than precious metals, all he would find would be his own tombstone. When he found payable silver, he reversed the joke by registering the location of his claim as 'Tombstone and Graveyard' (Tefertiller 1997). The resulting rush led to a boom town, which retained the extraordinary name of Tombstone. It sounds like a crazy frontier tall tale. Except it was true. And Tombstone became an eerily prescient name for one of the most violent and wildest places in the West.

Mining is an urban occupation. Rich mineral finds attract large numbers of people concentrated into small areas. Not only are there the miners, but if there is enough wealth to be had, it also draws in a panoply of merchants, administrators and service providers. All of these are concentrated in boom towns which seemingly spring up in a few weeks to service the mining bonanza. Bawdy, bustling and boozy, they epitomise the Wild West, with the hard-working miners being rapidly relieved of their earnings by equally hard-working prostitutes, saloon-keepers, card-sharps and other entertainers. As a recent empirical study has demonstrated, on average miners did not do any better than if they had stayed back East and worked as labourers. In contrast, those who benefited significantly from mining were merchants and service providers (Clay and Jones 2008).

All that money attracted trouble. Wherever there is vice, there is corruption and violence as the avaricious jockey for their cut of the take. Nor was this confined to just mining towns. Changing economic conditions led to a range of western boom towns with common features. The spread of railways generated variations on this theme, particularly with the boom in driving cattle from Texas to the railheads at Abilene, Dodge City and Wichita. Paid off after months on the trail, the cowboys became synonymous with drunkenness and gunplay.

The tangible and intangible cultural heritage of mining towns is often packaged up for tourist consumption (Frost forthcoming). In some cases, the boom-town architecture and streetscapes are ideal for artisans, shops, cafés and galleries. Examples include Bisbee (Arizona) and Nevada City (California). Others function as evocative *ghost towns*. Bodie (California) is a spectacular example of this (Figure 5.1). High in the Sierra Nevada, it is now operated as an open air museum by California State Parks (DeLyser 1999, 2003). A third variant is *living history* – with costumed characters, re-enactments and businesses modelled on those of the past. Examples include Tombstone and Dead-wood (South Dakota), both places famous for their violent stories and heavily mediated by cinema.

Figure 5.1 Once a bustling mining town, Bodie now attracts tourists as a ghost town (photo S. Frost).

Hollywood and *Town Westerns*

Hollywood drew heavily on the themes of violent gunfights and showdowns in urban areas, already well-established through dime novels. When Westerns took hold in 1939, films included gunfights in the streets of Lordsburg, New Mexico (*Stagecoach*), Tombstone, Arizona (*Frontier Marshall*) and Dodge City, Kansas (*Dodge City*). The latter emphasised that boom town's corruption and break-down of law and order, with Bruce Cabot playing a crooked villain who gets to be marshall. Thirty years later, Cabot was still playing that same role in *Chisum* (1970). The common trope in many Westerns was that the law was ineffective or tainted, forcing the heroes to take the law into their own hands. Thus was com-bined suspicion of government being the tool of big business and a justification for vigilantism (Calder 1974; Lawrence 2005; Slotkin 1992). The paradox of Westerns set in boom towns was that while urbanisation might be equated with civilisation, it also represented corruption and decadence. On the range, the cowboy could be free and primitive, whereas in towns rules applied, denying the benefits of the frontier.

As Westerns got more adult, the combinations vying for control of towns became more complex. Borrowing from *film noir*, the normal forces of law and order were often revealed to be in cahoots with the villains. The straightforward hero had to negotiate shifting alliances and be on guard for deception. In some cases, the hero had a murky past, drawing them into intrigue and danger, as in *Man of the West* (1958) and *Warlock* (1959).

These urban complexities were well illustrated in the Budd Boetticher film *Buchanan Rides Alone* (1958). The eponymous hero (Randolph Scott) rides into the border town of Argy. It is controlled by two brothers – Judge Simon Argy and Sheriff Lew Argy. Both detest and distrust the other. The law has become a plaything in their ongoing feud. Egging them on is the shadowy Carbo. All are suspicious of Buchanan, who they suspect is an agent of their adversary. Though nothing of the sort, Buchanan must use his wits to survive as he is drawn into the vendetta. The predictable finale is a main street shoot-out. The brothers kill each other. With the town now 'free' of its corrupt founders, Buchanan rides away and Carbo steps in to take over. Will anything change? This concept of a gunman riding into a town beset by two warring factions and then playing them off against each other would become a common theme in Spaghetti Westerns such as *A Fistful of Dollars* (1964).

Urban corruption has remained a strong theme in modern Westerns. In *Sil-verado* (1985), the sheriff (Brian Dennehy) is a former outlaw, he is in the pay of the wealthy rancher and owns the saloon. In *Unforgiven* (1992), the sheriff (Gene Hackman) is single-minded and ruthless in keeping the peace, but only to satisfy local ranchers and business interests. In *Open Range* (2003), the law is controlled by a rancher (Michael Gambon), who uses it to keep others off what he considers is his land. In all three films, the hero kills these villains in an urban shoot-out. The continuing popularity of this archetype reflects modern concerns about links between organised crime, big business and government.

Wyatt Earp and Tombstone

Like many Western mining towns, Tombstone drew in gamblers and prostitutes as well as miners. A multi-sided struggle developed over control of the
town, particularly over the elected position of town marshall and the opportunities offered by saloons and gambling. The Earp brothers (Wyatt, Virgil,
Morgan and James), with John 'Doc' Holliday, formed one faction. Increasing
tensions with a loose gang of rustlers and stagecoach robbers known as the
'Cowboys' escalated into a full-blown vendetta. The most well-known incident in the feud was the 'Gunfight at the OK Corral', at Tombstone on 26
October 1881, in which the Earps and Holliday shot and killed Cowboys Billy
Clanton, Frank McLaury and Tom McLaury. However, this was not the end.
After the controversial acquittal of the Earps for murder, reprisals came when
Morgan was shot in the back while playing pool in a saloon and Virgil
ambushed in the street. The final reckoning came when the remaining Earps
and Holliday rode out to confront the Cowboys. In the resultant *man-on-man*
showdown Wyatt gunned down Cowboy leader 'Curly Bill' Brocious. The
other notorious Cowboy leader, Johnny Ringo, was later shot dead by an
unknown assailant (in films, this is often Doc Holliday, though the evidence
places him elsewhere).

Wyatt Earp in cinema

The story of Wyatt Earp has been heavily mediatised by cinema. Even when
touted as authentic, these films have often been highly fictionalised. The examples outlined below illustrate two important principles in how the Western myth
has been constructed by film. The first is the influence of *intertextuality*, with a
great deal of cross-referencing in evidence. Certain characters, scenes and
images keep reappearing, almost as if expected. Over time this results in a
layered story, seemingly true due to its elements, being constantly repeated. The
second concerns authenticity. As in many period films, the emphasis has been on
the look – particularly clothing – rather than historical veracity (Rosenstone
1995).

Frontier Marshal (1939)

This was filmed at Lone Pine (California) and a town set on the Fox lot in Hollywood. Randolph Scott (Wyatt) and Cesar Romero (Doc) are wooden and one-
dimensional. In contrast, the film is dominated by the two female leads. Sarah
(Nancy Kelly) arrives from the East searching for Doc. A refined nurse, she
represents the civilisation that Doc has rejected. Also interested in him is rough
saloon singer Jerry (Binnie Barnes). She represents the Wild West. While that
sounds simple, both are played as complex characters who eventually develop a
grudging respect for each other. For its day, this is a highly unusual Western
with its focus on strong women.

Doc is on the verge of choosing when he is killed by Curly Bill. In turn, Jerry grabs Doc's gun and shoots the villain. With the Cowboys defeated, Sarah (civilisation) decides to stay. In contrast, Jerry (wild times), chooses to leave. Pointing to a sign announcing the building of a bank, she wryly comments, 'when people start saving their money, it's time for me to vamoose'. Jerry is loosely based on Doc's girl Kate Elder. However, as she was still alive at the time, there was sense in providing her character with a different name. Sadie Earp – Wyatt's wife – was also still alive and she was hired as a technical adviser (Tefertiller 1997). This might explain her absence and that Wyatt lacks any romantic interest.

Life in Tombstone is painted as carnivalesque. Nearly all the action takes place either in two feuding saloons or the street between them. One gains the advantage by importing dancing girls from Chicago. The customers are either drunk (on champagne!) or gambling. The top-hatted proprietor of one hires famous Eastern comedian Eddie Foy to perform, adding that he has aspirations of obtaining actress Lily Langtry and opera singer Jenny Lind. His disgruntled competitor kidnaps Foy and forces him to perform in his saloon. Foy was one of a number of entertainers who toured the West; he claimed he played Tombstone, though that is disputed (Blake 2007). The kidnapping incident may have really happened, though in Dodge City.

Frontier Marshal is nowadays mostly forgotten. Made in the year of the boom in A Westerns, it still followed the budget, casting and conventions of a B-grader. Nevertheless, it was influential in fixing an image of Wyatt. As Blake argued:

> The Wyatt Earp in *Frontier Marshal* is the kind of hero that children at the movies would look up to. Audiences, and the Western genre, needed that in 1939. World events were beginning to make them nervous; spending a few hours in a movie theatre watching a story about an actual person who vanquished lawbreakers gave audiences a sense of hope and welcome relief. The cinematic myth of Wyatt Earp, upholder of law and order, was just beginning.
>
> (2007: 46)

Dodge City (1939)

Released a few months before *Frontier Marshall*, this A Western tells the story of Wyatt in Dodge City, but gives him a different name. A hugely successful film for Warner Brothers, it utilised their number one action star in Errol Flynn. Under the name Wade Hatton, he cleans up the infamous cattle town. Initially reluctant to get involved, he changes his mind after a small boy is killed by crossfire. As with many Warner Brothers movies of the time, the message is strongly against ideas of American non-intervention in world affairs (Barr 1996).

Wade/Wyatt is the catalyst for civilisation. The lawless elements must be defeated so that families will settle and a community develop. The choices are exemplified by Wade's offsider Rusty (Alan Hale Sr). Joining a Temperance

League, he takes the pledge to quit drinking and fighting. Of course he fails, becoming involved in the spectacular saloon brawl that was the action highlight of the film. Indeed, so impressive was the fight, Warner Brothers kept using it as stock footage in film and television up to the 1960s (particularly *F Troop*), further reinforcing the stereotype of the saloon brawl as a common occurrence in these towns.

My Darling Clementine (1946)

Filmed by John Ford with a town set actually constructed in Monument Valley, this starred Henry Fonda as Wyatt and Victor Mature as Doc. Based on the same book as *Frontier Marshall*, it followed a similar plot. Wyatt and Doc meet in Tombstone and become friends. Doc is faced with the choice between his old Eastern girlfriend Clementine (Cathy Downs) and a wild Hispanic saloon singer Chihuahua (Linda Darnell). The main plot difference is that Wyatt is given a back-story. He only takes on the job of marshall after his brother is murdered. The killer is Old Man Clanton (Walter Brennan) and the reckoning comes at the OK Corral.

In Ford's hands this is a much superior film; indeed, one of the most popular Westerns of all time. However, it is a highly fictionalised account, a source of some criticism (Peary 1983). Ford rarely made movies about actual historical figures and here he follows little more than the basics. For Kitses, this is 'one of the masterpieces of classical American film ... while purporting to rework one of the more violent confrontations to the Wild West's storied bad men, *My Darling Clementine* constructs a loving hymn to the values of civilisation' (2004: 55). As in *Stagecoach*, Ford used a standard plot with stock characters as a foundation, but then layered it with his nuanced artistic style.

Accordingly, Wyatt is good and honest, the epitome of the mythical Western hero. He could simply seek vengeance by killing the Clantons. Instead he takes the job of marshall. He can only truly revenge his brother's death by operating within the law and becoming part of the process of civilising the wild town of Tombstone. Wyatt's journey towards redemption is exemplified in the famous church social dance, shot outdoors to take advantage of Monument Valley. The Clantons are simply evil and uncouth, even though they kidnap a Shakespearian actor for entertainment, they do not really enjoy it. Strongly bound by family ties, they symbolise what the Earp brothers could be if they slipped. Doc represents a fallen hero. Educated and cultured, he now leads a dissolute life. The arrival of Clementine shocks and embarrasses him. He is too far gone to re-enter civilisation, but can achieve redemption through sacrificing himself helping Wyatt in the gunfight (Peary 1983).

Gunfight at the OK Corral (1957)

The action takes place across three infamous towns: Fort Griffin, Texas; Dodge City, Kansas and Tombstone, Arizona. All three places are introduced by a group of riders entering town and passing the Boot Hill Cemetery. At Fort

Griffin, Wyatt and Doc meet; at Dodge City, a friendship develops and at Tombstone they aid each other at the infamous gunfight. Doc (Kirk Douglas) is garrulous and explosive. In complete contrast, Wyatt (Burt Lancaster) is stoic and taciturn.

The unlikely bromance between the introverted Wyatt and extroverted Doc is the core of this movie. Little is said by either about their feelings. They are strong and silent – the epitome of 1950s masculinity – but also crippled by their inability to let their guard down. Both are unable to maintain their relationships with women, seemingly finding each other's company more desirable. Both are drifting, the classic Western archetype. The similarity of the towns is an important motif. Each is introduced by its identical Boot Hill Cemetery (Fort Griffin and Tombstone were both shot at Old Tucson). There is nothing distinctive about them, nothing to anchor either Wyatt or Doc – a striking contrast to Ford's imagined community in *My Darling Clementine*. The film ends with Doc playing cards and Wyatt riding off alone to California.

Women seem marginal to the story and, accordingly, this film has often been criticised as misogynistic. Kate (Jo Van Fleet) may be interpreted as a passive victim. Though often drunk and with little self-respect, there is a complexity to her portrayal, particularly through her intense loyalty. Symbolising her marginalisation, this supposedly true account changes the story of how Doc escaped from a lynch mob in Fort Griffin. In this film, he is helped by Wyatt; whereas in reality it was Kate.

Wyatt's romantic interest is Laura (Rhonda Fleming). For half the film it is a conventional love story, but then Wyatt decides to abandon her to venture to Tombstone. Tompkins (1992: 40) argued she was 'the shadow of the more important male [fellow gambler Doc] … masking the fact that what the men are really interested in is one another'. This may be the intention, but if so, her character fails in distracting the audience. Sergio Leone was also particularly critical of this role, arguing her character was superfluous and slowed the story down. Instead, he argued, if a film needs such a gorgeous female part, then she should have a central role in the plot, as he did with *Once Upon a Time in the West* (Frayling 2005). Despite the slightness of her part, there are some interesting variations. Unlike earlier versions, she is not respectable; being a professional gambler. In previous films, Wyatt's romantic interest was a nurse or school-teacher, here we are taken closer to the reality of Sadie as an actress. Gambling provides Laura with independence and it is notable that she imposes conditions on Wyatt. Unfortunately, he rejects these and leaves her in Dodge City. Here, we disagree with Leone, the character of Laura *is important*. She demonstrates Wyatt's inability to commit to their relationship. A similar rejection of marriage and domesticity occurs in *Will Penny* (1968).

A running theme is of the dual nature of these towns. On the one hand, they only exist to service cowboys and miners, come to town for a spree and wild times. The respectable townspeople, trying to build a civilised community, are economically dependent. The two groups are connected but distant. In Dodge City, guns are banned, except in the south side, a red light district on the other side of the railway tracks. The rowdy cowboys are corralled there and not welcome in the main part of town. Snubbed by the townsfolk the cowboys rebel, shooting up a local dance. Their leader, Shanghai Pierce, eloquently states 'you're happy to take our money, but we are not good enough to dance with your women'. Wyatt disarms him, but nobody argues against what he has said. In Tombstone, Wyatt and his brothers are employed to keep the Clantons out of town. When they do come to town, it's to see Eddie Foy perform. However, they are stopped at the door to the Birdcage Theater. Inside, the entertainment is only for those who conform to the town's rules.

Wyatt is the agent of the respectable class, keeping the cowboys under control. However, while a loyal servant, he can never join their community. He is tainted. There are snide remarks about his friendship with a killer like Doc. Sheriff Cotton Wilson dogs Wyatt, offering a pessimistic vision of his future. In Fort Griffin, Wyatt is disgusted that Wilson had not tried to detain Clanton and Ringo. Wilson justifies his inaction with 'I've been a lawman for 25 years and all I've got to show for it is a room at the back of a cruddy boarding house'. Later Wyatt finds that Wilson is now county sheriff in Tombstone. Once a good lawman, he is now corrupt, boasting of $25,000 in the bank. He offers Wyatt a huge bribe, adding he should take it as he will never get much from the town. It is a bleak depiction of Western towns, in line with the cynicism of the Adult Westerns of the 1950s. And the gunfight offers no resolution.

Tombstone (1993)

This modern attempt to be as authentic as possible has come to be regarded as the definitive cinematic telling of the gunfight at the OK Corral. In Tombstone, it is referenced in posters and other imagery far more than any other film. Its popularity is a combination of its narrative complexity, excellent ensemble cast and high attention to detail in costuming. All these factors come together to provide a film that – rightly or wrongly – is perceived as authentic.

Wyatt Earp (Kurt Russell) arrives in Tombstone. He's quit his job as a marshall in Dodge City and now just wants to make money. With him are his brothers Virgil (Sam Elliott), Morgan (Bill Paxton) and friend Doc (Val Kilmer). Though the town has aspirations of progress and sophistication, there are daily shoot-outs involving the Cowboys. When Wyatt asks 'what about all these saloons?', the marshall responds: 'the fact is – Cowboys are good for business, that's the real Mother Lode in Tombstone, 24 hours a day you got liquor, hostesses, gambling'.

Wyatt wants a piece of this action. It's a new start, but he still carries the psychological scars of his former job. Steeped in violence, he shows no reaction to the gunplay all around him. In order to make a start in the new town, he casually enters a saloon and sadistically humiliates and then beats up the card dealer. He then takes his job.

His brothers, however, cannot stomach the violence. After the Marshall is killed by Curly Bill, Virgil takes his place. If this is to be their home, he argues, they need to take a stand. Wyatt reluctantly agrees to help. This is not because he has changed his mind, but rather he must support his brothers. The gunfight at the OK Corral sparks a blood feud. In retaliation, Morgan is shot in the back and Virgil wounded in an ambush. Enraged, Wyatt hunts down and kills the Cowboys.

Unlike previous films, Wyatt is not about law and order. He chats and jokes as Cowboy Johnny Tyler (Billy Bob Thornton) shoots a drunken miner down in the street in broad daylight. It is only when his family is threatened that he takes action. He becomes a vigilante. Personal vengeance is presented as equivalent to justice and this probably struck a chord with audiences. Having cleared out the Cowboys, Wyatt leaves Tombstone. He has neither interest nor connection with the community.

The relationship between Wyatt and Doc is very different to *Gunfight at the OK Corral*. They have a strong bond, but this has no impact on their other relationships. Wyatt falls in love with actress Sadie Marcus (Dana Delaney) and at the end, he rides off with her. Matching them, Doc and Kate (Joanna Pacula) are also a strong couple. The intriguing pairing is of Doc and Johnny Ringo (Michael Biehn). Both are surprised that the other is as well educated as they are – a highlight of the film is their Latin 'duel'. Matched against each other, they must engage in the ultimate gunfight.

Modern Tombstone

Today, Tombstone is a successful tourist town. Business and employment flow from the myth and imagery of its heyday, over 130 years ago. In examining how the Wild West is imagined, we focus on Tombstone during Helldorado Days, a carnivalesque festival held each October.

Establishing liminal space and time

The festival commences each morning with the national anthem. This is a solemn ceremony, starkly contrasting with the fun and fantasy to come. In the main street, the festival marshall calls on the audience to remove their hats. Men are instructed to place their hand on their hearts and former service personnel to provide their salute. That so many do so is a reminder of how militarised a society the United States is. The anthem is sung with gusto. Even though there are foreign tourists in the crowd, no leeway is allowed. The marshall gives the orders, there is no concept at all of anyone being allowed to opt out.

Such a ceremony accords with the *ritual structure* of festivals outlined by Falassi (1987). In this seminal work, he proposed a series of ten rituals that were commonly found in festivals around the world. While rarely planned as such, these rituals evolved as a reflection of basic human needs and beliefs, ceremonially framing the components and actions of an event and providing meaning and structure. The singing of the national anthem functions as a *rite of valorisation*, the first of Falassi's rituals. This communal singing claims the time and space for the festival; it will now become a liminal experience, markedly different from normal time and space.

Helldorado Gunfight Theater

Tombstone hosts a number of theatrical attractions, with professional actors performing daily shows. In addition to the OK Corral (Figure 5.2), there are the Helldorado Gunfight Theater, Tombstone Gunfighters and Doc Holliday's Gunfight Palace. During the festival, the actors – dressed as 'cowboys' with the distinctive red sashes – wander the streets drumming up customers.

The Helldorado Gunfight Theater is a block off main street. The audience grabs a beer and sits on bleachers. The cast consists of three actors (Figures 5.3 and 5.4). One is a sheriff, the others cowboys, their act is comic. Laughs come from the cowardly drunk sheriff, who ultimately turns the tables. The interplay is reminiscent of the Three Stooges. There's no attempt at historical veracity, just a simple satisfying entertainment.

Main street skits

Over the weekend, a full program of short performances takes place in the main street. Described as *skits*, all involve amateurs – a contrast to the professionals of the commercial attractions. Props are minimal, but great care is taken with the

Figure 5.2 Entrance to the OK Corral (photo W. Frost).

Figure 5.3 Performances at the Helldorado Gunfight Theater (photo W. Frost).

Figure 5.4 Performances at the Helldorado Gunfight Theater (photo W. Frost).

authenticity of costume, weaponry and frontier vernacular. Such authenticity is qualified, in many cases it is highly mediated by film. Nonetheless, the audience and performers share common expectations of what is acceptable in terms of this perceived authenticity. Getting it wrong, through including a jarring modernism, might expose the performers to unwelcome ridicule. Underpinning this quest for Western authenticity, the skits are bounded by an array of storyline tropes, again heavily influenced by the interplay of myth and cinema.

Many of the skits involve the Earps in gunplay. Nobody tries to follow history exactly. Rather, the heroic lawmen face off against sundry villains. The common trope involves the smartly dressed Earps trying to make an arrest. In accordance with myth, the Earps must make a speech about the need for law and order and call on the malefactor to surrender. In turn, their opponents must refuse, usually with appropriate bravado and cussing. This leads to the inevitable shoot-out. Real guns are used, loaded with blanks. The villains are vanquished. Occasionally, one of the marshall's sidekicks also bites the dust, but Wyatt Earp is always unharmed.

A few skits steer away from the Earps and are more adventurous in their narrative. Two are considered, as they touch upon some subversive elements in the mythology of the West.

The Mexican

A Mexican walks into a saloon. Dressed in a Vaquero outfit, he's quiet and bespectacled. The patrons yell for him to get out – they don't like Mexicans in Tombstone. They roughly throw him into the street. There's some nervous laughs from the audience, who are mainly Anglo-Saxon in origin. The Mexican returns with a pistol and calls to his tormentors to come out and face him. As they emerge, he shoots them down. Those remaining inside argue about who should take him on. Their growing panic is contrasted with their continued macho language and posturing. None will back down and apologise. As in childhood games, their deaths are exaggerated, as each performer seeks to outdo the others (Figure 5.5).

The widows

Two middle-aged widows arrive in Tombstone. Dressed in black, they are on their way to California, but have lost all their money (Figure 5.6). The women from a saloon suggest that they can earn some money as dancehall girls. At first the widows are hesitant. They are, after all, respectable. With seemingly no other choices, they agree and change into colourful and revealing costumes. One, in particular, dons pink underwear and a blonde wig (Figure 5.7).

Three miners come in for a good time. The experienced women coach the widows in their new roles. They need to encourage the miners to spend big. The widows are successful. The miners drink too much and lapse into semi-consciousness, thereby avoiding any possibility of sex (Figure 5.8). There is much laughter from the crowd at the hopelessness of the inebriated miners. The widows warm to their job and decide they will stay in Tombstone.

Figure 5.5 Those shot by the Mexican die in an exaggerated performance (photo W. Frost).

Figure 5.6 The transformation of the widows (photo W. Frost).

Figure 5.7 The transformation of the widows (photo W. Frost).

Figure 5.8 The transformation of the widows (photo W. Frost).

Figure 5.9 Dressing up as Wyatt and Sadie Earp (photo W. Frost).

Figure 5.10 Taking on the persona of the saloon girl (photo W. Frost).

This is a transformative parable. At first the widows are meek and passive – *invisible* in their sombre black clothing. Once changed into more revealing clothes, they are sexualised and desirable. Their age is now unimportant. In their new roles they are in charge. It is the male miners, desperately willing to pay for company and drink, who are passive, powerless and objects of the crowd's scorn.

La passeggiata

Hundreds of costumed participants promenade the wooden sidewalks in their finest. It is an informal parade that echoes the spirit of the past, where there was entertainment and status in seeing and being seen. Unlike the skits, there are no scripts, though it is still a performance.

For men the most common look is the Earps, but this is mediated through the film *Tombstone* (1993), the popularity of which is evidenced through the number of film posters on display and the copying of costumes from that movie (Figure 5.9). Participants aim to channel Kurt Russell (and intriguingly *not* Henry Fonda, Burt Lancaster or Kevin Costner).

However, there are just as many women and men in this passeggiata. Many of these women are influenced by the fashions in the film *Tombstone*. Just as men want to look like Kurt Russell or Sam Elliott playing the Earp men; women aspire to represent the Earp women (played by Dana Delaney and Joanna Pacula). The Earps were complex moral characters. Though often represented as soberly dressed lawmen, they were also involved in saloons, gambling and prostitution. Their common law wives were also involved in prostitution. Such shades of grey are well-known and seemingly embraced by participants at Helldorado Days. A further subversive element comes with the popularity of Kate Elder. A Hungarian whose real name was Mary Harony, she was a prostitute who was also romantically involved with Johnny Ringo (Tefertiller 1997). Foreign, duplicitous and permissive, she has evolved to become the iconic Tombstone woman. Accordingly, many participants want to dress like the *bad* woman and lean towards corsets, feather boas and fishnet stockings (Figure 5.10). While Tombstone's infamy rests on being a violent macho town, its modern imagining has been mediated by films and role-playing in such a way that it is now distinguished by fluid interpretations of masculinity and femininity.

6   Fort Sumner

Mama, put my guns in the ground
I can't shoot them anymore.
('Knockin' on Heaven's Door',
written and performed by
Bob Dylan for *Pat Garrett and
Billy the Kid*, 1973)

The more bastards I dust, the more news stories they write.
(Billy the Kid, played by Emilio Estevez, in *Young Guns*, 1988)

Introduction

While Tombstone and Dodge City celebrate the lawman, it is the outlaw that is the hero in the New Mexican towns of Fort Sumner, Lincoln and Mesilla. Billy the Kid is fêted in films and by tourists. Enigmatic and romanticised, despite the protests of those who view him as a cold-blooded killer, his legend remains firmly entrenched.

Such iconography is paradoxical. A lawbreaker and quintessential outsider, films and other media have elevated the Kid so that he now receives official approval through having a national scenic byway and tourism marketing brand bearing his name. More than any other outlaw of the Wild West, he has been reimagined as an American Robin Hood, unjustly wronged and standing up for the marginalised. Indeed, he continues to make news through ongoing attempts to grant him a posthumous pardon (Wheeler *et al.* 2011).

Fort Sumner, site of his death and grave, provides an extraordinary example of the selective imagining of the West and its mythology. It is a poignant and disturbing *Dark Tourism* destination. While Billy the Kid draws tourists, his end is juxtaposed with this being the final location for the Long Walk of the Navajo, often referred to as the Navajo Trail of Tears (Figures 6.1 and 6.2). In 1864, the US government forcibly removed the Navajo from their lands in Arizona and western New Mexico and relocated them at Bosque Redondo on the Pecos River. Approximately 9,000 Navajo walked 500 kilometres to their new home, which

Figure 6.1 Contrasting stories at museums in Fort Sumner (photo W. Frost).

Figure 6.2 Contrasting stories at museums in Fort Sumner (photo W. Frost).

quickly turned into a death camp. In 1868, no longer able to ignore the high mortality rates, the government decided to abandon the Navajo reservation at Fort Sumner and the survivors were allowed to walk back to their ancestral lands (Sides 2006). As is often found in the West, such historical episodes are often marginalised and largely forgotten. Certainly, while Billy the Kid has been the subject of many films, there have been none dealing with the Navajo Long Walk.

The outlaw myth

The myth of the romantic outlaw exists in many societies throughout history. With Robin Hood as a template, instances include the *Social Bandits* of colonial Peon societies and the *Frontier Outlaws* of nineteenth-century Anglo settler societies. The following discussion draws on four intersecting bodies of literature. The first is an historical analysis of the outlaw phenomenon, generally comparative and encompassing historians, sociologists and folklorists (including Hobsbawm 1969; Kooistra 1989; Seal 1996). The second examines how outlaws have been represented in cinema (Calder 1974; Lawrence 2005; Slotkin 1992). The third considers their place in tourism (Beeton 2004; Frost 2006; Wheeler *et al.* 2011). The fourth is the literature on hero myths and their role in society (Campbell 1949) – which we have previously applied to travel narratives (Laing and Frost 2012, 2014). This last field is particularly important (though often overlooked), for if an outlaw is viewed as a hero, does that require them to fit the patterns of heroic mythology and folklore?

Drawing on this extensive literature, the outlaw myth comprises the following common elements:

1 The outlaw hero comes from humble origins. He is a member of a dispossessed or marginalised underclass. This may be on the basis of ethnicity, religion or class.
2 Injustice and oppression rules. The state/authority fails to remedy this and is often an active agent in this inequity. The police, courts and government are the puppets of big business interests such as landowners and railways.
3 The hero is young, consequently innocent and naive, but also headstrong. He has personal qualities that make him a natural leader. His ability to stand out may be epitomised in physical prowess or wearing distinctive *flash* clothing.
4 Initially he tries to avoid trouble. There may be a past history of a brush with the law, even time in jail, when he was younger.
5 There is an incident that forces the hero to change. Often it is a cruel injustice against his family, particularly a mother or sister. This is akin to Campbell's *Call to Adventure*, which unwittingly forces the hero to embark on a journey.
6 In a corrupt and decadent society, the hero must go outside the law to take revenge.

7   In taking personal revenge, he unwittingly seeks justice for all who are oppressed.

8   Action is only taken against the oppressors and this aids others who are suffering ('robbing from the rich to give to the poor'). The common people are sympathetic and provide assistance.

9   The outlaw is bold and fearless – sometimes a cunning trickster (Seal 1996) – and his daring exploits expose the inadequacies and impotence of the authorities.

10 The heroic outlaw is 'a symbol of social and political discontent, and this is what separates them from common robbers and murderers' (Kooistra 1989: 37–38). A legend develops, disseminated through traditional media such as stories and songs (Seal 1996).

11 The outlaw is betrayed and destroyed. The traitor is often someone he trusted (a strong Christian allegory). Despite his destruction, the outlaw has succeeded in drawing attention to the injustices. His oppressors are exposed and defeated. His sacrifice was worthwhile.

Applying this to the Western context leads to a few further qualifications. The frontier is a zone of uncertain behaviour and morality. Economic opportunities abound, but government is weak and uneven. Property rights are confused and fluid, tempting the powerful and ruthless to attempt to monopolise them. Such conditions provoke conflict and injustice, so that the frontier and outlawry are intertwined. The period immediately after the Civil War propelled a large flow of former soldiers westwards, both seeking new opportunities and leaving their past behind. Displaced, violent, damaged; they attracted trouble. The outlaw hero is a White myth and he usually cannot be Black, Hispanic or Native American, though he may have supporters and allies from these groups (Wheeler *et al.* 2011).

An intriguing Western variation is the parallels between the lawman and the outlaw. Both may have similar backgrounds and outlooks and it may only be the accidents of fate that have set them against each other. Wyatt Earp, for instance, may be seen this way. This is a particularly strong theme in *Tombstone*, where the shooting of his brothers forces him to operate outside the law. There are also parallels in that former outlaws – perhaps even past associates of the hero – are recruited to work as hired guns to do the dirty work for landowners and railways.

Hollywood utilised a variety of outlaw archetypes. *Bad* outlaws function as out-and-out villains. Often these were played as charismatic, flamboyant and ruthless; dangerous opponents who will not be easily defeated. Some actors specialised in these roles, such as Eli Wallach, Lee Marvin and Lee Van Cleef (who wore a black frock coat in the style of Wyatt Earp). Then there are outlaws whose *Time is passing*. With a violent past that is catching up on them, they cannot change their ways. Sympathetically portrayed, they are nevertheless doomed. Examples include the title characters of *The Gunfighter* (1950), *Shane* (1953) and *The Wild Bunch* (1969). Finally, there is the *good* outlaw. Films 'based on a true story' of a real outlaw often take this perspective. Even if completely fictionalised, Hollywood saw the advantage in making such an appeal to authenticity. The two most common instances were Jesse James and Billy the Kid and it is the latter that we focus on.

Billy the Kid

He was probably born Henry McCarty, probably in 1859 and possibly in New York (for biographical details we follow Gardner 2011). Following the death of his father, the family moved West – Indianopolis, Wichita, Denver, Santa Fe, Silver City. His mother died when he was about 14. Hanging around mining camps and military outposts, he became known as Henry Antrim (after his stepfather) or simply as the Kid due to his slight physique. He had a few scrapes with the law, each getting progressively more serious, until in 1877 he shot a man in a saloon brawl in Fort Grant, Arizona.

With a murder charge hanging over him, he skedaddled to New Mexico. Now calling himself William H. Bonney, he fell in with a group known as 'The Boys'. Arrested for stealing a horse from an Englishman called John Henry Tunstall, he was surprised to be offered a job by Tunstall as a ranch hand.

Tunstall was immersed in what came to be known as the Lincoln County War. Commerce in the area was monopolised by Lawrence Murphy and James Dolan. To break their grip, Tunstall joined with Alexander McSween and John Chisum in opening a rival store and bank in Lincoln. Matters came to a head when Tunstall was murdered by Dolan's men. The Boys now became 'The Regulators' and sought revenge. Even though the Kid had only known Tunstall for less than three months, they had formed a close bond. As the vendetta unfolded, the Kid took part in the killing of Sheriff Brady (who was in Dolan's pay) and others who had murdered Tunstall. In turn, McSween was killed in a shoot-out involving over 100 men in Lincoln.

The Kid shifted to Fort Sumner and engaged in rustling. Further shootings occurred. When he was wrongly accused of killing a lawyer, he struck a deal with Governor Lew Wallace (who had just written *Ben Hur*) to give evidence against the real killer in return for a pardon. With this coming to nothing, he remained an outlaw. Just before Christmas 1880, the Kid was captured by Sheriff Pat Garrett. Convicted of the murder of Sheriff Brady, the Kid was sentenced to hang. However, in April 1881, he broke out of Lincoln Jail, killing two deputies. With the Kid rumoured to be in the vicinity of Fort Sumner, where his girlfriend Paulita Maxwell lived, Garrett and his posse rode there on the night of 14 July 1881. When the Kid entered a darkened room in the Maxwell house, Garrett shot and killed him.

Pat Garrett is often portrayed as the Kid's friend who ultimately betrays him. However, while they knew each other, they were not friends. There is an interesting parallel between the two. In 1876, Garrett was 26 years old and engaged in buffalo hunting. One morning he got into a fight over washing-up water with his friend Joe Briscoe. As their punch-up escalated, Garrett shot Briscoe.

Turning himself in at Fort Griffin, the sheriff decided there could be no charges as there were no witnesses. Garrett was free to go. In contrast, when the Kid killed a man in a fight a year later, there were witnesses and charges laid (Gardner 2011).

What dogs Garrett's reputation is the manner of the Kid's death. It was a darkened room. The Kid, who spoke fluent Spanish, asked 'Quién es' (Who is it?). Garrett knew the Kid well enough to recognise his voice and let off two shots. The Kid was armed and may have gone for his pistol. Or he may not have. Garrett took no chances and fired at the dangerous gunman. Under the conventions of Western mythology, this was no fair fight, no brave gun duel in the sun. This was nothing like the direct confrontation at the OK Corral. Accordingly, Garrett has tended to be criticised, sometimes even villified as a cowardly assassin or Judas.

Dead at 21, the Kid was romanticised to fit the legend of the outlaw hero. Young, handsome, charismatic. Fast and fearless with a gun. Popular with the Hispanics, he spoke their language fluently. He loved dancing and dressed flashly. Befriended by Tunstall, he was duty-bound to seek vengeance to repay the Englishman's trust. Through his actions, he exposed the corruption of the authorities, forcing Washington to intervene. Whether or not this is exactly true, this is the popular interpretation that continues through to the current day.

The cinematic Kid

We consider five films. Some are mostly fictional and fanciful, others claim authenticity. As with films regarding Wyatt Earp, there are recurring storylines and plot twists, with film-makers conscious of previous representations of the myth.

The Outlaw (1943)

Legendary for all the wrong reasons, this Howard Hughes production is actually quirky and engaging. It is dominated by Jane Russell and her revealing outfits. She is Rio, who has a love–hate relationship with Billy the Kid (Jack Beutel). For both, it was their first starring role, but the fame they gained was negated by Hughes keeping them on contract and not allowing them to work elsewhere. Russell would eventually become a noted musical comedy star, she is excellent as Calamity Jane in *The Paleface* (1948); but Beutel's career stalled.

The film starts in 1881 in Lincoln, New Mexico. A deputy tells Sheriff Pat Garrett (Thomas Mitchell) that Doc Holliday (Walter Huston) has arrived in town. Garrett is not concerned as Holliday is his friend. He's more worried for the horse thief Holliday is chasing. The Kid has unwittingly bought the stolen horse and its ownership is a source of friction throughout the film. Wary of each other's reputation, they won't fight. Garrett is disappointed, he dislikes the Kid and is upset that Holliday has a new friend. The Kid kills a man who draws first, a critical scene foreshadowing that he is doomed to always be a target. When Garrett tries to arrest him, Holliday helps him escape, but the Kid is wounded. Holliday takes him to Rio's house to recover. She is Holliday's girl, but falls for the Kid.

The film is odd for its inclusion of Holliday. He belongs in a completely different storyline in another state (Chapter 5). This alternate history gives *The Outlaw* an unreal fairytale atmosphere. Adding further confusion, in 1881 Holliday was 30 years old and Garrett 31. However, Huston was 60 and Mitchell 51 when the film was released. It is jarring that they are too old. Furthermore, Mitchell always played the good guy, such as Doc Boone in *Stagecoach*. Here, he is bitter, surly and untrustworthy.

The twist comes with Garrett shooting Holliday (who actually lived to 1887). The Kid takes the opportunity to disappear with Rio. Garrett is convinced to tell people that the Kid lies in the grave. He is given the Kid's distinctive pistols to verify the story that he has rid the Territory of the dangerous outlaw. That Holliday will take part in the gunfight at the OK Corral three months later is conveniently disregarded.

Jane Russell returned to outlaw territory by playing Belle Starr in *Montana Belle* (1952). This was an example where Hollywood abandoned all pretence of following a true story. Instead the focus is on Belle's double life – a variation on the outlaw as trickster. As Belle, Russell is dressed as a man, leads the outlaw gang and is a crack shot. However, when she puts on a blonde wig, she is transformed into sultry saloon singer Montana and nobody can see her true identity. Yes, this plot was copied for the television series *Hannah Montana* (2006–2011).

The Left-Handed Gun (1958)

Cheaply made in 12 days on Hollywood sets, this is a dark, allegorical tale. In essence, it follows the basic structure of the true story. The Kid (Paul Newman) is befriended by Tunstall and takes revenge for the rancher's murder. Arrested by Garrett (John Dehner), the Kid escapes from Lincoln Jail, killing two deputies. Finally, Garrett shoots him at night as he comes through a doorway. There are, however, liberties. Garrett and the Kid are portrayed as very good friends. This changes after the Kid shoots up Garrett's wedding. At the end, the Kid goes against Garrett with an empty holster. With all his friends dead or rejecting him, he just wants to end it.

Despite its low budget, this was a film with strong artistic pretensions. The script by Gore Vidal is heavy with biblical allusions. Method actor Newman grunts and wails, signifying that the illiterate Kid is inarticulate and child-like. Thirty-three years old at the time, Newman was embarrassed that he was too old for the role and this particularly shows in the second half of the film. The Kid is an emotionally immature child in a man's body. Highly adept with a gun, he is unable to control his use of it, constantly making poor decisions (Bignell 1996).

Though the allegories and acting now seem dated, this is a powerfully bleak vision of the West. The Kid shoots six men in cold blood. All plead for him to stop, begging for their lives. Even a wedding degenerates into a bloody shoot-out. In turn, the Kid's two comrades are both shot down just at the moment they decide to give up their outlaw's path. The Kid is shot in a lit doorway, with Garrett hidden in the dark. There are no heroic gunfights, no evenly matched duels. The townspeople are just as bloodthirsty. When the sheriff is shot, they turn into an angry mob, killing the innocent McSween, burning his house and wantonly smashing up his store. The Kid is not separate from this community, they are just as savage and hot-headed as he is.

Observing all is Moultrie (Hurd Hadfield), representing the voyeuristic audience. A young fey drifter, he begins to follow the Kid around. Gradually his character and role builds. When the Kid disarms a marshall, Moultrie pockets the bullets. Later, he brings the Kid shortbreads and books in jail. The books are dime novels, stories of the Kid's exploits. In the end, he boasts to the Kid that he has done very well out of their friendship; selling souvenirs and writing letters that have been turned into dime novels. When he shows the outlaw the photographs of the bodies of his friends that he is selling, the Kid is sickened and chases him off. Rebuffed, Moultrie turns, telling Garrett where the Kid is. Moultrie, more than Garrett, is the Judas in this telling of the outlaw myth. In his single-minded pursuit of knowing the gunfighter, Moultrie functions like a *parasocial fan* (Kim 2012), obsessively stalking and constructing a connection with a celebrity.

Moultrie also functions as a troubadour, disseminating and retelling the Kid's story. He is a Will Scarlett to the Kid's Robin Hood. Similar roles occur in later movies regarding fictional outlaws. In *Cat Ballou* (1965), Nat King Cole and Stubby Kaye literally tell the story though song. In *From Noon Till Three* (1976), the outlaw's story is turned into a romantic novel by the woman (Jill Ireland) he has a quick fling with. In *Unforgiven* (1992), gunfighter English Bob (Richard Harris) has Beauchamp (Saul Rubinek) as a biographer in his retinue. When English Bob is beaten up by Sheriff Little Bill (Gene Hackman), the writer switches to writing his stories about the victor. Such roles provide a layer of authenticity, a story-teller within the story who the audience knows is embroidering the legend.

In this cheaply made film, nearly all the action takes place in two towns, Lincoln and Modero (essentially Fort Sumner). The two places are strongly contrasted. Lincoln, the American town, is violent and dysfunctional. Modero, its Hispanic neighbour, is a strong community. Here the Kid is safe, for the locals will protect him. It is a place of fiestas and weddings, a romanticised view of Hispanic culture quite different from what is normally portrayed in Hollywood films.

Chisum (1970)

A rare film in which John Wayne played a real life person. Evoking an alternative narrative to *The Searchers*, Wayne's Chisum was in love with his brother's wife. In frustration, he left Texas and went West to New Mexico to establish a ranch. Twenty years later, he is joined by his niece Sally (Pamela McMyler). Though wealthy, Chisum is upset by Murphy (Forrest Tucker) and Sheriff Brady (Bruce Cabot) driving out competitors. With Tunstall (Patric Knowles) and McSween, Chisum sets up a rival business.

Sally attracts two suitors: Pat Garrett (Glenn Corbett) and William Bonney (27-year-old Geoffrey Deuel). She is more taken with the latter, but her uncle is worried as he recognises that the Kid has a dangerous wild streak. When Tunstall is murdered, the Kid reverts to his outlaw ways, shooting down the perpetrators and Sheriff Brady in cold blood – thereby settling the issue of the romantic triangle. With Chisum finishing off Murphy, order is restored. However, there is no place for the bloodthirsty Kid and he rides off with a price on his head.

Chisum is aware that the relationships between Sally, Pat and Billy are a replay of his own youth. A generation ago, he was the wild brother. Now, he feels the girl should choose stability. Sally realises this when Billy starts his vengeful killings (in this he is reminiscent of Ethan in *The Searchers*). Pat and Billy are positioned as 'brothers', very different in temperament, but with a strong friendship. Billy rides off an outlaw and there is the hint that they have unfinished business. The character of the uncertain youngster was common in many of Wayne's films in the late 1960s and early 1970s. They were usually male, such as Robert Carradine in *The Cowboys* (1972) and Ron Howard in *The Shootist* (1976); though probably the most well-known is Mattie (Kim Darby) in *True Grit* (1969). The standard trope in these Vietnam-era Westerns was that the older Wayne would guide these troubled and confused youths towards common sense. Billy in *Chisum* almost makes it, but ultimately takes the wrong path.

Pat Garrett and Billy the Kid (1973)

Pat Garrett is hired as sheriff and ordered to hunt down Billy the Kid. There is practically no back-story. Tunstall is not mentioned. Chisum is the rapacious villain (perhaps a dig at the recent John Wayne film). How and why the Kid became an outlaw is not explained, perhaps director Sam Peckinpah assumed viewers knew most of the story.

Garrett (James Coburn) was formerly an outlaw in the Kid's gang (a completely fictional invention for this film). He is the Judas figure, self-loathing and shunned by nearly everyone. In the end, he shoots the Kid in a darkened room in Fort Sumner, making this the only one of these five films to attempt an authentic representation of what happened. In focussing on Garrett, Peckinpah is revisiting a similar plotline in *The Wild Bunch* (1969). In that film, former gang member Deke Thornton (Robert Ryan) is recruited to hunt and kill former comrade Pike Bishop (William Holden). Deke takes the job as a way of getting out of Yuma Jail, where he was savagely whipped. He has made a promise to himself that he is never going back to jail. Pike respects that decision, which is in line with the gang's code of self-preservation. In contrast, no motivation is ever explained for Garrett changing sides. There is no coercion and the money does not seem sufficient. Garrett clearly hates the job and, as the film progresses, he hates himself more and more.

The Kid (Kris Kristofferson) is handsome, articulate and charismatic. Everyone likes him. He is a natural leader of his gang. As befits the outlaw myth, he is a trickster. Running into Deputy Alamosa Sam (Jack Elam), they decide to settle matters with a proper showdown. Back to back, they will walk ten paces and then fire. Sam cheats, turning at the count of eight. Except, the Kid knows Sam will cheat. He turned and aimed at the count of one and so already has the drop on Sam.

Like *The Left-Handed Gun*, this is a film rich in symbolism and allegory, particularly from the New Testament (Stevens 1996). Our favourite scenes are linked by the Bob Dylan song 'Knockin' on Heaven's Door'. Dylan contributed an evocative soundtrack and played one of the Kid's gang, essentially functioning as the outlaw's minstrel. Garrett recruits husband-and-wife team Slim Pickens and Katy Jurado to attack a hideout. Jurado, a Mexican actress who came to prominence in *High Noon* (1951) does most of the killing, but Pickens is mortally wounded. As he sits down to die, 'Knockin' on Heaven's Door' is played. It is repeated when Alamosa Sam lies dying. These powerful scenes, dominated by what would become such an iconic song, are reserved for two well-known older character actors in Slim Pickens and Jack Elam. It signifies their special place in the Western genre and that their lawmen characters, while flawed, are heading for heaven. Surprisingly, the Kid receives no musical farewell. As referred to symbolically and explicitly throughout the film, while many see him as a good person, he is still going to hell.

Young Guns (1988)

This final film sticks more closely to the known historical facts than the other four. In telling the story of the Kid, it covers the period from his arrival in Lincoln up to the massive shoot-out in which McSween was killed and which ultimately ended the Lincoln County War. Accordingly, it finishes almost where *Pat Garrett and Billy the Kid* started.

The selling point for this production was in casting six members of the *Brat Pack* to play the Regulators. Emilio Estevez is Billy the Kid. At the time he was 25 years old and had recently had major successes with the youth-orientated films *The Breakfast Club* (1985) and *St Elmo's Fire* (1985). Co-starring were equally wild-partying Brat Packers: Charlie Sheen (Dick), Kiefer Sutherland (Doc), Lou Diamond Phillips (Chavez), Dermot Mulroney (Steve) and Casey Siemaszko (Charlie). Warming to a theme of Hollywood youngsters reimagining the Western for the youth market, the cast includes the sons of well-known actors including brothers Estevez and Sheen, Sutherland, Patrick Wayne and Cody Palance.

Tunstall (Terence Stamp) has 'a soft spot for runaways, derelicts and vagrant types', the 'flotsam and jetsam of frontier society'. His six boys – somewhat reminiscent of J.M. Barrie's 'Lost Boys' – are treated with respect and encouragement. He tells newcomer Billy that he expects him to learn to read, for 'you need more than skill with a firearm to succeed in the new world'.

Murphy (Jack Palance) is competing with Tunstall for government contracts. The Irishman tries to frighten the Englishman off, invoking old country enmities:

> Do you see our good sheriff sitting up there on his horse? Do you know how much money he has invested in my store? His life savings. This is a new country, we won't be bowing down to you no more Englishman. Get ready for Hell.

When Tunstall is murdered, the boys seek revenge. Dick, the mild and sober one (interesting casting of Charlie Sheen) wants to operate within the law. Billy, increasingly a Peter Pan for the Lost Boys, wants blood vengeance and eventually kills Murphy and all his henchmen. While the film is mainly historically accurate, here it deviates; Murphy actually died from cancer before the Kid got to him.

As the gang pick off the villains, the newspapers focus on their exploits. Tunstall's reading lessons come in handy, allowing most of the boys to revel in the publicity. Dick is the exception, he hates it. He gets even angrier when he sees that his picture has appeared in the newspaper with the title of Billy the Kid. The Kid loves it, even when Dick complains 'you ain't no Robin Hood'. Doc muses over how supportive the newspapers are, commenting that 'this country needs a hero'.

Conforming to the outlaw myth, the Kid is a trickster, often sneaking up behind his victims and laughing while he shoots them. In a cantina, he sidles up to a stranger who is boasting that he will kill the Kid and claim the reward. Feigning interest in his fancy pistol, the Kid asks to look at it. What the hapless newcomer does not realise is that the Kid removes the bullets. Revealing that he is the Kid, Billy calls on him to draw. When the man's gun does not fire, the Kid shoots him dead. The Kid actually killed Joe Grant in similar circumstances to this, though it was some months later than the period covered in this film (Gardner 2011).

With the success of this film, a sequel was shot – *Young Guns II* (1990). Estevez, Sutherland and Diamond Phillips reprised their roles. Its twist was that Pat Garrett helps fake the death of the Kid, who reforms and lives happily into the twentieth century. In 1950, 'Brushy Bill' Roberts had made this claim and a museum dedicated to him as the Kid still exists in Hico, Texas. The other distinction of the sequel was an anthemic theme song: 'Blaze of Glory', by Jon Bon Jovi. The producers had approached Bon Jovi about using his earlier song 'Wanted Dead or Alive'. However, the singer explained that its references to cowboys were metaphorical, that song was about being a rocker on the road ('a steel horse I ride ... a loaded six string on my back'). A fan of *Young Guns*, he offered to write a new song for the film.

A tourist icon?

Fort Sumner is a dusty nondescript town. Except for Billy the Kid, it would attract little traffic. Even with him, it has a rundown ambience, with a marginal tourist trade. In the main street, the Dazend Movie Museum and Fort Sumner Film Office is closed, with no sign of opening hours (Figure 6.3). It does, however, feature a colourised replica of the iconographic photo – and only known picture – of the Kid (Figure 6.4).

Figure 6.3 Main Street Fort Sumner, the Movie Museum is closed (photo W. Frost).

The original fort is a few kilometres out of town. The museum draws in a few tourists, but it is nothing comparable with the celebration of Wyatt Earp in Tombstone. Next to the museum is the Kid's grave. A sign explains that the tombstone was stolen in 1950 and not recovered until 1976. It was then stolen again in 1981. After that, the grave was guarded by a steel cage (Figure 6.5). A stone marker reads 'Pals' and lists William H. Bonney, Tom O'Folliard and Charlie Bowdrie. In this cemetery, they are now together behind bars.

Figure 6.4 Life-sized cutout of the only known photo of the Kid (photo W. Frost).

Figure 6.5 Grave of Billy the Kid (photo by W. Frost).

7   The good outlaw

> We're suspicious of strangers. That's all. A hangover from the old days. The Old West.
>
> (Reno Kelly, played by Robert Ryan, *Bad Day at Black Rock*, 1956)

> Where I came from, if one did not want to die of poverty, one became a priest or a bandit.
>
> (Tuco, played by Eli Wallach, *The Good, the Bad and the Ugly*, 1966)

Introduction

The hero returns home after fighting in the war. The community is fractured, his father disowns him. Law and order have broken down, powerful and corrupt interests rule. Disguised as outlaws, the villains kidnap his girl and commit other outrages. To fight back, the hero enlists the help of a *good outlaw*. Together, they defeat the evil-doers and restore law and order.

It sounds like a Western. But it's not. It's *Ivanhoe* by Walter Scott (1819). Set in thirteenth-century England, the good outlaw who helps the eponymous hero is Robin Hood. As the myth of the West developed, he crossed the Atlantic and became the template and justification for a central character in many stories. Even real outlaws, such as Jesse James, claimed affinity with Robin Hood (Stiles 2002). When the boom in Westerns began in 1939, it was simple for Warner Brothers to take the actors, directors and most of the plot from the very popular *The Adventures of Robin Hood* (1938) and transfer it to the new genre.

Recent historical research has challenged the notion that Robin Hood was just a myth. Studies of court records have revealed a number of defendants named Robin Hood or similar, all in the right place and at the right time. Seemingly the name was applied – like a nickname – to a range of malcontents; implying that there was an original outlaw with a certain degree of notoriety (Knight 2003). Such ambivalence was recognised in a recent episode of *Doctor Who*; where the timelord is surprised to encounter Robin Hood, as he was sure he was only a myth.

In contrast, such niceties do not apply in Hollywood. A host of historical personages have been heavily fictionalised in film. As discussed in the previous chapter, *The Outlaw* (1943) has Pat Garrett killing Doc Holliday and allowing Billy the Kid to escape. While such liberties were commonplace, film-makers were constrained by certain core facts when dealing with history. As Elliott (2007) points out, *The Royal Tenenbaums* (2001) plays with the idea of a writer (Owen Wilson) discovering that George Custer actually survived the Battle of Little Bighorn, but only gets away with it as it is a comedy.

To avoid the restrictions of history, Hollywood has tended to focus more on fictional outlaws. This allows for a full scope in terms of incidents, characteristics, romantic entanglements and location. Nonetheless, the conventions of the *outlaw myth* are still followed more often than not. In this chapter, we extend the discussion from Chapter 6, moving on from real to fictional outlaws. In particular, our focus is on some of the great outlaw films of the 1950s. Not only were the 1950s a Golden Age of Westerns in both quality and quantity, the films of this period were distinguished by their adult themes, which included a strong emphasis on law-breaking and its consequences. As a result, the outlaws seeking a new start became a major part of the Western myth.

Shane (1953)

Shane begins with a small boy watching a lone horseman riding towards his home. The rider is a small, insignificant speck in the midst of a vast landscape fringed by the Grand Tetons of Wyoming, seemingly innocuous when juxtaposed with the grandeur of nature (Miller 1983). From a distance the boy cannot tell anything about him except he is mystery. When the stranger arrives, he introduces himself as Shane (Alan Ladd) and he will bring chaos and disorder to a small ranching community, affecting almost every character through both his actions and inactions.

Such imagery is repeated again and again in Westerns. In *Hondo* (1953), it is a stranger; in *The Searchers* (1956), it is the long lost brother and while in *The Tall T* (1957), it turns out to be a friendly neighbour, the wary father has picked up his rifle just in case. The arrival may be a cause for hospitality or reunion, or it may be that they bring death. The landscape out of which these riders emerge is vast and unforgiving, making mockery of any claim to mastery over the environment. Nature is the great leveller, even for the strongest and the bravest. Despite Tompkins' claim that 'when a lone horseman appears on the desert plain, he dominates it instantly, his view extends as far as the eye can see, and enemies are exposed to his gaze' (1992: 74), the rider is in fact at his most vulnerable and conquest is at best illusory. This is a landscape that portends death. While there is initial hospitality, tragedy is coming.

The young boy Joey (Brandon De Wilde) is instantly beguiled by the glamour of the stranger. The contrast between Shane's fringed buckskin plainsman shirt and trousers and a fancy Indian gun belt of silver and the plain farming clothes of Joey and his father Joe (Van Heflin) is stark. Joe's wife Marian (Jean Arthur) is also wide-eyed, as she spies him through the window of their log cabin. We get the first hint that Shane is a wanderer, with his comment 'I'm heading north.

Didn't expect to see any fences around here'. The family are oblivious to the likelihood that Shane will not stay long, so seduced are they by this unexpected visitor. But there is a sense of doom around Shane, that he will never be able to stop wandering the plains, which unfolds with the narrative. It is notable that he is played by Ladd, an actor more well-known for his work in *film noir*.

For Joe, Shane represents another pair of hands ('we're going to make a farm out of this place yet!'), although he distrusts him at first. Joe fears that Shane is connected to rancher Ryker and his gang, who are terrorising the farmers, to get them off the land. They take out a stump together, which has beaten Joe to date, symbolising his final clearance of the land and taming of nature. Shane is also handy with his fists, and as Joe finds out later on, with a gun, and is a support to Joe when his neighbours are keen to flee. The young Joey sees Shane as the ultimate hero, although Shane never glorifies his past to the boy. For Marian, Shane is a romantic interest, and she is captivated with his softly spoken demeanour.

Ladd is not the typical Hollywood Western leading man. Unlike Gary Cooper, John Wayne, Charlton Heston and later Clint Eastwood, he is short, just 5 foot 6 inches, and with his blond wavy hair, almost effeminate at times in appearance. He is arresting, however, with his direct glance and enigmatic smile. His lack of dialogue squares with the Western hero as a man of few words, who has eschewed affection and family life to the point that this 'ethic of self-denial ... turns the hero to stone. He becomes the desert butte' (Tompkins 1992: 214–215). When asked where he is bound, on arrival, Shane's reply is tautly ambiguous: 'One place and another. Some place I've never been'. Flora (1996) argues that despite the economy of language displayed, Shane is eloquent when he needs to be.

Fear over Shane prompts Ryker to bring Wilson (Jack Palance), another gunfighter, to town. He appears to be the antithesis of Shane, certainly in terms of his clothing – black Stetson, black boots and a black waistcoat – but also in the menace that he conjures up. But are the two men all that different in terms of their past? We get the feeling that the two men are acquainted, by the way they interact when the gang turns up at the farm, but also because of Shane's warning to the farmers to be careful of Wilson. As one of the farmers astutely comments: 'You seem to know an awful lot about this kind of business, Shane'. Horrocks (1995) suggests that they each recognise the other as an angel of death – Wilson in black and Shane his white counterpart, the avenging angel. Their meeting is the *dance of death* that all Westerns exult, an almost erotic (or homoerotic?) fascination with and yearning for death and dying. These men 'can't literally ravish each other ... instead they kill each other' (Horrocks 1995: 54). In contrast, the farmers are not fighters, although willing to help each other by rebuilding a burnt cabin. Their strength, unlike Shane's, lies in *community*. Horrocks (1995: 68) refers to this as an example of how 'male potency and sociability are inversely related' in the Western.

Marian realises what is at stake, crying 'Don't let [Joe] go Shane. Don't *anybody* go!' This is a classic scene in Westerns, where 'a man defies a woman's wishes by fighting with another man' (Tompkins 1992: 131), which can be traced to Wister's *The Virginian* (1902), along with the staged shoot-out as the narrative climax (Murdoch 2001). Tompkins (1992) argues that this defiance of feminine (maternal?) authority is consistent with the Western's male-centric focus, which casts domesticity to the shadows and marginalises the role of women on the frontier.

Back in his buckskins as he enters town, Shane has lost his farmers' garb, symbolic of his return to his gunfighting past. It is however fleeting, as he is all too aware. He tells the old man Ryker that his days are over, and when Ryker retorts 'What about yours, gunfighter?' Shane replies: 'The difference is, I know it'. As Horrocks (1995: 69) observes: 'the coming of civilization will wipe out such men as Shane: their romantic existence cannot exist in ordinary society'. They are an anachronism, along with 'the classic western legend of home and heroism' (Wallmann 1999: 150), given that Shane, despite his altruistic deeds on behalf of the community, has no place to settle down. He is the classic outlaw, protecting the weak from injustice, but too violent and dangerous to ever be a part of it (Kooistra 1989; Seal 1996; Wheeler *et al.* 2011).

Shane shoots Wilson, Ryker and the rest of the gang. He has cleaned up the threat that they represent and life is now apparently safe for the farmers, but at the cost of Shane's happiness – he must move on. As he says to Joey: 'There's no living with a killing. There's no going back for me'. He tasks the boy to look after his parents, another example of Shane's selflessness (Flora 1996). Like the outlaw, the gunfighter can be 'both dangerous and very good' and thus 'the transient killer becomes the struggling farmers' savior' (Prassel 1993: 290). Tompkins (1992: 220) describes this as the 'tragic sacrifice' of the gunfighter as hero – 'Having hardened himself to do murder, he can no longer open his heart to humankind. His love is aborted, cut off'. Joey's final call to Shane as he departs has entered Hollywood legend: 'Come back Shane! Pa's got things for you to do. And mother wants you, I know she does!' Joey is too young to realise the sacrifice that Shane has made.

Johnny Guitar (1954)

This is an inverted Western, where women fight it out to the death and good men – wearing black – watch on. Robertson (1995: 33) labels it *feminist camp*, in that it provides a critique on the 1950s view of women's place in society through exaggerating or subverting gender roles. The film begins with Johnny Guitar (Sterling Hayden), a wandering musician, witnessing a stagecoach robbery and riding away without taking any action. This establishes his character as weak and essentially passive. We soon find out that Johnny Guitar is an alias. Years ago he was a notorious gunfighter.

Johnny turns up at a hotel owned by Vienna (Joan Crawford). First viewed at the top of a staircase, legs apart, Vienna is garbed in a black shirt, belt and boots and brown breeches. This is the first of many scenes where she is in masculine dress, reflecting not only her power as the owner of the hotel, but also her dominant personality. One of her staff comments: 'I've never seen a woman who's more like a man. She thinks like one, acts like one, and sometimes makes me feel I'm not'. Vienna emasculates many of the men she encounters (Robertson 1995), including the Dancin' Kid, whose infantile name reflects the power imbalance in his relationship with Vienna.

The director, Nicholas Ray, intended the film to be an allegory of McCarthyism and this influenced some of his casting. Sterling Hayden was known to have been contrite over the evidence he gave to the House Committee on Un-American Activities, while Ward Bond, who played the leader of the lynch mob, was an infamous anti-Communist. The twist to the story is that Bond apparently perceived his role in *Johnny Guitar* to be that of 'the good guy' (Peterson 1996). Ray also plays with Western traditions, in which the bad guy always wore black. Initially, Vienna is faced with a posse of men in light clothing. Later, as the townspeople became more vengeful and irrational, they are all dressed in black, having come from a funeral.

Vienna and Johnny were once lovers. The possibility of rapprochement is interrupted by the arrival of a posse. While Sheriff Ward Bond is ostensibly in charge, it is Emma (Mercedes McCambridge) who is their real leader. They blame the Dancin' Kid for the hold-up of the stagecoach, in which Emma's brother was killed. They are also suspicious of Vienna and Johnny, even though they have no evidence of their involvement in the crime. Part of the feud between Emma and Vienna is economic – regarding control of land that the railroad needs – but more importantly there is jealousy and possibly even attraction.

Emma is almost comically vengeful, an overblown and at times magnificently psychotic performance by McCambridge. It has been argued that her repressed spinster is the lightning rod for the 'film's disgust for McCarthyist hysteria' (Peterson 1996: 6). The men, led by the sheriff, are less certain of Vienna's complicity in the deed, but are still happy to label her an outlaw and go along with the lynching. Vienna is a match for Emma, answering her threat to kill her with the retort 'Not if I kill you first'.

Both women are front and centre of the action, and neither appears willing to back down. Their role in this film is interesting, given the often passive characterisation of women in many Westerns. Horrocks (1995: 65) notes that *Johnny Guitar* is one of the few Western films where a woman is given 'any psychological depth', although the actions of Emma appear wildly overblown, especially when she burns down Vienna's hotel and cackles madly at the sight (as the film progresses, she resembles in costume and manner the evil witch from *The Wizard of Oz*). The motivation behind her relentless vengeance and hatred of Vienna appears to be a simple case of sexual jealousy, linked to the Dancin' Kid (Peterson 1996; Robertson 1995). Emma clearly wants him, as Vienna taunts, but she also appears to desire Vienna as well, an emotion she is both attracted to and repelled by. For this reason, Emma is often read as a (closet?) lesbian, another example of an individual who resides outside 1950s societal conventions (Peterson 1996; Robertson 1995). Vienna appears to understand this, with her comment 'You want the Kid and you're so ashamed of it you want him dead. And you want me dead too. Then maybe you can sleep at nights'.

Emma's suspicions of Vienna's complicity in the stagecoach robbery never seem convincing, and it is difficult to avoid the conclusion that Emma's envy has left her unhinged. This adds to the film's *camp* effect, defined by Robertson (1995: 33) as 'a sensibility committed to artifice and exaggeration, particularly with respect to sex and gender roles'. Strangely, art mimicked real life here, in that Joan Crawford and Mercedes McCambridge hated each other on the set, leading Joan to throw her fellow actress's clothes onto the road (Spoto 2010).

Vienna's clothing changes at various points in the film, becoming less masculine and more conventionally feminine, but always carrying a deeper meaning. It is designed to make her less threatening, which Peterson (1996) describes as a *masquerade*. Her slash of red lipstick is toned down and we get scenes of her in a white crinoline dress as she awaits the posse coming to kill her; a symbol of her purity/ innocence in contrast to their black garb and almost laughably impractical in the Western setting. At another stage, she is dressed in a scarlet gown in a scene with Johnny Guitar, reflecting Emma's label of her as a 'railway tramp' but also allowing their seduction to re-ignite. Questions might be asked as to how she got the money for the hotel. Vienna does not hide from her murky past, but wants to change and start anew. She asks several men to help her on this quest, including Johnny, seemingly unable to move forward without a man by her side.

Johnny Guitar's previous romantic history with Vienna is apparent from her glances at him, much to the envy of the Dancin' Kid. Johnny lets her walk all over him, including her comment 'That's pretty strong talk for a man who doesn't wear a gun'. He notes 'You're the boss', another illustration of her dominance over the male characters (Peterson 1996; Robertson 1995). Johnny's intention is to settle down after years spent wandering, and as he observes: 'A man's got to plant a root somewhere. This seems like a good place'. His passivity however appears to have its limits, and when he has to, he fights, reminiscent of *Shane*, shooting the gun out of the young Turkey's hands. It is only later that we find out his true identity – he is the famous gunslinger Johnny Logan. Vienna tells him that he is still 'gun crazy', suggesting the reason why they broke up as a couple some years ago.

Vienna is taken to a spot near the bridge to be hanged, but the men find that they have little stomach for it, leaving only Emma to bay for Vienna's blood. Johnny saves her by shooting the rope. Here we see a common outlaw convention, dating back in cinema to *The Adventures of Robin Hood* (1938). The Good Outlaw uses his special powers (either superior marksmanship or tricksterish disguise) to rescue the helpless in the nick of time. This occurs in many films. Our favourite is Joe De Rita in *The Bravados* (1958). Made just prior to joining *The Three Stooges*, De Rita is an outlaw who kills the hangman and takes his place. Garrulous, brightly dressed and quite odd, most of the townspeople avoid him; allowing him to break the other gang members out of jail. James Stewart would play a very similar role in *Bandolero!* (1968).

For Johnny Guitar, rescuing Vienna is the 'first chance I've had to be a hero', suggesting a transformation from his gunslinger past. Vienna changes her white dress for blue jeans and a red shirt, becoming masculine again when she needs to be active, alternating between *femme* and *butch* (Peterson 1996; Robertson 1995). The posse chase Vienna and Johnny to the Kid's hideout behind a waterfall. When the showdown between Vienna and Emma finally occurs – two women fighting over one man (the Kid) – it 'mimics a catfight more than it does a shootout' (Peterson 1996: 15). Vienna triumphs over her rival and ends up in Johnny's arms, dressed in pants and still in control. This revisionist Western thus concludes, in a direct reversal of the ending of *Shane*, with the passive former gunslinger being saved by the actions of a *good* woman.

3:10 to Yuma (1957)

While this movie was remade in 2007 with Russell Crowe and Christian Bale in the lead roles, it is the original film that we focus on here. The title song, played during the opening credits, highlights one of the themes lying at the heart of the film: 'A man may meet his fate, for fate travels everywhere'. Even a wanderer can't escape his destiny. The film also extols the virtue of standing up for what is right and the message this sends to others, particularly the young. Like many Westerns, *3:10 to Yuma* is a morality tale and resembles *Shane*, in that it suggests that some men are beyond redemption, and are fated to remain outside the law, never able to integrate into a community, however much they long for stability. A similar trope occurs in *Bend of the River* (1952), where two former outlaws (James Stewart and Arthur Kennedy) keep their pasts secret from the decent folk in the wagon train they are guiding. They want to prove to this community that they can change and thereby be worthy to join it. While one achieves this, the other reverts to his old ways.

The film begins with a stagecoach hold-up, witnessed by Dan Evans (Van Heflin) and his two sons. Evans, rather like the character Heflin plays in *Shane*, is a good man, but seemingly weak and put upon. He doesn't get involved in the shootings, justifying his actions to his boys: 'And get myself shot too?' The outlaw leader, Ben Wade (Glenn Ford), is a complex and charismatic character. While he is prepared to shoot through a human shield, he later requests that the body of the driver he shot be sent back to where he lived. There are other instances of his humanity throughout the film, such as his conversations with Evans' wife, juxtaposed with a wiliness and single-minded determination to escape justice that makes him capable of anything. In this way, the audience never quite knows how to take Wade, nor whether to cheer on his attempts to escape or hope for his comeuppance.

Evans reacts sharply to his wife's questioning about the robbery. His pride is wounded, and perhaps his conscience is hurting him too. The boys now echo what their father said to them at the time of the shootings, thus sharing the morality of the decision that was made with the use of the collective word *we*: 'What else could we do? Do you want us to get shot?' Evans is firm: 'That's life, we have to watch a lot of terrible things. Can't go chasing after outlaws'. This apathy clearly disappoints his wife but also sets an example for his sons that one should not get involved in other people's troubles. The shame that accompanies this inaction will later motivate Evans to bring Wade to justice and thus show his sons a different role model for living their lives.

Wade, in a bar in Bisbee, opens up to the saloon girl about his need to keep wandering: 'I never stay long in a place'. Evans comes into the bar and tells Wade: 'You drove off my cattle'. He is paid for the time it took him to round them up, but it is clear to both protagonists (and the audience) that this is a bribe to stop Evans going to the law. Wade even goads him about this ('Anything else you want to get paid for?'). When the marshall enters and captures Wade, Evans volunteers to transfer the prisoner at his house to custody and gain a $200 reward for his trouble. The money will help him get back on his feet, but there is a sense that he wants to redress his inactivity at the hold-up.

Evans' wife Alice (Leora Dana) is kind to Wade and is told a story about a woman that Wade once met. There is a suggestion that the two might have met on another occasion, although this is never explored in the film. Evans is very jealous and reproves Alice: 'Why did you have to sit there listening to him like that for?' When she demurs, he spells it out: 'All big-eyed and listening to him'. Like *Shane*, the outsider (in this case an outlaw) is a threat to the sanctity and security of the household. This prompts the husband in both cases to want to be a hero, and win back their wives' respect. Alice underscores this with her praise, aimed at making Evans see how his previous conduct was unacceptable: 'The boys are so proud ... proud of you. Their own father catching Ben Wade. Didn't you see them looking at you? I'm proud too'. Wade's comment after supper, however, jolts Alice and their elder son into realising the risks Evans is running: 'I'm obliged to you for your hospitality, ma'am, I really appreciate it. Your husband too. Hope I can send him back to you alright!'

The action thereafter chiefly revolves around the question of what is driving Evans to put his life in danger in this way, and whether it has its limits under pressure. He says to Wade: 'I'm just doing this for the money', to which Wade replies 'I know'. Is this Wade's comment on Evans' values? He is constantly testing Evans, looking for signs of weakness, or perhaps awake to them. When he tells Evans 'I didn't think you'd shoot', Evans' response ('You know I will next time') is met with an almost imperceptibly soft retort: 'Do I?' There is a long pause as the men stare at each other. There are hints of *High Noon* (1952) in these scenes, with both men watching the clock, aware of the impending arrival of the 3:10 train to Yuma. Wade offers him double the money to let him go. While Evans doesn't take up the offer, the temptation is huge, as the outlaw probes his weak spots: 'Cowpokes like us, we just don't belong in that kind of business ... killing ourselves trying to make a go of it alone. You've got to have money backing you'. He plants the idea of being a silent partner, and Evans shows how close he is to accepting the bribe ('How do I know I'll get it?'), before ordering Wade to be quiet, fearful of how long he can hold out against temptation.

Again like *High Noon*, others lack the moral fibre to help. The brother of the murdered stagecoach driver uses his family as an excuse for not avenging his brother's death. Evans asks for five townspeople to help him. These men come on board, but they are old and not likely to be very useful in a shoot-out. Some of them leave when they realise the size of the posse trying to rescue Wade. They also try to assuage their guilt at their cowardice by trying to argue that the case has nothing to do with them. The one man who shows bravery is the town drunk Alex, who warns Evans that there is someone on the roof, and sacrifices himself in the process. This galvanises Evans. Not everyone can be bought or fails to keep their word.

Even though Evans is released by Mr Butterfield, the stage line owner, who says he is under 'no obligation' to continue and can still get the money, he refuses to give up. Alice is also not able to make him change his mind. Her conscience is clearly troubled and she apologises if she left the impression she was complaining: 'I don't want a hero, I want you'. Evans responds to his wife that even though he could never give her very much in material terms, 'Maybe this will be something worth remembering'. He is also inspired by Alex's example, 'The town drunk gave his life because he believed that people should be able to live in decency and peace together. Do you think I can do less?'

We see a different, more wistful side to Wade, as the tension ratchets up. He hears Evans' wife singing and observes: 'I like a girl singing. It kinda keeps a man from working too hard, puts his mind at rest'. He tells Evans that while he was having supper at his house:

> I was thinking that maybe one day I'd like to have a wife. Must be real nice having a couple of boys like that to ride out every morning. And a woman like that, every night, real close. I'd treat her a lot better than you do!

Wade is playing mind games, banking on making Evans realise what he stands to lose, and touching a nerve with respect to Alice, but this is not the whole story. Wade also reflects that he can't settle down and have what Evans has. This is what the outlaw desperately wants.

Wade tells Evans: 'Do me a favour. Run before they chop you down'. Later he amends this to: 'Let us get out of here'. Evans responds: 'What's this *us*? Why did you do that Ben? I don't like owing anybody any favours'. Wade simply tells him that he saved his life back at the hotel. The men are aware that each is capable of nobler behaviour than they originally thought, and there is now a shared bond of grudging respect. The film ends with Wade on the train bound for Yuma. Both men see Alice riding alongside, but Wade sees her first. There is a faraway look in his eyes. It begins to rain, the drought is breaking (farmer Evans' reward?). He doesn't now need the money, but also has not sold his soul for nothing. While he notes 'My job is finished when I get you there', Wade's cool response suggests that the game is not over for him: 'I've broken out of Yuma Jail before'. Again, the outlaw is a trickster.

The swinging Sixties and beyond

The outlaw films of the 1950s, focussed on moral issues of redemption and sacrifice. Often they were allegorical. In the 1960s that changed. The outlaw was

100 The good outlaw

single-minded, violent and avaricious – an *anti-hero*. However, they were still constructed as having some redeeming qualities. As Peary (1989) noted, charismatic and likeable actors were intentionally cast as the ambivalent villains, as in the case of William Holden as the outlaw leader in *The Wild Bunch* (1969). In that film, the outlaws are vicious murderers of innocent people, but lay claim to a code of honour, a trope distinguishing many crime films of recent years.

In *The Good, The Bad and the Ugly* (1967), Tuco (Eli Wallach) is given a back-story justifying his *ugliness*. Growing up poor was tough. His brother chose to be a priest to escape, Tuco chose to be an outlaw. In the search for the gold, the three outlaws (Wallach, Clint Eastwood and Lee Van Cleef) seem to be uncaring about the Civil War occurring around them. That's if you watch the original US cinematic release. The restored version provides a different story. It shows that they are all appalled by the slaughter and suffering. Yes, they want the gold, but that's their private matter. The first to indicate his disapproval is intriguingly the vicious killer played by Van Cleef. At the end, it is Eastwood's character who philosophises that all this killing is a waste for he has 'never seen so many men killed for no good purpose'.

In recent years, Hollywood has come full circle. The outlaw has once again become constructed in 1950s terms, with *Shane* in particular highly influential. *Silverado* (1985) drew on classic Westerns in spinning a tale of former outlaws hoping to make amends. In doing so, they have to battle a former gang member who has now become a corrupt sheriff. *Open Range* (2003) was an effective reworking of *Shane*. In this case, the former gunslinger (Kevin Costner) has settled down as an anonymous cowhand, but has to return to his old ways to avenge the murder of his comrades. *The Homesman* (2014) has an outlaw (Tommy Lee Jones) rescued from hanging, but with the price that he must commit a good deed of escorting three women home. Redemption through a dangerous journey across a hostile landscape remains a key element of the Western myth.

8   Lone Pine

A man needs a good reason to ride this country. What's your's?
(Ben Brigade, played by Randolph Scott,
Ride Lonesome, 1959)

Introduction

Lone Pine, a small town of about 2,000 people, is 300 kilometres north of Los
Angeles. Just past the turn-off to Death Valley, an old art deco cinema sits on
the outskirts of town. Except, it is not an old cinema. It was purpose built in
2006 to house the Lone Pine Film History Museum. This permanent attraction
arose from the Lone Pine Film Festival, held annually since 1990. Built with
donations and profits from the festival, the exterior of the museum building is a
replica of a real 1930s cinema in Nebraska (Frost 2008).

IMDb.com lists 343 productions as having been shot around Lone Pine. The
majority were B-grade Westerns, with a heyday from the 1930s through to the
1950s. Film crews were drawn to Lone Pine as the rocky Alabama Hills added dra-
matic effect (Figures 8.1 and 8.2). More spectacular than the hills around Hollywood, they could be used to represent anywhere in the West. Furthermore, the high
mountains of the Sierra Nevada allowed Lone Pine to stand in for more exotic
locations, particularly the North-West Frontier of India and Afghanistan in films
ranging from *Gunga Din* (1939) to *Iron Man* (2008). While the setting for a large
number of B Westerns, serials and television shows, Lone Pine is also closely associated with a series of tough, realistic and bleak Westerns made by Budd Boetticher in the 1950s. Starring Randolph Scott, these are seen as the ultimate in the
Adult Westerns of the period and were highly influential on the 1960s *Spaghetti
Westerns*. Paying homage to these milestone films, recent Westerns such as *Django
Unchained* (2012) and *The Lone Ranger* (2013) had scenes filmed at Lone Pine.

Lone Pine is significant in Western tourism as a special example of a place
that has utilised its cinematic heritage to leverage strong flows of tourism. In this
case, we stress it is the film heritage that is important. Established in the mid-
nineteenth century, Lone Pine's history is similar to many other small towns
around the California and Nevada border area. There has been mining, but not of

Figure 8.1 The Alabama Hills, Lone Pine, California (photo W. Frost).

Figure 8.2 The Alabama Hills, Lone Pine, California (photo W. Frost).

sufficient scale or longevity to develop a townscape of impressive mining boom architecture. Agriculture has been limited by the scarcity of water and what little Lone Pine had was diverted to Los Angeles early in the twentieth century (Reisner 1986). No charismatic outlaw made this his base. Astride a major highway, Lone Pine has survived as a service centre for passing trade. Its only point of difference is its use in a wide range of films.

The Lone Pine Film Festival

The annual festival was established in 1990, intriguingly during a period when Westerns were thought to be well and truly dead and buried. Its genesis was in the activities of Dave Holland, a Hollywood film production company manager and film history enthusiast. In the early 1980s, Holland organised two tours of Lone Pine for 20 or so of his family and friends. Hiring a bus they headed into the Alabama Hills and tried to match locations to photographic stills from films of the 1930s and 1940s. The highlight of the tour was a formal dinner amongst the rocks (Ogburn 2009). Somewhere along the line, one of the participants suggested he write a book (Holland 1990).

Holland's activities stimulated local interest. Townspeople were puzzled by 'this man who ordered dinners in the rocks for groups of friends, who booked multiple rooms at the Dow [Hotel] and seats in cafes around towns – yet was not doing any filming' (Ogburn 2009: 15). The town economy was geared for the occasional windfall of film production, but this was something very different. Kerry Powell, a local, had previously developed an idea of a film festival and she made contact with Holland. Together, they developed the idea of extending Holland's private tours to a public festival (Ogburn 2009).

The key features were the tours to film locations, the twilight barbecue dinner amongst the rocks and the screening of films in the high school auditorium. Quickly added to this were Guest Star Panels. They found that actors and filmmakers were keen to return and reminisce. Amongst those who came were Gregory Peck, Budd Boetticher, Ernest Borgnine, Leonard Maltin, Jack Palance, Douglas Fairbanks Jr, Harry Carey Jr, Ben Johnson, Roy Rogers and Dale Evans. As the festival evolved, some years were marked with special themes. These included:

1991   A Tribute to Hopalong Cassidy
1993   A Tribute to John Wayne
1996   Tribute to Randolph Scott, Budd Boetticher and Burt Kennedy
1997   Salute to Republic Pictures
1998   Salute to Director William Wellman
2003   Women of the Westerns
2005   Cowboy Heroes and their Horses
2006   Return of the Badmen
2007   Singing Cowboys
2012   100 Years of Universal and Paramount Studios

Inside the museum

The museum opened for the 2006 festival. While there is a lot of discussion in the events literature regarding legacy (Frost and Laing 2011), Lone Pine provides an instructive example of a festival that has succeeded in developing a complementary year-round attraction. In addition to housing an extensive collection of costumes, props, posters, vehicles and artefacts, it includes a cinema for festival and regular screenings. Our fieldwork took place in 2012, when the museum was now well established. At that time, pride of place went to the most recent donation of the dentist's wagon from *Django Unchained* (2012) and the staff were excited to relate that Quentin Tarantino had personally visited the museum to present it (Figure 8.3).

What is most eye-catching within the museum is the emphasis on Western costumes. Of particular note are the colourful and elaborate costumes for women of the 1930s and 1940s (Figures 8.4 and 8.5). Juxtaposed with these are film posters from the 1950s featuring both men and women in tight clothing and suggestive posing (Figure 8.6). In these we see the sexualisation of the Western during this period, as target audiences were shifted from juvenile to adult markets. We discuss such issues in relation to clothing in more detail in Chapter 13.

Figure 8.3 Dentist's wagon from *Django Unchained* (2012), Lone Pine Film History Museum (photo W. Frost).

Figure 8.4 Elaborate costumes for Dale Evans, Lone Pine Film History Museum (photo W. Frost).

Figure 8.5 Cowgirl outfit by Nudie Cohn, Lone Pine Film History Museum (photo W. Frost).

Budd Boetticher and the Ranown Cycle

While Lone Pine is usually associated with B Westerns and serials, it was from time to time used for higher quality productions. For example, John Ford used the area to great effect in *3 Godfathers* (1948). On the run after a bank robbery, three small-time outlaws (John Wayne, Pedro Armendariz and Harry Carey Jr) are forced into the desert. In pursuit, the sheriff (Ward Bond) uses a train to post men at strategic waterholes. The scenes utilising the narrow gauge Carson and Colorado Railroad struggling through the fine dust of the wasteland were a highlight. Another example was the use of Lone Pine as a spectacular location for the Indian attack on the wagon train in *How the West was Won* (1962).

Figure 8.6 Suggestive poster for *The Return of Jack Slade* (1953), Lone Pine Film History Museum (photo W. Frost).

Of these higher quality films, those made by director Budd Boetticher (pro-nounced Bet-tikker) and writer Burt Kennedy stand out. Seven films were made, all starring Randolph Scott (Figure 8.7). These became known as the Ranown Cycle, after Boetticher's company. Gritty, violent and vengeful, these films made good use of the arid Lone Pine location; with the rocky and inhospitable landscape mirroring the existentialist hero's struggles. With their emphasis on violence and bleakness, they became a strong stylistic model for many of the Spaghetti Westerns of the 1960s (Cumbow 2008).

The first film in the series was *Seven Men From Now* (1956). This was made for John Wayne's Batjac company and the initial intention was for the Duke to star in it. However, supposedly Wayne had just finished *The Searchers* and did not want to make another film about a man obsessed with revenge. With Wayne out, Boetticher tried to recruit Gary Cooper, but eventually had to settle for Scott. Years later, Burt Kennedy revealed that he wrote all the scripts with the view that John Wayne would play the lead roles (Eyman 2014). A slightly different version was told by Boetticher and Kennedy at a panel Q&A session at the Lone Pine Film Festival. According to them, Wayne initially did not read the script as one of his staff said it was too similar to *Hondo*. When Warner Brothers tried to buy the project, Wayne perversely became interested. Agreeing that it was not right for him, Wayne offered it to Joel McCrea and Robert Preston, before trying Randolph Scott (Smith 2009).

Figure 8.7 Poster for 1996 Film Festival focussing on Randolph Scott, Budd Boetticher and Burt Kennedy (photo W. Frost).

Scott had appeared in Westerns since 1928. According to Peary (1982: 336), he 'was considered a reliable, sturdy hero, but nothing more significant'. Scott was 58 years old at the time and 'though his career was certainly not in decline, it was in need of a boost' (Smith 2009: 89). Playing a straightforward character, such as Wyatt Earp in *Frontier Marshall* (1939), he could be dreadfully wooden. In contrast, where he was matched against a strong villain and there was some ambiguity, he was more effective. An example of this was *Colt .45* (1950), where his protagonist was a flamboyant and unstable outlaw played by Zachary Scott. Teaming up with Boetticher, Randolph Scott excelled. A style that had previously come over as wooden, now seemed to indicate strength and integrity. That he was in his fifties also helped, for while still ruggedly handsome, his lined face suggested both sadness and determination.

We consider four of Boetticher's Lone Pine films. All were characterised by pitting Scott against charismatic villains. Boetticher was obsessed with bullfighting and in both films the protagonists engage in an interplay of bluffs and taunts, while the Lone Pine landscape provides an heroic arena, suggestive of the bullring. While Scott's hero is laconic and reserved – often because he is caught in a situation beyond his control – the villain is more flamboyant and talkative. As the two circle each other, Boetticher plays with their similarities and mutual attraction. Given the right circumstances, they could be close friends and ride off together. Boetticher has often been likened to Ernest Hemingway in his focus on rugged individualism. His films were dominated by an heroic quest, an odyssey in which integrity is paramount and no compromise is possible (Kitses 2004).

Seven Men From Now (1956)

The first in the series, with Scott playing a role intended for John Wayne. Ben Stride (Scott) comes across John and Annie Greer (Gail Russell), whose wagon is stuck in mud. Helping them out, he keeps riding with them towards Villa Flore. Along the way, they are joined by Bill Masters (Lee Marvin). Ben and Annie are attracted to each other and Masters begins to needle them about the developing relationship.

Slowly, Ben's back-story comes out. He is hunting seven men who robbed Wells Fargo. During the robbery, Ben's wife was killed. He doesn't know who the men are, but has a hunch they are heading towards Villa Flore. Ben is a former sheriff and the robbers know he is coming to get them, so this manhunt is the reverse of a normal one. Even though Ben is doing the chasing, the outlaws will come to him. That he does not know who they are adds a feeling of paranoia to the pursuit. He has already killed two men while drinking coffee around a fire. They panicked and talked too much about the robbery, if they had kept quiet they would have been safe. When they rescue a lone rider from the Apaches, he immediately tries to shoot Ben. Masters kills the robber, saving Ben. Masters knows about the robbery and makes it clear that he is after the loot. Adding further to the menace and paranoia, Masters holds a grudge from when Ben was a sheriff and locked him up.

Masters rides ahead into Villa Flore and tells the outlaws that Ben is coming for them. They reveal that the strongbox is hidden on the Greers' wagon. The Greers tell Ben this and he takes the money. The robbers will now have to come to him to get it. Ben kills two of them, but it is Masters who kills the final two. Masters now challenges Ben to a showdown in the desert. Ben is the quicker draw.

The Tall T (1957)

Pat (Scott) is a good fellow, likeable and honest, a bit of a dreamer. Riding into town, he drops in at a stage station to see widower Hank and his son Jeff. There's a strong bond between Pat and the boy, Jeff is the son Pat wishes he could have had. Later in town he jokes with stage-driver Rintoon, but cries off drinking in the saloon as he wants to buy some candy for Jeff. He also wants to buy a bull from his former employer. Here, the dreamy Pat gets sucked in to a foolhardy bet that he can ride the bull. Having lost his horse in this wager, he hitches a lift home on Rintoon's stage.

For the first 20 minutes, the film has been an old-fashioned lightweight comedy with Pat joking and laughing with his friends. Now all that suddenly changes. Stopping at the stage station, they are confronted by outlaws Frank (Richard Boone), Chink (Henry Silva) and Billyjack (Skip Homeier). They shoot Rintoon and it is quickly revealed that they have killed Hank and Jeff. In an instant, the only three people Pat cares about are dead. He will not smile again for the rest of the film.

The other passengers are newlyweds Willard and Doretta Mims. Mrs Mims (Maureen O'Sullivan) is the daughter of a wealthy mine-owner. When Frank talks of killing them all, Willard convinces them to hold his wife for a ransom of $50,000. He returns to town to arrange it, while the outlaws take the prisoners to their hideout in the rocks.

Once the ransom is arranged, Willard is killed. Pat realises that when the money is delivered, then he and Doretta will be killed. He hatches a plan to create disharmony amongst the gang. While Frank collects the ransom, Pat convinces the suspicious Chink that Frank will not come back. Chink sneaks after Frank. With Billyjack alone, Pat jumps him while Doretta distracts the bandit. Hearing gunfire, Chink returns, but is shot by Pat. When Frank returns with the money, there is a shoot-out, from which Pat emerges victorious.

Ride Lonesome (1959)

Bounty hunter Ben Brigade (Scott) captures young Billy and is taking him in to Santa Cruz (i.e. Nogales). At a lonely stage station they run into Sam (Pernell Roberts) and Whit (James Coburn). Brigade is suspicious of them as he knows they are minor outlaws. Also at the station is Mrs Lane (Karen Steele), her husband runs it. Attacked by Mescalero Apaches, they find that Mrs Lane's husband has been killed. For protection they must all ride together. As they proceed, Sam and Whit reveal that they want Billy. If they can take him into Bisbee, the territory governor will grant them a pardon and they can start afresh.

Trailing them is Frank (Lee Van Cleef), Billy's older brother. Sam and Whit are puzzled why Brigade is travelling slowly and leaving a clear trail. They realise he wants Frank to catch up. Brigade explains his actions. Years ago he was the marshall in Santa Cruz. He had put Frank in jail and the outlaw swore vengeance. When Frank got out, Brigade waited for him (shades of *High Noon*). However, instead of a showdown, Frank went to his house and killed his wife. Billy is the bait, allowing Brigade to fight and kill Frank. That done, he hands Billy over to Sam and Whit.

Comanche Station (1960)

Cody (Scott) rides into a Comanche camp and trades for the release of Mrs Lowe (Nancy Gates). Returning to Lordsburg, they run into Ben (Claude Akins) and his gang. They tell Mrs Lowe that her husband has put a $5,000 bounty on her head, dead or alive. She is disappointed that Cody is nothing more than a bounty hunter. As they proceed, they are attacked by Comanche (who strangely have Mohawks, whereas the Comanche wore their hair long). One of the gang reveals that Cody is not a bounty hunter. His wife was captured by Comanche ten years ago and so he is on a self-appointed mission to release as many captives as he can. As they near Lordsburg, Ben tries to kill both Cody and Mrs Lowe. The temptation of such a big reward is too much. Cody kills him and returns Mrs Lowe to her husband. They live on a rundown farm, implying the huge reward was a fiction. Cody doesn't hang around. This was meant to be Scott's last film, so it ends with a long elegiac shot of him heading into the rocky hills.

Themes and tropes

Randolph Scott's character is always a loner. In *The Tall T*, he has left his job on a ranch to set up his own spread by himself. In the other three films, he is a widower and the death of his wife provides both a motivation for his wandering and an explanation of his solitary character. As a loner, Scott has to be self-reliant. In each film he is beset by dangers that are outside of his control and can only rely on himself to win through.

He is a man of few words. In both *Ride Lonesome* and *Comanche Station* his behaviour is misinterpreted by the female leads. They find it difficult to reconcile indications of strength and integrity with the idea of him as a money-grubbing bounty hunter. The true explanations only come late in the films. In *Ride Lonesome*, his lack of dialogue is taken to such extremes that it becomes a source of humour. For example, when Sam tells him that Mrs Lane is the most beautiful woman he has ever seen, Brigade's response is 'she ain't ugly'. Tompkins' contention that 'westerns are full of contrasts between people who spout words and people who act' (1992: 51) is exemplified in these films. Whereas the other characters are talkative, Scott, as the hero, is quiet.

The villains, in contrast, are gregarious and charismatic. They ride with gangs, of which they are the natural and unquestioned leaders. Their motivations are clear and they are quite happy to tell others what they are doing and thinking. For example, Ben in *Comanche Station* tells Cody that he wants the reward. In *Seven Men From Now*, Masters indicates straight away that he is after the strong-box. There is no subterfuge, they both know there will have to be a fight. Despite these contrasts, there is a strong bond between villain and hero. Playfully, Boetticher highlights these connections through the interchange of names throughout the series. In *Seven Men from Now* and *Ride Lonesome*, Scott plays characters called Ben, whereas in *Comanche Station*, Ben is the villain.

In *Seven Men From Now*, villain Masters constantly baits everybody. He enjoys causing dissension and mistrust. He gets no advantage, it is just a game he plays. He quickly sizes up John Greer as weak and that Annie is strongly drawn to Ben. Like a bullfighter he plays and teases, knowing that the final confrontation is coming. Masters then plays the outlaws off against Ben, biding his time before jumping in to finish off the last two. With only Ben left between him and the money, their showdown is a *tour de force*. With the rocks forming a natural amphitheatre, they face each other, waiting for the other to make a move. This powerfully stylised action and venue would be copied again and again by Sergio Leone.

In *The Tall T*, the connection between villain Frank and hero Pat is a major theme. While Pat hates the outlaw, Frank really likes Pat, perversely for his honesty. Pat is passively resigned to his fate, until Frank tells him that he detests the two young guns that he rides with. This provides a glimmer of hope. Pat will work to set the gang members against each other. To do this, however, he must be cunning, deceptive and ruthless – qualities we might usually associate with the villains. Whereas Frank killed Willard because he was a *talker* he orders Pat to *talk* to him and tell him about his ranch. The outlaw admires what Pat has achieved, commenting that he would like a place of his own someday. Playfully, Frank argues that Pat and Doretta are the ideal match, partly a macabre joke given he intends to kill them, but partly because he likes the idea of settling down. Pat must see something in Frank, for at the end he offers him the chance to ride off. Frank does not take this as he wants the money. Once the outlaw is dead, the stony-faced hero has everything Frank desired – the woman, the money and the ranch. The suggestion is that Pat has become like Frank.

The bullfight motif is clear in *The Tall T*. The villainous Frank is the bull. Strong and powerful, he feels fully in control, toying with his prisoners and killing them when he feels like it. Whereas Pat is quiet, Frank is full of life and laughter. His downfall is in under-estimating the hostages. As their elaborate game progresses, he is deceived and makes mistakes. Pat gets more powerful as he knocks off the bandits one by one. Nonetheless, the outlaws still believe they are the stronger. Even at the end, Frank charges directly at Pat – like a bull – confident he can outshoot him.

In *Comanche Station*, Cody and Ben are ex-soldiers with bad blood between them from the past. However, gradually Cody realises that he has misjudged Ben and finally apologises to him. When attacked by the Comanches, Ben rides in and rescues Cody. According to Kitses (2004), this is to save Cody for a final confrontation. However, we disagree. At this stage they have made their peace and are essentially partners. It is the temptation of the huge bounty, rather than any malice, that later drives Ben to want to kill Cody.

In *Ride Lonesome*, the killing of Brigade's wife makes the gulf between hero and villain too great to bridge. Nonetheless, both may be seen as motivated by commitment to family to take great risks. Just as Frank hung Brigade's wife, Brigade is prepared to hang Frank's brother Billy from the same tree to lure Frank into the open. Lacking a strong connection between the protagonists, Boetticher provides a second pair of villains in Sam and Whit. Talkative and likeable, they back Brigade against Frank, even though they also discuss killing him to take Billy. In the end, Brigade smiles (for the first time in the film) and hands Billy over as a reward for their help.

The women are strong characters in all four films. Central to the plot is that they need to be rescued. The interplay between them and Scott is often ambiguous. Scott's sexuality has been the subject of much discussion, particularly his sharing of a house with Cary Grant. Nott (2004) rejects the idea that he was homosexual or bisexual, but it is often repeated. Generally, gay actors attracted little attention in Hollywood as long as they were not too open and the studios happily provided publicity that they were on the verge of marrying (Eliot 2006; Eyman 2014; Nott 2004). In Westerns, gay subtexts sometimes sneaked it, most notably in *Red River* (1948). In *Buchanan Rides Alone*, the eponymous hero (Scott) forms an attachment with Pecos (L.Q. Jones); turning the young gun who is meant to be guarding him. Together they plan to escape to Texas and share Scott's homestead. Perhaps in line with Hollywood's code regarding illicit relationship, Pecos is killed before anything further develops.

Seven Men From Now has a sort of a conventional Western romance, perhaps because it was written for John Wayne. Annie and Ben are strongly attracted to each other. Annie is married, to a 'good man' as she says on a number of occasions. However, the others dismiss him as weak, unmanly and unworthy of such a wife. Masters bullies him and Ben has little time for him. In typical Western fashion the matter is resolved. John proves himself a man by standing up to the outlaws and as a result is conveniently killed. The film ends with Annie in her widow's black, but deciding she will stay. Smiling, she looks at Ben. Scott also gets the woman – once again recently widowed – in *The Tall T*. This is the only film in which the lead female is a mature woman. At the time it was made, Scott was 59 years old and Maureen O'Sullivan was 47. Both had been stars in the 1930s, when O'Sullivan played Jane in the *Tarzan* movies. Thrown together, romance develops quickly and the film ends with them arm in arm. Nott (2004), however, argues that their chemistry is unconvincing and that Pat is deceiving her, feigning interest in order to gain her assistance.

In the last two films in the series, Scott was matched with young starlets, resulting in a large age gap. In *Ride Lonesome*, he shows absolutely no interest in the stunningly attractive Mrs Lane. This makes sense in that he is on an obsessive quest to avenge the murder of his wife. Accordingly, the hints of romance are between Mrs Lane and Sam. *Comanche Station* finishes the series with an unfulfilled romance. Cody and Mrs Lowe are attracted to each other. A running discussion about her husband not personally searching for her suggests that Cody might win her in the end. However, when they arrive in Lordsburg, he is stunned to find that she has a small child and that her husband is blind. Without saying a word, Cody rides off.

The ending of *Comanche Station* and its plot of kidnapping suggests John Ford's *The Searchers* (1956). Throughout these films there is much evidence of intertextuality, with Boetticher borrowing heavily from Ford. Nott (2004) suggests that this was partly an in-joke amongst the film-makers. If Scott was a poor-man's Wayne, then it was appropriate to imitate scenes from his films. In addition to the juxtaposition of *The Searchers* and *Comanche Station*, the Comanche attack on the Rangers in *The Searchers* is recycled for *Ride Lonesome* and the army's abandonment of the stage in *Stagecoach* appears again in *Seven Men From Now*.

One last ride

Comanche Station was meant to be Scott's farewell. However, he was coaxed out of retirement for *Ride the High Country* (1962). Boetticher was offered the job of directing it, but was busy; so instead it was given to a young director called Sam Peckinpah. He had mainly worked in television and this was only his second film. It would make his reputation.

It is *circa* 1910 and Steve Judd (Joel McCrea) is a former lawman. As he has got older, work has dried up and he has mainly been employed in bars. He has been contacted by a bank, who want him to escort a gold delivery. When he turns up, the slimy bank manager is disappointed, saying 'I expected a much younger man'. Steve replies, 'well I used to be'. The bank manager is unimpressed and bawls him out, 'we're more than familiar with your reputation, but that was made many years ago and we're dealing in the present not the past'. He gets the job only because there is nobody else, six guards have been killed in recent months.

He runs into his old partner Gill Westrum (Randolph Scott). Dressed in imitation of Buffalo Bill, Gill works in a carnival, conning gullible cowboys. Gill agrees to join him, though his plan is to steal the gold. They ride up into the Sierra Nevada towards the mining camp of Coarse Gold. Along the way they reminisce. Gill keeps coming back to the idea that they were never properly compensated for all the risks they took. He packages this up in joking banter, lightly sarcastic, but with a clear message. For example, Gill compliments Steve on:

> all the other rewards you've gathered during your years of loyal service. A blue-grass thoroughbred, silver mounted saddle, magnificent wardrobe. I'm envious. What more can a man expect? What more can he hope for?

Eventually, Gill tries to sneak off with the gold. Steve stops him and angrily slaps him. Distraught, Steve reveals his doubts about Gill, 'all that talk ... what we had coming but never got paid. I knew in my bones what you were aiming for, but I wouldn't believe it. I kept telling myself you were a good man, you were my friend'. Gill tries to argue that it's only the bank's money. Steve yells back that it doesn't make it OK, 'what they don't know won't hurt them? Not them, ONLY ME!' Steve says he will turn Gill into the sheriff, but lets him escape one night. Gill keeps tailing him, looking for an opportunity. When Steve is ambushed by the Hammond brothers, Gill charges in to help him. In the shoot-out, Steve is mortally wounded. Gill promises that he will do the right thing and take the gold to the bank. The dying Steve smiles and say, 'hell, I know that. I always did. You just forgot it for a while'.

Originally, the idea was that Scott would play Steve. This would make it a very similar role to most of his Boetticher films. However, McCrea did not want to play Gill and threatened to pull out. Scott defused the situation, saying:

> well, I'll play either one, but if I had my choice I'd rather play Gill. I've played the straight, honest guy so damn long that it would be more interesting.
>
> (quoted in Peary 1989)

It was an inspired decision. Scott excels as the swaggering, talkative, morally compromised Gill. Though he was often seen as the poor man's John Wayne, it is impossible to imagine the Duke playing so effectively against type as Scott does. Director Peckinpah went further and changed the ending, so that the good Steve dies, with Gill promising to complete his mission. That changed the dynamics of the story, with both Gill and Steve on a quest. Their journey through the high country is then one of redemption for Gill. For Steve, his task is to set an example for his friend and hope he will return to his former ways. Having completed the film, Scott reasoned this was a perfect ending to his career and retired for good (Peary 1989; Weddle 1996).

Ride the High Country was critically acclaimed for providing an elegiac vision of the closing of the Western frontier. Comparisons were made with another 1962 production in *The Man Who Shot Liberty Valance*, which also was seen as the swansong for Western faithfuls in John Wayne, Jimmy Stewart and John Ford. It too focussed on old-timers looking backwards, mythologising what the West was like before it was tamed.

The release of these two films marked a crossroads in the Western. The generation that had seen the rebirth of the Western in 1939 and the dominance of the Adult Western was getting old. Randolph Scott and Joel McCrea retired. John Wayne and Jimmy Stewart would no longer play young men (both were now in their mid-fifties). *The Man who Shot Liberty Valance* was seen as Ford's last great film. Wayne did not make another film with Ford. Budd Boetticher would not direct another Western. Nor would Anthony Mann. Ward Bond died in 1960, aged 57; Gary Cooper and Gail Russell died in 1961, he was 60, she was only 36. Veterans Thomas Mitchell and Michael Curtiz died in 1962, both in their seventies.

What came next was a direct legacy of Budd Boetticher and Randolph Scott. In 1964, Sergio Leone released *A Fistful of Dollars,* an Italian film, made in Spain, set in the West and starring an American television star in Clint Eastwood. The Spaghetti Western would dominate the rest of the 1960s. Highly stylistic, with ambivalent good guys, talkative and flamboyant villains versus silent heroes; these new films lovingly drew on Boetticher and Scott at Lone Pine.

9 Yellowstone

> What a beautiful and thrilling specimen for America to preserve and hold up to
> the view of her refined citizens and the world in future ages! A *nation's Park*,
> containing man and beast, in all the wild and freshness of their nature's beauty.
>
> (George Catlin 1841: 263)

> Today I am in the Yellowstone Park and I wish I were dead.
>
> (Rudyard Kipling 1899: 72)

The adventures of George Catlin

George Catlin was born in the Wyoming Valley of Pennsylvania in 1796.
Wyoming is a Native American word and for no discernible reason it was
applied in 1865 to a newly established and largely unknown territory straddling
the Rockies. Catlin started out as a lawyer, but was restless and dissatisfied. In
1823 he chucked in the law and moved to Philadelphia to commence a career as
a portrait painter.

His life took an extraordinary change in direction when he saw a delegation
of Native Americans from the West en route to Washington, DC. He had
encountered Native Americans before and had grown up hearing tales from his
mother of her capture by Iroquois during the Revolutionary War. However, this
was a transformative moment. Many travel narratives may be viewed in terms of
Campbell's *Hero's Journey* (Laing and Frost 2012, 2014). Applying that structure to Catlin, his encounter with Native Americans at Washington formed his
Call to Adventure, starting him on a Western odyssey. He decided to leave
behind his wife and family and head westwards to paint Indians (Matthiessen
1989). As Catlin later justified his decision:

> I have for many years past, contemplated the noble races of red men ... their
> rights invaded, their morals corrupted, their lands wrested from them, their
> customs changed ... and I have flown to their rescue – not of their lives or
> of their race (for they are '*doomed*' and must perish), but to the rescue of
> their looks and their modes ... [so they may] live again upon canvass, and

stand forth for centuries yet to come, the living monuments of a noble race. For this purpose, I have designed to visit every tribe of Indians on the Continent, if my life should be spared; for the purpose of procuring portraits of distinguished Indians, of both sexes in each tribe, painted in their native costume.

(Catlin 1841: 10–11)

A child of the Age of Enlightenment, Catlin was entranced by the concept of the *Noble Savage*, though equally convinced of their future extinction. Leaving Pennsylvania, he travelled to St Louis and was introduced to General William Clark, Superintendent of Indian Affairs for the West. Thirty years previously Clark and Merriwether Lewis had famously crossed the continent. With Clark's help, Catlin travelled up the Missouri River. Over the next decade, Catlin made a series of journeys into the West – accompanying either trappers, traders or military expeditions. He painted hundreds of portraits of a wide variety of tribes. In addition, he wrote a series of 58 letters, specifically for publication in Eastern newspapers and journals. Highly readable and engaging, they form one of the great exploration travel narratives of the nineteenth century and complement his paintings. While Hollywood made no film of Catlin's adventures, he may be seen as a rough template for the painter Langdon Towne (Robert Young) in *North-West Passage* (1940), even though that film deals with an earlier period in American history. Catlin's paintings served as one of the major sources for costuming details of the Native Americans in *Dances with Wolves* (1990).

Catlin followed a simple modus operandi. At each village he enlisted the help of the European operator of the local trading post. This gave him status as an important visitor, but beyond that, it was his painting that excited curiosity: 'perhaps nothing ever more completely astonished these people than the operations of my *brush*. The art of portrait-painting was a subject entirely new to them' (Catlin 1841: 103). At the Mandan village, he started by painting the two principal chiefs. At first they showed little interest, they were tolerating the imposition to curry favour with the trading post operator. However, when Catlin had finished, 'it was exceedingly amusing to see them mutually recognizing each other's likeness, and assuring each other of the striking resemblance' (Catlin 1841: 103).

When he showed his portraits to the crowd gathered outside, their reaction seemed like those out of the movies (though, it was probably the later script-writers who drew on Catlin for such ideas). Those assembled could recognise their chiefs, but had no way of explaining how the paintings had been done. Accordingly, 'they pronounced me the greatest *medicine-man* in the world; for they said I had made *living beings* – they said they could see their chiefs alive in two places'. Some however, exclaimed that his medicine was too great, 'that such an operation could not be performed without taking away from the original something of his existence' and that he was stealing some part of the chiefs to 'carry it home with me amongst the white people and that when they died they would never sleep quiet in their graves' (Catlin 1841: 105–106). Generally, Catlin was fêted for his efforts. The one exception was amongst the Sioux. When his portraits led to jealousy between two warriors, one was killed and a vendetta commenced. Hearing that some blamed him for starting it with his *bad medicine*, Catlin quietly slipped away before vengeance was visited upon him.

More than a painter, Catlin evolved as an advocate of the Native Americans. His letters actively pleaded with his Eastern readers to change their attitudes. For example, in Letter 26 he wrote:

> There has gone abroad, from the many histories which have been written of these people, an opinion which is too current in the world, that the Indian is necessarily a poor, drunken, murderous wretch; which account is certainly unjust ... I have travelled several years already amongst these people and I have not had my scalp taken, nor a blow struck me; nor had occasion to raise my hand against an Indian; nor has my property been stolen.
>
> (Catlin 1841: 205)

At the root of Catlin's travels was the notion that the Native American way of life was doomed. Apart from recording their customs and dress, Catlin earnestly hoped that something could actively be done to save them from extinction. How that could be achieved was a topic he returned to continually. Turning over the possibilities, some radical ideas began to form and be conveyed back East to his readers.

Having stayed with the Crows at the junction of the Yellowstone and Missouri, Catlin proposed that:

> It is for these inoffensive and unoffending people, yet unvisited by the vices of civilized society ... it is time ... that our government should raise her strong arm to save the remainder of them from the pestilence that is rapidly advancing upon them. We have gotten from them territory enough, and the country which they now inhabit is most of it too barren of timber for the use of civilized man.
>
> (Catlin 1841: 62)

At the Mandan village, he considered possibilities of assimilation. He saw them as good material for civilization, for they already were mainly sedentary and raised crops. They were:

> The best opportunity for such an experiment of any tribe in the country. The land about their villages is of the best quality for ploughing and grazing ... I deem it not folly nor idle to say that these people *can be saved* ... if they would introduce the ploughshare and their prayers ... presenting a nation of savages, civilized and Christianized.
>
> (Catlin 1841: 182)

Ultimately, Catlin retreated from this vision of the Jeffersonian ideal. It was in Letter 31 – one of his lengthiest – that he fully developed the idea that he is famously known for. Written at Fort Pierre, in modern-day South Dakota, he started with a description of the buffalo, for he saw this as, 'the very heart or nucleus of the buffalo country ... the finest animals that graze on the prairie are to be found in this latitude'. However, he warned that the buffalo were 'hurrying on their final extinction' (Catlin 1841: 250).

Catlin described and painted the Sioux hunting the buffalo. He also noted the large numbers of wolves on the prairie. Modern estimates are of around 30 to 60 million buffalo on the Great Plains at this time and that they supported high predatory populations of 400,000 wolves and a similar number of humans (Flannery 2001: 318–319). However, it was the influx of White men that Catlin viewed as spelling doom for the buffalo. He recounted that recently a party of Sioux had brought into the trading post 1,400 fresh buffalo tongues – typically viewed as the most tender meat – which they exchanged for a few gallons of whisky. The rest of the animal was wasted. In a later letter, while accompanying a military expedition to the Comanche, he wrote of how on one restday, the soldiers killed several hundred buffalo for sport, taking the meat from only half a dozen.

Modern ecological thinking sees the buffalo as 'a human artefact, for it was shaped by Indians and its distribution determined by them' (Flannery 2001: 227). Surprisingly, they were only a recent arrival in the New World. Following the end of the Ice Age, they spread from Europe down through the Arctic about 13,000 years ago. This put their arrival at roughly the same time as human and their adaptation to the new environment was probably heavily influenced by their interaction. Archaeological work at Folsom in New Mexico – at a site discovered by Black cowboy George McJunkin in 1908 – showed that Native Americans were hunting buffalo there about 12,500 years ago. Up until about 1600, there were no horses in North America, so hunting was on foot with spears. At some stage a more productive method was discovered in driving herds over clifftops. At Head Smashed In Buffalo Jump Park in Alberta (Canada) this was regularly done from about 5,000 years ago until the arrival of Whites. Faced with predation from humans and wolves, buffalo evolved to live in vast herds for protection. There expansion was also probably aided by Native Americans burning woodlands to encourage grasslands (Flannery 2001).

Though he knew none of this science, Catlin was a keen observer and could see that changes were rapidly occurring. Perceptively, he tied the slaughter of the buffalo to the future prospects of Native Americans on the plains. Whilst at the time ecology was little understood, he contemplated that the buffalo 'is soon to be extinguished, and with it the peace and happiness (if not the actual existence) of the tribes of Indians who are joint tenants with them, in the occupancy of these vast ... plains' (Catlin 1841: 263). What could be done? Catlin outlined his vision which had slowly evolved as he journeyed through the West:

> When one ... imagines them as they *might* in the future be seen (by some great protecting policy of government) preserved in their pristine beauty and wildness, in a *magnificent park*, where the world could see for ages to come,

the native Indian in his classic attire, galloping his wild horse, with sinewy bow, and shield and lance, amid the fleeing herds of elks and buffaloes.

(Catlin 1841: 263)

Catlin wrote that this could be a *'nation's Park'*. Preserved for all time, under the protection of the US government, protecting an ecosystem and focussed on its wildlife; this is the first reference by an American to the concept of a national park. In 1872 – the year Catlin died – the world's first national park was established at Yellowstone in Wyoming. Whilst he did not specifically call for a national park in that area, Catlin has come down in history as the pioneer of the idea. Indeed, according to national parks historian Alfred Runte (1979), Catlin was well ahead of his time, going beyond simple monumental scenery, he advocated ecosystem protection. As Runte noted, at the time he was writing in the late 1970s, the US National Parks Service had still not established any national park to protect grasslands. Furthermore, while some have been uncomfortable that Catlin's park was to include both humans and wildlife (Matthiessen 1989), such ideas of indigenous people remaining within national parks are nowadays increasing in popularity (Zeppel 2009).

A Yellowstone campfire

The catalyst for the world's first national park was an 1870 exploring party. They were a group of businessmen, local officials and journalists from Helena in Montana. They had come south to Yellowstone to follow up vague reports by fur-trappers of its natural wonders. Partly tourists, partly explorers, partly economic opportunists; nowadays they would be characterised as *explorer travellers* (Laing and Frost 2014). Their leader was Henry Washburn, a Civil War general and lawyer who had recently been appointed Surveyor-General of Montana. Keeping a record of their adventures was Nathaniel P. Langford, a businessman and sometime government official. His account was published the next year in a new magazine called *Scribner's Monthly* (Langford 1871). The output of such publications was booming in a growing United States. Highly popular in the East, they often contained exciting stories of Western adventures and exploration. Langford – and possibly others on the trip – had connections with the Northern Pacific Railroad, which was interested in publicising visitation to areas like Yellowstone which were along its under-construction route (Frost and Hall 2009).

Langford's two-part magazine story was a chronological account of their adventures, as was an expanded book version published in 1905. He effectively conveyed the dangers of Indians, wild animals and getting lost and also the sense that around each corner was another surprising natural feature. At the beginning, his account emphasised that they were leaving civilisation behind, crossing over a frontier into an unknown region. Armed with rifles and revolvers, they 'resembled more a band of brigands than sober men in search of natural wonders' (Langford 1871: 2).

For the first part of their journey, 'the old mountaineers and trappers who preceded us had been particularly lavish in the use of the infernal vocabulary' (Langford 1871: 7). Passing the Devil's Slide, they ventured on to the Devil's Glen and Hell Roaring River. Entering into the spirit of things, they assumed the explorers' prerogative in naming the Valley of Desolation and Devil's Hoof. Reaching the first thermal springs:

> we suddenly came upon a hideous-looking glen filled with the sulphurous vapor emitted from six or eight boiling springs of great size and activity. One of our company aptly compared it to the entrance to the infernal regions. It looked like nothing earthly we had ever seen, and the pungent fumes ... filled the atmosphere [with] ... a disagreeable sense of possible suffocation.... The springs themselves were as diabolical in appearance as the witches' caldron in Macbeth.
>
> (Langford 1871: 10)

Langford followed a standard nineteenth-century trope in describing and appreciating nature. Both the cultivated writer and reader were familiar with the concept of the *sublime*. Emerging from the Romantic tradition, this led travellers to seek out wild places, particularly mountains, canyons and waterfalls, which evoked feelings of awe, exultation, mortality and even terror. These were experiences so profound that people were almost incapable of describing them. This understanding and appreciation of the sublime marked travellers – and the readers of their travel narratives – as sophisticated and discerning (Frost and Hall 2009; Nash 1967). On reaching the Grand Canyon of the Yellowstone, Langford appropriately recounted:

> The brain reels as we gaze into this profound and solemn solitude. We shrink from the dizzy verge appalled, glad to feel solid earth under our feet. ... The stillness is horrible.... The solemn grandeur of the scene surpasses description. It must be seen to be felt. The sense of danger with which it impresses you is harrowing in the extreme. You feel the absence of sound, the oppression of absolute silence.
>
> (Langford 1871: 12)

However, as Langford proceeded in his account, the tone changed. Rather than continuing to view the landscape as infernal or terrifying, the encounters with geysers and thermal springs evoked feelings of wonder and joy. The geysers in particular seemed to be something that none of them had expected. Nor had any of them seen the like before. The numbers and variety astonished and entranced them. One they measured as reaching 219 feet in height and its eruption lasted for 18 minutes. Another was only 140 feet, but expended a greater volume of water. One erupted at such regular intervals that they gave it the name of Old Faithful.

Having discovered the Upper Geyser Basin, with nearly 100 geysers, the adventurers have an animated discussion around the campfire one night. As

Langford recorded in his later book: 'the proposition was made by some member that we utilize the result of our exploration by taking up a quarter section of land at the most prominent points of interest, and a general discussion followed'. One suggested that buying land near the falls would 'eventually become a source of great profit to the owners'; another suggested speculating near the geysers as they 'could be more easily reached by tourists'. Finally, Cornelius Hedges, a Yale-educated lawyer, spoke up. He argued that:

> he did not approve of any of these plans – that there ought to be no private ownership of any portion of that region, but that the whole of it ought to be set apart as a great National Park, and that each one of us ought to make an effort to have this accomplished.

The others enthusiastically agreed and joined in a lobbying campaign that was successful in the declaration of the national park 18 months later (Langford 1905: 117–118).

Whether or not the idea for a national park was actually conceived around the campfire has been hotly debated. Indeed, in the 1960s National Parks Service management became so worried about the veracity of the story that it cancelled the annual re-enactment of the campfire discussion (Frost and Laing 2013). Nonetheless, members of the expedition were involved in the campaign to protect and promote Yellowstone.

In Langford's *Scribner's Monthly* article there is no mention of the national park idea, though he referred to the potential for tourism resorts. Tellingly, he concluded his tale with a prediction:

> By means of the Northern Pacific Railroad, which will doubtless be completed within the next three years, the traveler will be able to make the trip to Montana from the Atlantic seabord in three days, and thousands of tourists will be attracted to both Montana and Wyoming in order to behold with their own eyes the wonders here described.

> (Langford 1871: 128)

Thomas Moran goes West

Those on the Washburn Expedition were not just amateur explorers; they also dabbled in writing and art. The magazine *Scribner's Monthly* planned to publish some articles about their adventures. These were written by Nathaniel Langford. A number of the party had sketched various sights around Yellowstone, but these were not up to publication standard. Accordingly, the editors hired artist Thomas Moran to rework them. As the US government put together an official scientific expedition under Ferdinand Hayden to survey Yellowstone, the idea evolved that Moran should join it. *Scribner's Monthly* and the Northern Pacific Railroad lent Moran $500 to head to Montana to offer his services. It was the first time Moran had been West (Kinsey 2006).

Hayden's was a scientific expedition. Its aim was to professionally evaluate and justify the claims of the amateur Washburn party (Frost and Hall 2009). Nonetheless, it was also heavily involved in boosterism of the region and its potential railroad. Apart from its scientific report, more popular media was utilised. Hayden himself wrote articles for *Scribner's Monthly*. Moran's drawings were critical in verifying the authenticity of what the writers in official and popular accounts were claiming.

Most audaciously, Moran went beyond line drawings. As the movement to declare a national park gained momentum, he produced a 7 by 12 feet oil painting, entitled *The Grand Canyon of the Yellowstone*. It was purchased by Congress and hung in the lobby of the Senate in the Capitol, Washington, DC (it is nowadays displayed in the Smithsonian) (Kinsey 2006; Runte 1979). In breathtaking colour, Moran captured the monumentalism of Yellowstone. Those who had read Langford's account of its sublime scenery could see it fully represented. Catlin had focussed on painting people, but Moran's success drew artists to concentrate on the Western landscape.

The travel writers come to Yellowstone

With the national park established, a steady stream of tourists began to flow into Yellowstone. The accoutrements of tourism developed – as the Washburn party had predicted around their campfire. The railway brought visitors to the park boundary and within there were hotels, tented camps, coaches, horseback tours and tour guides. As Yellowstone grew in popularity, travel writers began to add it to their Western itineraries. We conclude this chapter by considering two examples of late nineteenth-century travel narratives featuring Yellowstone.

Yellowstone Land of Wonders (Jules Leclercq, 1886)

Like Catlin, Leclercq was originally a lawyer. A Belgian, he travelled and wrote extensively. Most of his output was in French and he was popular in Europe. He is a strong reminder that as far back as the nineteenth century, many Europeans were fascinated by the West and its frontier mythology. Leclercq had previously written a book of his travels in the United States in 1877. In 1883, he was back in North America with a view of a follow-up based on a trip to Mexico. However, faced with extreme heat in late summer, he decided to take a detour into the cooler mountains.

As with many travel writers, Leclercq grappled with the problems of how to pay for his adventures. In constructing a travel narrative, it is often desirable to highlight independence, even if all or part of the expense is being paid for by tourism operators. The essential paradox is of maintaining trust with the reader and not appearing to be simply an advertising copywriter. Accordingly, Leclercq merely recorded that while he suffered from the oppressive heat in St Louis, 'I let myself be persuaded' to go to Yellowstone instead of Mexico (1886: 10). Then, travelling to St Paul (Minnesota), he visited Charles Lamborn, General Manager of the

Northern Pacific Railroad. 'Learning that I wanted to compare the geysers of the Rocky Mountains to those of Iceland' – where Leclercq had just previously been – the enthusiastic Lamborn offered to help, 'In the end he obliged me to accept a free ticket worth one hundred dollars' (Leclercq 1886: 29).

Behind this offer was the rationale that the Northern Pacific had just extended its line to reach Yellowstone and Leclercq could provide valuable publicity in the European market. Accordingly, Leclercq repaid his obligation, describing how:

> The train was composed of brand-new reassuringly solid, and irreproachably comfortable cars. The smoking car, with its straw-bottomed seats, was deliciously cool. At mealtimes, one went to the dining car to eat especially good things while devouring the miles.... When night came one could savour the delights of the 'sleeping car'.
>
> (1886: 30)

This emphasis on comfort and reliability was important for tapping the continental market. The contrast with, for example, the highly popular Jules Verne is particularly instructive. In *Around the World in 80 Days* (1873), Phileas Fogg's train journey through the West is dangerous and risky. In one episode the train is attacked by Indians. In another they are only able to cross a jerry-built bridge at full speed and they just get across before the bridge collapses. While an exciting read, it was hardly the publicity that the railroad companies wanted. Verne had not actually been to America, but he was convincingly inventive. Leclercq's account was an important counterpoint.

However, this left Leclercq with a problem. What interest was there in a safe travel narrative? His contemporaries sold stories of adventure and derring-do, often constructed as an altruistic and hazardous quest. Richard Burton, for example, donned a disguise to undertake his pilgrimage to Mecca. Fred Burnaby journeyed across forbidden borders in Russian Asia to demonstrate that an Englishman should be able to go wherever he pleases. Henry Morton Stanley ventured into unknown Africa to find the missing Livingstone. How could Leclercq justify himself?

What he seized upon is what today we call *last chance tourism* (Forsdick 2005; Laing and Frost 2014). Arriving at Mammoth Springs, he stayed at a half-finished hotel, and was woken by the carpenters starting work early in the morning. This hotel, he explained was the first of many that would open in the next few years, and they would all be linked by a system of roads. He was proceeding through the national park on horseback and camping in tents and adventure that would soon be replaced by modernity. Leclercq's national park visit allowed that, 'I was still able to contemplate it in its glorious virginity, just as it appeared only a few years ago to the first explorers' (1886: 44–45).

His account was studded with references to this last opportunity for an *authentic* frontier experience. Jack, his guide, seemingly came straight out of a dime novel: 'he wore an outfit that was half-Indian, half-European: buffalo-skin trousers plunged into oversized yellow boots ... elk-hide vest, colossal felt hat shading a bearded face, and on his belt an enormous American pistol' (Leclercq 1886: 59–60). As with many of his contemporaries, he followed the trope of the sublime, reinforcing that this is a special place he has journeyed into. For example, visiting the geysers, he 'experiences an inexpressable feeling of horror in the presence of these convulsions of nature ... nowhere else, not even in Iceland, had I felt such impressions of dread' (Leclercq 1886: 70).

From Sea to Sea (Rudyard Kipling, 1899)

Rudyard Kipling journeyed across the United States in 1889, when he was only 23 years old and still relatively unknown as a writer. He wrote a series of articles for the Indian newspaper *The Pioneer* and these were compiled into book form a decade later. For the modern reader, his writing seems clunky, the humour forced and the anti-Semitism is shocking and grating. Clearly Kipling was still learning his craft, but his account provided a valuable insight into how Yellowstone had developed in the six years since Leclercq visited.

Travelling on a Thomas Cook tour, Kipling could hardly pretend he was on a dangerous adventure. Instead he followed two paths in his writings. The first was a focus on the American soldiers stationed at Yellowstone, particularly the cavalry. The army had been drafted in to protect Yellowstone in 1883, for while Congress had created a national park, it had put little thought into how to manage it. Until the First World War, the army would provide protection and administration, with its legacy apparent in the distinctive military-style uniforms of NPS rangers. Kipling knew that his readers in imperial India would be interested in the US cavalry, particularly how they compared to British troops. In time American readers would become familiar with Kipling and his emphasis on the frontier and writers like Owen Wister were influenced by the British writer to pen similar stories of the West (Murdoch 2001).

Kipling's second tactic was to criticise. Particularly how dreadful the other tourists were. Famously wishing he was dead, he claimed that while on a coach ride on a winding road, 'even at the risk of my own life, I did urgently desire an accident and ... massacre' of his fellow passengers (Kipling 1899: 74). Throughout his account, Kipling juxtaposes the horror of the whining and vulgar Eastern tourists with the dignity and authenticity of Westerners such as the soldiers. He was not alone. Others made similar observations. For example, Margaret Long, visiting Yellowstone in 1890, observed in her diary: 'how the advance of modern civilization has divested this spot of most of its romance' (quoted in Riley 1999: 135–136). Then, as now, those who identified as travellers bemoaned the influence of tourists.

10 Grand Canyon

No building of any kind, not a summer cottage, a hotel … to mar the wonderful grandeur, the sublimity, the great loneliness and beauty of the Canyon. You can not improve it. The ages have been at work on it and man can only mar it. What you can do is keep it for your children.

(Theodore Roosevelt, quoted in Rothman 1989: 65)

Introduction

The Grand Canyon was simultaneously protected (initially as a national monument) and developed for tourism at the beginning of the twentieth century. It is still one of the great iconic destinations for visitors to North America, attracting 4.5 million visitors in 2013 (NPS 2014). In this chapter, we focus on the role of the railway in both its protection and development, along with Fred Harvey, who brought a high standard of hospitality to the Grand Canyon and more generally throughout the American West with his 'Harvey Girls', and promoted the Canyon as a cultural as well as natural heritage site. The Harvey Company engaged architect Mary Colter to develop iconic structures such as the El Tovar Hotel and the Hopi House, whose style drew heavily on Native American and Hispanic culture. We will consider how this tourism development and marketing influenced national identity through an alternative narrative of the American West.

Films and television have also contributed strongly to the image of the Grand Canyon, as we explore in this chapter. For example, the climax of the film *Thelma & Louise* is one of the great scenes of modern cinema – the two women accelerate their car into oblivion, and the T-bird convertible is frozen in mid-air, with the terrifying abyss of the Grand Canyon below. It is the ultimate symbol of escape, but also of the terrible price Thelma and Louise pay for it. Everyone recalls this part of the film, however it was not filmed at the Grand Canyon, but rather further up the Colorado River, near Dead Horse Point State Park in Utah. Yet in the minds of movie-goers, where else could it logically be?

The choice of the Grand Canyon as the setting for this film's denouement added to the shock value, seeing the lead characters drive over the edge of one of the most iconic natural features in the world. Is it perhaps because this is a primal fear when visiting the Canyon, looking down into the depths and imagining what would happen if a visitor fell down? It is possible to see people straying beyond the fences and ignoring the warning signs to get a better photograph or possibly just to experience the thrill of getting close to danger. The shudder this elicits is part of the extraordinary experience of visiting the Canyon, as is its jaw-dropping size (Figure 10.1).

The birth of a national park

In 1903, President Theodore Roosevelt visited the Grand Canyon in Arizona. He was on a tour of the West, which included national parks at Yellowstone and Yosemite. At this time, the Grand Canyon was nothing more than a federal forest reserve; though it was well-known, particularly through the monumental paintings of Albert Bierstadt and Thomas Moran (Nash 1967). Our modern image of Roosevelt, through the media of photography and silent film, is of a portly and bespectacled man in formal frock coats. Such an image is deceptive. When he came to the presidency in 1901, Roosevelt was only 42 years old and he still

Figure 10.1 The Grand Canyon (photo J. Laing).

holds the distinction of being the youngest ever president of the United States. Furthermore, while born to a patrician New Yorker family, Roosevelt had ranched in North Dakota and written extensively on his experiences. Indeed, perhaps more than any other person of his time, Roosevelt created and popularised the myth of the West (Cutright 1985; Murdoch 2001).

Late in the nineteenth century, massive and rapid urbanisation sparked a crisis in American identity (Nash 1967; Tompkins 1992; Watts 2003). As the average American shifted from being a farmer to a sedentary city worker, concerns grew about the potential for physical, moral and national degeneration. Reacting against modernity:

> Eastern men began to romanticize aggressive male endeavour and to appropriate its symbols, its rhetoric, and its psychological rewards. They were increasingly drawn to all-male leisure activities such as sport and hunting ... the cult of the cowboy soldier arose in art, drama and fiction, popularizing exaggerated and violent forms of masculinity.
>
> (Watts 2003: 7)

Roosevelt both exemplified and promoted this trend. When in 1884, his wife and mother both died on the same day, he moved from New York to his ranch in North Dakota. Long interested in the outdoor life, he went West searching for healing and transformation. During the resultant sojourn, he reinvented himself as a Westerner – rugged, self-reliant, a man of action. Returning to state, and ultimately federal, politics, he took advantage of the point of difference his Western background gave him. A prolific writer, his circle grew to include the novelist Owen Wister, the painter Frederic Remington and the historian Frederick Jackson Turner. The latter, Nash (1967) argued, was strongly influenced by Roosevelt in his seminal essay on the closing of the frontier, which in parts was strikingly similar to Roosevelt's previous writings.

With his love of the West and the frontier, Roosevelt emerged as a committed preservationist. In 1887, he founded the Boone and Crockett Club. Its members were the wealthy and powerful elite. Passionately interested in hunting, they paradoxically championed the creation of national parks and nature reserves. Through international connections, the Boone and Crockett Club became a major force in the global environmental movement. And once Roosevelt became president, he was in a position to act on these beliefs.

Roosevelt at the Grand Canyon

At the time of the president's visit, the Atchison, Topeka and Santa Fe Railroad (ATSF) had commenced a railway line from Williams, nearly 100 kilometres to the Canyon rim. Furthermore, they planned a grand hotel, called El Tovar, and constructed in mock Swiss chalet style. Roosevelt used his visit to voice his displeasure at such a development (see the epigram at the start of this chapter). In turn, the management of the ATSF assured the president that they had decided to build their hotel an appropriate distance away from the rim. Whether they were genuine or not in this sentiment, within a year the commercial prospects had swayed them back to their original plan and El Tovar was built (Figure 10.2). The area was only a forest reserve and seemingly there was nothing that Roosevelt could do to stop them (Rothman 1989).

El Tovar was a tasteful, upmarket operation, built at a cost of $250,000 (Rothman 1996; Weigle 1997) and duplicating grand hotels in scenic areas across the country. However, within a few years, other entrepreneurs announced tourist enterprises, including an electric railway to convey sightseers along the rim. Now Roosevelt acted, proclaiming the Grand Canyon a national monument in 1908. El Tovar could stay, but private development on the rim would be severely limited from now on. The ability of the president to declare national monuments came from the 1906 Antiquities Act. Depending on one's perspective, Roosevelt was either a scandalous political opportunist or a visionary. National parks could only be created by Congress. On a number of occasions, proposals for national parks were frustrated by vested interests. The Antiquities Act, however, gave the president the power to act quickly to save national treasures that were under threat.

The genesis for this legislation was concern with the activities of archaeologists in New Mexico, particularly at Chaco Canyon. Late in the nineteenth century, pre-contact art and artefacts had become very popular with collectors.

Figure 10.2 El Tovar Hotel, Grand Canyon (photo J. Laing).

In part, this was fuelled by major exhibitions at the World Fairs held in Chicago and Madrid in 1892 to commemorate the four-hundredth anniversary of Columbus. The concern was that commercially motivated pot-hunters were selling off the nation's heritage and often destroying sites before they could be scientifically examined (as depicted in the opening scenes of *Indiana Jones and the Last Crusade*, 1989). The Antiquities Act was intended to allow the president to declare such dig sites as national monuments and accordingly protect them. Once passed, Native American sites at El Morro, Chaco Canyon, Montezuma Castle Tonto and Gila Cliff were quickly protected.

Roosevelt went a step further. First, he declared Devil's Tower in Wyoming a national monument. A second natural national monument was the volcanic Lassen Peak in California. Then, in 1908, Roosevelt applied his discretionary power to protect the Grand Canyon. It would keep this anomalous status until 1919, when it was finally converted into a national park (Rothman 1989). Ironically, 'in the first full year of national park status for the Grand Canyon, 67,315 visitors came, up from the 37,735 that represented the first total tabulated by the National Park Service in 1919; by 1928, the number topped 150,000' (Rothman 1996: 529). Thus national park status bequeathed a large financial benefit to the railways and their associated companies such as the Harvey Company (Rothman 1996), as tourists flocked to see what the fuss was about.

Monumental landscapes, power and identity

The epic scale of the Grand Canyon made it an axiomatic choice for a national park. There is a paradox inherent in these grandiose landscapes, in that we tend to admire (and thus protect) natural features that most resemble the *monumental*, i.e. 'man-made space' (Tompkins 1992: 76). They are seductive as symbols of power, but emphasise at the same time the vulnerability of human beings in comparison to their size and bulk (Tompkins 1992). Countries which possess these massive natural features are often keen to protect them, as they contribute to feelings of national pride and identity.

In the early days of American cinema, Raoul Walsh became one of the first Hollywood directors to take his actors on location (Davis 1998). He chose some of the most iconic of monumental Western settings for his film *The Big Trail* (1930), including the giant redwoods in Sequoia National Park and of course the Grand Canyon. Walsh's lead was to be followed by other directors, notably John Ford in his movies set in Monument Valley (Chapter 2) and the plethora of movies filmed in the rugged grandeur of Lone Pine (Chapter 8).

The Big Trail (1930)

John Wayne's first A list film wasn't the breakout role that he had hoped for and changed his name for. The studios felt that his real name, Marion Morrison, wasn't manly enough, for a man who was later to become the personification of masculinity and the most popular male film star in the world. *The Big Trail* unfortunately didn't attract the audiences that everyone expected, partly because many theatres weren't equipped to show it in widescreen (Davis 1998). The acting didn't help. Wayne, while youthfully handsome, with his chiselled features, and a clear charisma, had a stilted wooden delivery in his role as Breck Coleman, who helps to lead a group of covered wagons along the Oregon Trail to safety. It would not be until *Stagecoach* in 1939 that Wayne was given a similar opportunity, although by then he didn't disappoint, the result of nine years of experience gained in the wilderness of B movies and a director (John Ford) who brought out the best in him. Wayne was not the only culprit, with some of the poor acting attributed to the requirement to yell into microphones. Marguerite Churchill, Wayne's leading lady, failed to overcome her role as Ruth Cameron in *The Big Trail*, ending up back in B movies, but unlike Wayne, she never emerged again (Eagan 2010).

Despite a series of underwhelming performances, the lack of critical success enjoyed by *The Big Trail* is puzzling, given its magnificent vistas and the epic nature of the journey from the Mississippi to Oregon; in cinematographic terms, a task akin to the exodus out of Egypt in Cecil B. DeMille's *The Ten Commandments* (1923), seven years earlier. Some of the scenes, shot in widescreen, with the cattle heading out across the plain, dust swirling as they go, a buffalo stampede, the perilous crossing of rivers and descending down into canyons, with the wagons hanging by ropes, and the circling of the wagons as the Native Americans attack, are particularly stunning, when one considers that CGI technology was not available in this era and the action had to be created from scratch. The film 'set a standard for realism in Westerns that has rarely been matched' (Eagan 2010: 172), thanks to six months' filming on location by cinematographer, Arthur Edeson and some stunts which must have been 'as foolhardy to re-create as it must have been for the pioneers to attempt' (Eagan 2010: 173). Interestingly, one scene taking place in front of giant buttes, reminiscent of Monument Valley, appears to be merely a painted backdrop, although part of the film was said to have been filmed in Monument Valley, well before John Ford claimed it as his own (Eyman 2014).

Several scenes involving Native Americans deliver wildly inconsistent messages. Breck Coleman appears to understand the Cheyenne and their ways and can speak their language. He tells his group of settlers that they will be unharmed so long as 'we travel through their land' without settling down. The reference to 'their land' suggests that he acknowledges their ownership, yet the pioneers are aiming to create a new life in Oregon, presumably on someone else's land. There is laughter rather than gratitude at the Cheyenne gift of ponies, after Ruth's horse has died, with the pioneers attributing this to a misapprehension that Ruth was Breck's 'squaw'. The motivation for the Native American attack on the wagon train is never provided and appeared to be nothing more than an excuse for a grandiose set piece, with the wagons filmed from above. When the Cheyenne are defeated and leave, the comment is made by a member of the wagon train: 'I guess we were just a little too much for them'. The priest follows this up with his pronouncement that some of the pioneers had perished 'at the hands of the savages'. Within the one film, we go full circle from acceptance to denigration of the Other.

Early tourism at the Canyon: Fred Harvey and Mary Colter

Before the arrival of the Fred Harvey Company, most of the tourism development at the Canyon was small-scale and inadequate for accommodating large numbers of visitors (Rothman 1996). It would take the vision of the English-born Fred Harvey to transform this natural marvel into a fully fledged tourist attraction, providing 'access to the capital needed to package and promote a tourist experience and the means to convey consumers to the site of that activity' (Rothman 1996: 526). He saw a niche in the market for serving good food on trains but also augmenting this with a series of hotels/restaurants throughout the American West, known as Harvey Houses, offering pleasant surrounds and high levels of hospitality to guests. Some of the Harvey Houses became upmarket resorts, including the Alvarado in Albuquerque and La Fonda (Figure 10.3) in Santa Fe. One of the most famous however was El Tovar at the Grand Canyon, designed by Charles Whittlesey.

El Tovar created a community at the Canyon, with its own laundry and power plant (Poling-Kempes 1989). It commanded wonderful views of the Canyon and guests enjoyed fine dining in its restaurant. Other Harvey properties could be visited nearby, such as the lounge called the Lookout, and two attractions designed by Mary Colter – the Hopi House in 1905, a gift shop of Native American handicrafts (Figures 10.4 and 10.5); and the Bright Angel Lodge in 1934, which provided a less expensive alternative to staying at El Tovar. Mary Colter was originally hired as an interior designer, but advanced to architect of a series of buildings for Fred Harvey, all in a distinctive South-Western style (Riley

Figure 10.3 La Fonda Hotel, Santa Fe (photo J. Laing).

Figure 10.4 Hopi House, Grand Canyon (photo J. Laing).

Figure 10.5 Promotional signage for Hopi House, Grand Canyon (photo J. Laing).

1999). Apart from the convenience of the railway spur from Williams, visitors could be transported to the Canyon in motor cars owned by the Fred Harvey Company, complete with their own chauffeurs and guides (Rothman 1996; Weigle 1989).

Those local businesses that failed to survive the slick onslaught of the Fred Harvey Company were understandably resentful and this resulted in the taking of legal and political action against the behemoth (Rothman 1996). However, they failed in their bid to shut down the competition, and by the mid 1920s, tourism at the Grand Canyon was largely controlled by the combined forces of the ATSF, the Fred Harvey Company and the NPS (Rothman 1996; Youngs 2011). The slogan 'Meals by Fred Harvey' became a source of competitive advantage for the ATSF (Poling-Kempes 1989).

In their heyday, the Harvey Houses and Harvey operations on the trains main-tained standards of professionalism and formality that their competitors couldn't or wouldn't match. Harvey Houses were located at regular intervals along the train-line and even though they mostly operated at a loss, this was subsidised by the railway, in recognition of the boost these operations gave to ticket sales (Curtin 2008; Poling-Kempes 1989). This meant that corners did not need to be cut. Service was quick, yet not impersonal, and random inspections of staff, sometimes by Harvey himself, kept them on their toes. The food provided was far beyond what most patrons had experienced elsewhere, with the best of produce brought in through the rail system:

> Harvey brought fresh whitefish from the Great Lakes to the deserts of Arizona and New Mexico; Californian cantaloupes, fresh and cold, to the humid prairie of Kansas; sage-fed quail to the mining towns of Colorado; and Texas beef to southern California.
>
> (Poling-Kempes 1989: 41)

Guests could always expect a varied menu, with generous servings.

Adeptness at marketing helped the ATSF and Fred Harvey Company become one of the most recognisable brands in the West. Postcards created by the Detroit Publishing Company and sold exclusively through Harvey's outlets often fea-tured images of tourist infrastructure such as the El Tovar hotel and the carriages that would take visitors along the South Rim. Even when views of the Canyon were the focus, they included a Harvey facility in the photograph or were labelled as the view *from* or *near* one of the Harvey properties (Youngs 2011). Internal promotion of the company to its staff emphasised the quality of their product and their customer service. Complaints were taken seriously, and there is an apocryphal story of Fred Harvey hearing a steward refer to a customer as a 'crank' and retorting 'It is our business to please the cranks' (Curtin 2008: 364).

The Hopi House at the Grand Canyon helped to create tourist demand for Native American products. Visitors could observe artisans making items such as pottery and jewellery (Poling-Kempes 1989) and buy the wares at the shop, with indigenous dancers and musicians providing entertainment in the open air. The company's interest in Native American and Hispanic arts and crafts can be traced to Fred Harvey's son Ford and Herman Schweizer, a Harvey employee who started collecting and selling items to the clientele, while Fred's daughter Minnie and her husband John Huckel were also keen collectors of South-Western art. A Fred Harvey Indian Department coordinated these activities, headed by Huckel (Poling-Kempes 1989). The Fred Harvey Company went further however than merely promoting sales of these artefacts; what it sold was an *identity* for the South-West, 'displaying it as a tourist attraction of sublime natural wonders, prehistoric and colonial historic significance, and colorful, tamed, native peoples, primarily Indians' (Weigle 1989: 115). Their chief archi-tect and interior designer, Mary Colter, used Native American and Hispanic motifs and designs throughout the Harvey Houses, with 'an entire room devoted to Indian arts and crafts' in the Alvarado in Albuquerque. The company's 'Indian Detours' were popular with guests, 'taking them to pueblos and villages in Harvey Cars guided by Harvey Couriers. The Harvey Company, then, inter-acted with Indians in a variety of ways, most notably as employees, suppliers, and participants in the tourist trade' (Curtin 2011: 370). The company's notion of the *authentic* 'allowed for cultural change' (Curtin 2011: 386). This is an important point to stress. The company appreciated the cultural heritage of Native Americans, but did not expect them to live frozen in time.

This stance by the Fred Harvey Company arguably reversed the marginalisa-tion of Native American culture, which is particularly resonant in the Western movie. The American Indian generally appears in the background of these stories, often there as a convenient but shadowy protagonist for the hero, sym-bolised by mostly being portrayed by White actors. Yet the Fred Harvey Company and its acolyte Mary Colter still have their critics. Even though Frankeberger and Garrison (2002: 10) note that the Hopi House was 'built by Hopi craftsmen with authentic materials (except for the hidden Santa Fe railroad rails used as beams) and real features such as doors brought from Oraibi', it has been slammed as a 'theme-park gimmick' (Weigle 1997: 167), representative of the Disneyfication of the South-West perpetuated by the company (Weigle 1992, 1997). The latter argues that visitors to the Hopi House enter a manufactured *backstage*, made to look like a place where 'real' Indians lived and worked. Even D.H. Lawrence described the South-West as the 'national circus-ground' in *Just Back from the Snake Dance – Tired Out* (1924). Yet the charge of com-modification against the company is more complex than these comments suggest. Curtin (2011: 387) notes that 'the Indians constructed and assumed their own identities, as well'. This was not necessarily a one-sided business transaction involving White hegemony over an indigenous culture. It appears that the company at least tried to include Native American culture in the national nar-rative it was promoting to Americans and senior Harvey managers, employees and family members had a genuine interest in and admiration of the indigenous art works that they collected and showcased at their properties.

In the wake of the Second World War, it became more difficult to keep the Harvey Houses operating. The company started to decline and 'by 1963, company operations consisted solely of the Santa Fe dining car service, the La Fonda and Alvarado Hotels in Santa Fe and Albuquerque respectively, and hotels and concessions in the Grand Canyon and Death Valley' (Curtin 2008: 361). The family business was finally sold in 1968. Today, El Tovar remains a viable business in the Grand Canyon, still a taste of what gracious travel at the turn of the twentieth century might have been like.

The Harvey Girls

Poling-Kempes (1989) argues that the history of the American West often privileges the masculine (White) experience, and has overlooked or dismissed the voices of women and Native Americans in this narrative. In her view, the story of the Harvey Girls is every bit as important to the American story as the cowboy or trapper: 'The Harvey Girls joined the ranks of American trailblazers when they set down their bags and settled into these early railroad communities' (Poling-Kempes 1989: xvii). She had the opportunity to advance in her career, and potentially could become a manager, even if this was comparatively rare in the company's history. Not every woman who worked for the company could aspire to be a Harvey Girl. As the public face of the Harvey company, she was almost exclusively White. Native American, Black or Hispanic women were largely relegated to jobs behind the scene (Poling-Kempes 1989), mainly the kitchens, unless they were selling or demonstrating the making of cultural artefacts to visitors.

Fred Harvey was clear in his vision – he wanted the best and 'set about recruiting women to waitress in the same way he had set about locating the finest food, furniture, chefs, and managers' (Poling-Kempes 1989: 43). He protected their image vigilantly, through strict rules of conduct and dress. While being a waitress in the East was looked down upon, being a Harvey Girl in the West was respectable, reflecting the high standards that were set in a Harvey House. Her clothing became a trademark of the Harvey Company. Each woman wore a uniform, rather like a nun's habit in its simplicity and austerity, featuring a black skirt and shirt, topped with a white starched apron. These were laundered off-site and were immediately discarded for a new uniform if stained during a shift. Occasionally the women would wear versions of Native American or Mexican dress for special occasions (Poling-Kempes 1989; Weigle 1992). The Harvey Girls worked long hours but a job that was portable and 'daily contact with passengers and employees of the Santa Fe Railway' led to many marriage proposals (Poling-Kempes 1989: 59). They were a godsend in places where eligible women were few and far between and many of them helped to found settlements throughout the American West.

The Harvey Girls (1946)

The Harvey Girls is a frothy musical from MGM, best known for its Oscar-winning song 'On the Atchison, Topeka and the Santa Fe'. It tells the story of

Susan Bradley (Judy Garland), who travels to the small town of Sandrock as a mail-order bride and comes to work for the Harvey Company when her intended marriage falls through. Based on a 1942 Dell novel of the same name by Samuel Hopkins Adams, despite the screen acknowledgement of the assistance of the Fred Harvey Company 'on many historical details', the plot intersperses real-life events with colourful invention, to make the story more appealing to post-war audiences. The real Harvey Girls, as noted above, mainly wore plain and prac-tical black-and-white garb, and we do see these outfits in various scenes, but mostly the women are dressed in pastel-coloured frills. At one stage they are clad in lavish ballgowns at a party given for the town by the new Harvey House, an excuse to show off costumes by Helen Rose, who designed Grace Kelly's wedding dress when she married Prince Rainier in 1956.

We are left in no doubt at the start of the film about the contribution of the Harvey Girls to the opening up of the West and the American national story:

> These winsome waitresses conquered the West as surely as the Davy Crock-etts and the Kit Carsons – not with powder horn and rifle, but with a beef-steak and a cup of coffee. To these unsung pioneers, whose successors today still carry on in the same tradition, we sincerely dedicate this motion picture.

This is echoed in the pronouncement made by Miss Bliss (Selena Royle) to her new charges: 'A Harvey Girl is more than a waitress. Wherever a Harvey House appears, civilisation is not far behind. You girls are the symbol and the promise of the order that is to come'.

The Harvey Girls are depicted as neat, industrious and resourceful. They sing of their hopes and dreams, taking this opportunity to build a future and overcome the boredom and conventionality of their backgrounds ('It's a Great Big World'). They are also easy on the eye. As a cowboy observes, 'Mr Harvey know exactly how to pick 'em'. The refinement of the Harvey Girls is contrasted with the girls who work at the Alhambra saloon across the street, headed by the sleepy-eyed Em (a young Angela Lansbury, far removed from her later *Murder She Wrote* days), and it is the latter who suffer by compari-son in the town's eyes. At the party hosted by the Harvey Company, the men of the town want to dance with the Harvey Girls, not the harlots. As the Rev-erend Claggett (Morris Ankrum) pithily puts it: 'They turned down a wild time in favour of a *good* time'. This is not to say that the Harvey Girls are overly demure. Susan stalks across the road with two pistols when she finds out that the Alhambra employees have stolen the Harvey's meat supply and Sonora Cassidy (Marjorie Main of *Ma and Pa Kettle* fame) knows how to slug a man who takes liberties with her. The country girl Alma (Virginia O' Brien), in a comic song and dance act watched by a bug-eyed and loose-limbed Ray Bolger, who seems to be reprising the role of the Scarecrow from *The Wizard of Oz*, bemoans the standoffishness of the men she meets ('The Wild Wild West'):

I was hopin' to be ropin' somepin' wild in the wild, wild west
I been sittin' till I'm getting' kinda riled at the wild, wild west
I read about them desperado guys
As desperate as men can be
I reckon it was just a pack o' lies
The only one who's desperate is me.

The existing businesses in town are envious of the Harvey Company's entrepreneurial ventures, highlighted by the corrupt judge (Preston Foster), who tries to make the Girls fearful and leave, and eventually sets the Harvey House alight. Most of the rest of the town bands together to put out the fire, including the saloon girls, and the Harvey House reopens in the Alhambra, thanks to its owner, Ned Trent (John Hodiak), Susan's love interest and eventual husband. There is a curious scene when Susan apologises to Em for being a snob about her job at the saloon: 'It's only a matter of style, isn't it?' Rather open-minded, especially for Hollywood of the times. Susan even says she is ready to join the ranks of the saloon girls, if it means she won't lose Ned. But virtue triumphs in the end – Susan gets her man *and* gets to keep her reputation intact.

In this fantasy of the American West, the Native American is excised, while the (White) main characters take centre stage. The former are either silent or sing along in the background of group numbers, essentially decorative window-dressing to create atmosphere, and play no role in the plot. This is the kind of film that Tompkins (1992: 10) has denigrated for its tokenism: 'The absence of Indians in Western movies, by which I mean the lack of their serious presence as individuals, is so shocking once you realize it that, even for someone acquainted with outrage, it's hard to admit'. *The Harvey Girls* stands in stark contrast to the greater foregrounding of the Native American in several episodes of the television series *The Brady Bunch* (1971), discussed later in this chapter.

The modern Grand Canyon experience

Domestic travel throughout the West burgeoned after the Second World War, due to greater disposable incomes, more leisure time and better highways (Rothman 1996). Driving to the Canyon became the norm, with the new interstate highways making it easier and more convenient to take a road trip. There are also a number of air-tours available from nearby destinations such as Las Vegas (Schwer *et al.* 2000), offering both airplane and helicopter flights, which can facilitate a day-trip to the Canyon, or even less, for the truly time-poor. This mode of transport however raises concerns over noise and air pollution, as well as safety issues related to shared airspace (Schwer *et al.* 2000). The National Park Service does not promote the air-tour option on its website, preferring to provide information on more environmentally friendly modes of transport (www. nps.gov/grca/faqs.htm).

While the railroad from Williams to the Canyon ceased to operate in the 1970s, it was reintroduced in 1989, when the Grand Canyon Railway decided to buy all the stock and remaining infrastructure and reopen the rail line as a tourist attraction (Collison 2014; Davis and Morais 2004). Visitors can now travel by rail again, departing from the historic depot in Williams, which has been modernised to include a café and gift-shop. The rail company also runs the nearby Grand Canyon Railway Hotel and an RV park.

This development has been welcomed by some members of the local community, although others have criticised it as leading to a sharp increase in rents in the town, while wages remain low, and not resulting in a great deal of tourist money spent in the downtown area of Williams: 'It was claimed that the railway was actively creating a tourist enclave that restricted interaction between itself and the downtown shops' (Davis and Morais 2004: 6). There was also disquiet when the railway moved its headquarters to Flagstaff in 1995 (Davis and Morais 2004).

The Grand Canyon Railway now runs a night-time Polar Express trip at Christmas, bringing *The Polar Express* book (1985) and film (2004) to life, where children can meet Santa Claus when they arrive at the Canyon. Special opportunities are provided throughout the year to travel to the Canyon by steampower behind a 90-year-old Locomotive 4960. Waste vegetable oil is used to fuel the train, thus reducing the carbon footprint and leading the company to label its product 'The Greenest Train in America' (see www.thetrain.com). Even though the Polar Express trip is not by steam train, these types of events tap into *fantasies* about steam travel, which are often a feature of much-loved children's books and films (Frost and Laing 2014).

With the growth of mass tourism, films and television ensured their characters visited the Grand Canyon and talked about going there, thus contributing to its modern myth as a must-see attraction. A notable example in the 1970s was the visit by the all-American family, *The Brady Bunch* (1969–1974).

The Brady Bunch (season 3, 1971)

In a trio of episodes, 'Ghost Town, U.S.A.', 'The Grand Canyon or Bust' and 'The Brady Braves', the Brady family are taking the typical American vacation, a camping trip at the Grand Canyon. They drive off in their Plymouth Satellite station wagon (room for six children and a housekeeper!) with tents and sleeping bags strapped to the roof and a trailer for their luggage. At the time of first airing of these episodes, *The Brady Bunch* did not enjoy high ratings, although years of global syndication have now earned it cult status. Children around the world for years to come thus unconsciously absorbed the message that a road trip and camping is what *real families* do, and the Grand Canyon joined many children's personal bucket list as a travel destination, along with riding down to the bottom of the Canyon on mules, like the Bradys did. Ironically, the National Park Service is now considering cutting back the number of mules transporting tourists on the trails, to minimise erosion, and has strict rules on who can take these rides.

Right from the start, the trip is sold to the Brady siblings, and hence to juvenile viewers, as a *cultural experience*, with numerous references made to connections between the Canyon and Native Americans (or 'Indians', the term commonly used then). Mr Brady (Robert Reed) tells his youngest son Bobby (Mike Lookinland): 'It's not just the Canyon, Bobby. We're going to learn all about the Indian tribes that live there'. His sister Cindy (Susan Olsen) also says that she wants to see the Indians. Mother Carol (Florence Henderson) is the only one who focuses on the adventurous side of their trip, travelling down to the floor of the Canyon: 'That's the most exciting part of the trip! One mile, straight down'.

The seriousness with which they take the idea of contact with Native Americans is juxtaposed with jokes at their expense (this is a sitcom after all). When the housekeeper Alice (Ann B. Davis) is taught the Indian phrase for hello, she quips 'That'll come in handy if I ever bump into Tonto'. Bobby uses all the clichés that he has seen in Westerns when he meets the Indian boy Jimmy (Michele Campo) at the Grand Canyon, such as 'How!', leading Jimmy to respond 'How what?' Jimmy tells him to 'cut out the paleface stuff'. We later find that Jimmy wants to be an astronaut, and runs away from his grandfather, who 'only thinks about the old Indian ways'. Mike explains that he can do both – 'you can be proud of your heritage'. This leads to the rapprochement between the boy and his grandfather, and an invitation to the Bradys to become honorary members of the tribe, complete with a special Native American name, bestowed at a ceremony. Bobby tells the park ranger at the gate when they are leaving 'Now we're the Brady Braves!'

There is a diversion on the way to the Canyon, when the family decide to camp overnight in a mining ghost town, Cactus Creek. Mike tells the children that it is called a ghost town because it is 'just a memory of what used to be'. A grizzled old prospector (Jim Backus) locks them up in an old jail, to avoid them jumping his gold claim, but later comes back to rescue them. It's a device that allows the Bradys to play at being in a Western. They are lured into the jail with the idea that it was the first place where the outlaw Jesse James was incarcerated, although Mike is sceptical. Before that, the children see an old stagecoach and Greg decides they are going to make a movie called 'The Great Stagecoach Robbery'. He tells Marcia (Maureen McCormack) 'You be the school marm who's coming into town', while Jan (Eve Plumb) and Cindy are to be 'two dance hall girls coming to work in the saloon'. Peter (Christopher Knight) plays the outlaw who holds up the stagecoach, complete with a bandanna over his face, while Bobby is the driver, who dies a prolonged death after being shot. Even the idea to break out of jail comes from the films they have watched. Peter describes a cowboy making a lasso and the family join their belts and socks together to drag the spare set of keys down from a peg on the wall. Back on the road, the Bradys sing old-fashioned songs in the car, such as 'O My Darling Clementine', and they later sing 'Home on the Range' while seated around a campfire. This is an instructive example of intertextuality. Viewers watch a television family enacting Western themes and rituals based on television and cinema.

Their first glimpse of the Canyon is one of thrilled amazement: 'Would you look at that!' (Greg) and 'I never imagined it could be this beautiful!' (Marcia).

There is no self-conscious attempt to be blasé about it, as occurs in some of the more recent films (*National Lampoon's Vacation, The Guilt Trip*). The focus on the sublimity of the landscape is balanced with some facts and figures for the viewers, with the characters taking turns to quote out of guidebooks or their general knowledge. We are told the dimensions of the Canyon, and Mike states the obvious: 'The Grand Canyon is a mighty big place'. Eldest son Greg (Barry Williams) observes as they gaze over the rim: 'That's the Colorado River. That's what dug this whole canyon', and Carol tells them that the Indian name for it is 'mountains lying down'. The natural as well as cultural heritage is highlighted when Bobby and Cindy look for dinosaur fossils in the rocks. Like those around them, the family take photographs of themselves beside the rim, look at the railway station and watch Hopi dancers perform in the outdoors ('Are those real Indians?'). Greg scoffs at Peter's question about whether 'this rain dance stuff really works', responding 'No, they just do it for the tourists'. A storm duly begins on cue, suggesting that this cynicism is misplaced and what happens here is *authentic*, even if it is not recognised as such by all visitors.

The Canyon is acknowledged as potentially dangerous ('This isn't a play-ground out here. This is a wilderness!'), emphasised by an aerial shot of Bobby and Cindy, lost when they wander off from their camp, which shows them as small, vulnerable specks in a vast and forbidding landscape. Conversely the Canyon is also depicted as a *paradise*. The quality of the air is remarked on, with Greg noting 'I bet our lungs are wondering what happened to all the smog'. The final scenes before they head home show the family reluctant to leave this won-derland ('You just never get tired of looking at it').

This tri-part story arguably entered pop culture and anecdotally was one of the best loved of the TV series, judging by the number of people we have met who remember it. It showed family travel as an opportunity for role play and adventure, as well as being educational. Jennifer finally got to the Canyon as an adult; years after she enjoyed watching these episodes as a child. While the mule ride wasn't an option, her sense of awe at its monumentality was every bit as strong as that expressed by the Brady Bunch. We see this as one of those travel experiences which doesn't disappoint, much like the first glimpse of the Taj Mahal or the Great Pyramids, which makes the modern predilection for making fun of it somewhat curious. As contemporary travellers, do we now regard the contemplation of the sublime as embarrassing, naive or a form of tourist trap? In the next two films we look at, the idea of a road trip is satirised, along with the obligatory stop at the Canyon.

National Lampoon's Vacation (1983)

ELLEN: I honestly don't think we're going to find the Grand Canyon on this road.

CLARK: Jesus Christ, it's only the biggest goddamn hole in the world!!!

AUNT EDNA: Clark, watch your language!

CLARK: Make that the second biggest.

The Griswald family are headed for the fictional theme park Walleyworld, driving from Chicago towards California. As Clark (Chevy Chase) observes 'Getting there is half the fun!' There are numerous jokes made at the expense of the road trip and the Western myth. At Dodge City, Kansas, they visit a tourist trap, where son Rusty (Anthony Michael Hall) is scornful about the lack of authenticity: 'That guy's a crummy Wyatt Earp! He's wearing jogging shoes!' They drive down a closed road in Monument Valley, crashing the car, and requiring Clark to traverse the desert to find help, observed by two Navajo on horseback, both dressed as cowboys.

Eventually they visit the Grand Canyon, staying at the El Tovar hotel. The jaded response to the question 'Don't you want to look at the Grand Canyon?' is 'Nice!' Clark's credit cards have been cancelled and he can't clear a cheque with the snooty hotel manager, so he makes a run for it, stealing money from the till in the process. After they leave, they find that Aunt Edna (Imogene Coca, Jan's Aunt Jenny in *The Brady Bunch*) has died ('She must have passed away somewhere near Flagstaff'), so they tie her to the roof of the car and keep driving, a parody of *The Grapes of Wrath*. The last straw is their arrival at the theme park, only to find it closed for renovations. The film ends with a photo montage, with the final one being a photograph of the Griswalds on a plane. We realise that they flew home.

The Guilt Trip (2012)

Joyce (Barbra Streisand) and her son Andy (Seth Rogen) take a detour to the Canyon during a road trip across America, to fulfil Joyce's dream. Even the cowboy they meet along the way in Texas tells Joyce that he hopes they get to see the Grand Canyon. When they get there, after staring at it for a bit, Joyce articulates what they both appear to be thinking: 'How long are we supposed to look at this?' While Andy protests a bit, mentioning the time it has taken to get there, Joyce laughs and they both run back to the car. The message is that they have fulfilled the sightseeing duties of a typical tourist, and now must move on.

The importance of a natural wonder

The Grand Canyon is one of the Seven Natural Wonders of the World, as Greg Brady tells his siblings in *The Brady Bunch*, and was designated a World Heritage Site in 1979. Park statistics of its dimensions are astonishing – 446 km in length, an average width of 16 km rim to rim and an average depth of 1.5 km (NPS 2014). North America needed its own tourist heritage and iconography, set 'apart from the European legacy that they had long revered and sought to emulate, yet to which they felt inferior' (Rothman 1996: 526), and it found what it needed in the Grand Canyon. The growth of visitation to the Canyon can thus be traced to its place in American *cultural identity*. It is unlike anything that other parts of the world can offer to tourists and makes Americans feel proud about themselves and their country.

Icons like the Grand Canyon made it easy to promote 'See America First' (Rothman 1996; Schaffer 2001). Its gargantuan size allows visitors to indulge in 'Euro-American fantasies of an unoccupied continent' (Klein 1993: 42). Film and television continue their fascination with the Grand Canyon, with modern road trips often featuring a visit, even if it is merely tokenistic. This adds to the myth that has grown around the tourist experience at the Canyon, started long ago by the declaration of a national park and the promotional activities of the ATSF and the Fred Harvey Company. The Native American story plays a key role in the narrative promoted to tourists (even if the level of commodification can be criticised in some quarters), which sets the Canyon apart from other places in the West. The Grand Canyon contributes to how we see the American West – but even more so, has had an impact on how Americans see themselves.

11 Ghost Ranch

> I climbed way up on a pale green hill and in the evening light – the sun under the
> clouds – the color effect was very strange – standing high on a pale green hill
> where I could look all around at the red, yellow, purple formations – miles all
> around – the colors all intensified by the pale grey green I was standing on. It was
> wonderful.
>
> (Letter from Georgia O'Keeffe to Alfred Stieglitz, 1937,
> quoted in Buhler Lynes 2004: 32)

Introduction

Artist Georgia O'Keeffe came to the West from New York, having fallen in love
with the simplicity, monumentality, changing light and earthy colours of New
Mexico. She was escaping many things, including the breakdown of her relationship with her husband, photographer Alfred Stieglitz, but found solace in the
wild hills and expansive skies. Her identification with this region, particularly
around Ghost Ranch, and the repetition of her subject-matter led to it being
dubbed 'O'Keeffe Country', yet what she painted was essentially an imaginary
landscape, which conveys the essence of what she found there.

O'Keeffe was not the only extraordinary woman to build a life in the South-
West, particularly around Taos. This chapter examines some other notable
examples, including Frieda Lawrence, the wife of D.H. Lawrence, aristocratic
English artist Dorothy Brett, one of the Bloomsbury Group, Mabel Dodge
Luhan, New York society hostess and patron and Millicent Rogers, the
fashion-plate oil heiress. It explores what drew these women to the South-
West, what encouraged them to stay, and why their presence and individual
narratives are commemorated by various tourist attractions, including
museums, memorials and galleries.

Northern New Mexico has a story in which strong women dominate and have
influenced the direction of art, clothing and literature, yet interestingly little of
this history has found its way onto the screen. The most surprising omission is a
film or television series centred on the life of Mabel Dodge Luhan – she only
plays a minor role in the two films analysed in this chapter. While New Mexico
has a history of attracting artists since the nineteenth century, much of the

creativity which found a home in and around Taos was due to her influence, and she attracted lost and creative souls like moths to a flame. She is thus a logical focal point to begin this chapter.

Mabel Dodge Luhan

It was Mabel Dodge Luhan's drive, *joie de vivre* and warm hospitality that formed the nucleus of an artists' colony in this outpost of the South-West. It was the equivalent of the Parisian salons of the seventeenth and eighteenth centuries and Mabel was an American Madame de Sévigné. Born Mabel Ganson in New York, and wealthy as the result of a fortune inherited from her banker father, she was notorious for her salons in Greenwich Village, patronage of the arts, multiple husbands and bisexuality. In 1919, she moved to Taos with her then third husband, Maurice Sterne, and later divorced him in favour of a local Native American, Tony Luhan, who was persistent in his wooing of Mabel: 'Tony erected a tepee out in front, and each night drummed from within until she joined him' (Byrne 1995: 269). At the time, Taos was a backwater, despite the fact that artists had been coming here for some time, and could only be reached by a difficult journey by horse or car if the weather allowed. The high altitude also made it challenging for visitors (Burns 2011). Mabel wrote about her attraction to this way of life in her 1935 memoir *Winter in Taos*, focussing on the rhythm of the seasons, the fascination of the wildlife and the small pleasures that can be enjoyed when one is not consumed by the hustle and bustle of urban life.

Mabel saw herself as a symbol of emancipation as 'society, especially female society, emerged from Victorian mores and restrictions' (Burns 2011: 254), and marrying Tony was part of that. She knew this interracial marriage would be controversial, but saw Taos as the wellspring for a new harmony between humankind (Palken Rudnick 1984). The controversy that was her life extends to her motives for doing this. Some saw her as attention-seeking and she has been labelled 'an undeniable snob, interested only in people distinguished by background or accomplishments who lent themselves to her circle and soirees' (Burns 2011: 255). Many of the people she invited to Taos eventually found her insufferable, chiefly the Lawrences, possibly an example of how the queen bee often attracts the jealousy of those who would like to be in a similar position of control. The fetid atmosphere created by her often highly strung guests probably didn't help social cohesion:

> Many who came to the Luhan House were at a critical point in their lives, physically, psychologically, or vocationally. For them, the house functioned as a kind of life crisis center, breaking down and healing, making – and sometimes unmaking – love affairs and marriages.
>
> Source (Palken Rudnick 1998: 8)

Perhaps some of these guests also resented the fact that Mabel must have been privy to some of their most intimate secrets?

What is undeniable is the impact that her patronage had on the culture of its time, regardless of its motives. The people she invited down to Taos to her house, Los Gallos, aside from those already mentioned, were eclectic to say the least, including psychiatrist and psychotherapist Carl Jung, playwright and novelist Thornton Wilder, photographer Ansel Adams, dancer and choreographer Martha Graham, and fashion designer Adrian, known for his creations worn by Joan Crawford, which gave her a distinctive and elegant style (Spoto 2010). Mabel introduced many of these people to the work and culture of the Native Americans and encouraged their intellectual and artistic endeavours. For that, and that alone, we think she deserves our praise, rather than censure.

Many of her house guests were tempted to stay on in the region and continued to travel back and forth from New Mexico, using the Taos region as a base, but often leaving during the harsh winters. The Lawrences were an example of that, often escaping to Mexico or Europe. Mabel however stayed on all year round, happy to be at the epicentre of what she had created. She died in Taos in 1962 and is buried in the Kit Carson Cemetery, alongside Carson and his wife. The Mabel Dodge Luhan House became a National Historic Landmark in 1991 and still welcomes the artistic and literary community. According to its website: 'As an historic inn and conference center which offers retreat-style meetings and artistic, literary, and personal growth workshops, the Mabel Dodge Luhan House continues to build on its 80-year history of personal, intellectual and artistic ferment' (Mabel Dodge Luhan House 2014).

The house had another interesting postscript before its current usage. Dennis Hopper stayed in her home while editing *Easy Rider* (1969) (see Chapter 4) and subsequently bought Los Gallos from Mabel's granddaughter in 1970. He saw this as a centre for his own drug-fuelled counter-culture and called it the Mud Palace (Leigh Brown 1997). It was eventually sold again but Hopper retained his love for Taos, and was buried there when he died in 2010 in the Jesus Nazareno Cemetery, following a Native American funeral. The sounds of motorcycles being revved could be heard in the distance, a tribute from his biker fans. Fourteenth May, Hopper's birthday, has been declared Dennis Hopper Day in the State of New Mexico.

Georgia O'Keeffe

> She wasn't really part of the Santa Fe cultural scene, except for the Chamber Music Festival. She loved chamber music and was very generous to them. She wasn't part of the New York art scene, either. She'd come out here in part to get away from all that. She was really a woman apart.
>
> (Joanne Phillips on Georgia O'Keeffe, quoted in Turner 2004: 111)

For Georgia O'Keeffe, life in New York had been disappointing, both in terms of her fractured relationship with her husband, Alfred Stieglitz, and the critical reception of her series of close-up paintings of flowers, which were interpreted as having sexual connotations (Buhler Lynes 2004: 11). New Mexico offered a fresh start – and new inspiration for her artwork. Although she was invited to New Mexico by

Mabel Dodge Luhan, she generally stayed aloof from Mabel's circle of friends. Rather than living in Santa Fe or Taos, she chose Abiquiu and Ghost Ranch. O'Keeffe was caught up in her work and preferred solitude to do this (Turner 2004). She did however make new friends, such as Maria Chabot, who started the Indian markets on the Plaza at Santa Fe in the 1930s, and the pair often travelled together on painting trips. In her old age, she became friendly with a much younger man called Juan Hamilton (there was almost a 60-year age gap), who was left most of her fortune, leading to legal action from Georgia's family to try to claim it back. He ended up keeping her house at Ghost Ranch (Glueck 1987). The nature of their relationship remains a mystery, like much of Georgia's private life.

Most of her paintings were made when she lived around the area known as Ghost Ranch, 'a vast panorama of contrasting forms and colors shaped over millions of years by water and wind erosion' (Buhler Lynes 2004: 12). This is a timeless landscape (Figure 11.1), and its age is emphasised by the presence of a Museum of Paleontology, showcasing dinosaur fossils that were found in the area (Figure 11.2). The buttes and mesas are solid, unyielding, as far removed as is possible from the delicacy of the calla lilies she painted, with their petals and stamens presented in detail. Whereas her flower paintings are clearly feminine, her paintings of the rugged landscape of New Mexico, including the detritus of animals such as cow horns and skulls, are more ambiguous, depicting the sublimity of nature as a strong and powerful force and a confronting reminder of our mortality.

Figure 11.1 Ghost Ranch landscape (photo J. Laing).

Figure 11.2 Museum of Paleontology, Ghost Ranch (photo J. Laing).

While O'Keeffe is known for her realistic landscapes, Buhler Lynes (2004: 13) argues that they are essentially imaginary creations:

> the opposite of verisimilitude. Paintings that may appear at first to adhere faithfully to their subjects are, in fact, highly subjective explorations that are as dependent on the manipulation of color and shape as they are on the forms that inspired them.

The landscape of specific sites is thus used as a departure point by the artist, and O'Keeffe's work contributes to the imagery we have of the South-West, through these iconic images of mountains and sky, full of colour and bold strokes. Interestingly, the same sexual motifs can be interpreted in her buttes and mesas as in her flowers, despite O'Keeffe's reticence on the subject. She continued her work into old age, despite her failing eyesight, and died in 1986 at the age of 98. Her ranch, Rancho de los Burros, is not open to the public, but tours are available of her house at Abiquiu, which is managed by the Georgia O'Keeffe Museum in Santa Fe (Figure 11.3) and has been designated a National Historic Landmark. The museum opened in 1997 and their collection incorporates over 3,000 of her artworks, the largest single collection in the world. In 2001, the Georgia O'Keeffe Museum Research Center was established, dedicated to the study of

Figure 11.3 Georgia O'Keeffe Museum in Santa Fe (photo J. Laing).

American Modernism (Georgia O'Keeffe Museum 2014). Her paintings are also to be found in leading art galleries around the world, and there have been a number of retrospectives of her work, including the first retrospective exhibition by a female artist staged in the Museum of Modern Art in New York in 1946.

A telemovie in 2009 on Georgia O'Keeffe focussed mainly on her life in New York with Stieglitz, exploring the reasons why she fled to New Mexico as a kind of sanctuary in her darkest days but providing less exposition about what made her stay there and what she achieved in the latter half of her career.

Georgia O'Keeffe (2009)

We first encounter Georgia O'Keeffe (Joan Allen) in her old age, with a voiceover that shows how this very private person used her art to communicate with others: 'I don't trust words.... Just look at the paintings.... That's all I will allow you to see'. As a young artist, she meets Alfred Stieglitz (Jeremy Irons), a New York gallery owner and photographer, and he is quickly established as her mentor and later her lover. Wealthy heiress Mabel Dodge Luhan (Tyne Daly) meets Georgia at Stieglitz's gallery and calls her 'Alfred's latest plaything'. Georgia brushes this off but will later realise that Stieglitz will always lose interest in a new talent once they outgrow their need of him. Mabel invites her to visit her house in Taos – 'It's heaven'. This invitation will be a haven for Georgia in due course, although she doesn't yet realise it.

Georgia is ensconced in a flat by Stieglitz, who eventually marries her. He admires her gifts as an artist but also her determination to succeed. When he is horrified at her destruction of some of her artworks, she says that she knows that these are not the best she can do: 'I've been absolutely terrified my entire life and I've never let it stop me from doing a single thing!' Their relationship at this stage is symbiotic – he photographs her while she paints. It appears to be a true meeting of minds.

Georgia is struggling to express what she feels inside through her art. When Stieglitz asks her what she misses about living in New York, she answers: 'I miss the sky'. He takes her to his family estate and even here, we can see the beginnings of her craving for privacy and space to create. She finds a small cabin to paint in and tells Stieglitz: 'I'm working. Find your own place'.

Georgia is outraged when nude photographs taken of her by Stieglitz are exhibited in his gallery. She feels violated, 'a freak in a sideshow' – 'those pictures were my love for you … not for the world'. Stieglitz tells her that this publicity is part of a campaign to get her work known through her notoriety. Georgia is uncomfortable with this: 'Have I made a bargain with the Devil?' Stieglitz is also frank about their precarious financial position and thinks that the success of the photographs will put them on a more secure footing. We hear voiceovers of some of the reviews of her famous flower paintings, which emphasise her gender: 'Her art is gloriously female'. The implication is that the explicit photographs taken by Stieglitz have coloured the way that her work is received, perhaps to its detriment. The marriage starts to develop some cracks. When Georgia says that she wants a baby, Stieglitz is angry at the potential waste of her talent: 'You are here to paint, not to breed'. When he starts an affair with Dorothy Norman, a Sears Roebuck heiress, Georgia is devastated. A fellow artist, Rebecca Strand, seeing her despair, takes Georgia to Mabel's New Mexico home: 'You'll love it in Taos. It's like being on the Moon'. They arrive at night, with a storm in progress. Georgia is emotionally exhausted and bundled into bed. While the film is deliberately coy about the relationship between Rebecca and Georgia, recent biographies have claimed that the pair were in a lesbian relationship (Eisler 1991; Garber 2013). There are similar rumours about relationships between Georgia and Mabel Dodge Luhan, as well as her Native American husband Tony, which made Mabel jealous and eventually turn away from O'Keeffe. We see the writer Jean Toomer in the background (not a single word of dialogue!), but the film never explores Georgia's relationship with him, or whether this contributed to her decision to stay and paint in New Mexico.

When Georgia awakes the next morning and opens the curtains on the glorious mountain vistas that surround her, it is like a veil has lifted. The light is extraordinary. She has a renewed interest in life and is excited at what she sees all around her, learning to drive and travelling to paint, even in extreme temperatures. These scenes are filmed in Abiquiu and the producers had permission to shoot inside her actual house, allowing the audience a bird's-eye view of her life there. Tony Luhan introduces her to the Native Americans around Taos and she is fascinated by their culture. She starts to dress in clothes inspired by the Native Americans she meets, just like Mabel. Georgia writes to Stieglitz and is glowing about her experiences: 'I know I belong here. My head's filling up with pictures just waiting to jump onto the canvas'. The landscape is an inspiration: 'I look at the hills and the sky and I think half your work's done for you'. When Stieglitz comes to visit, she shows him a cow's skull, which will become one of her best-known motifs in her paintings.

While Georgia goes back and forth to New York, coming to visit Stieglitz when he falls ill, she is clearly suffering when she is close to him. His own brother calls him a 'bully' and says that Stieglitz is 'killing' Georgia. She has a complete break-down and it takes her almost 18 months to start painting again. One of her paintings is sold to the Metropolitan Museum of Art, evidence of the critical acclaim of her paintings of New Mexico. Georgia is grateful to Stieglitz for his support of her work, but must live life on her own terms. The story jumps ahead now to the end of Georgia's life. We are told that she lived to 98, and made sure that Stieglitz's legacy as a photographer was never forgotten. There is also a reference to O'Keeffe's growing blindness in her old age, which meant that she began to paint from memory, based on those 'pictures' in her head.

Frieda Lawrence

Frieda was the muse for her second husband, the writer D.H. Lawrence, who is known for a body of work including *Sons and Lovers* (1913), *Women in Love* (1920) and *Lady Chatterley's Lover* (1928). She was a German aristocrat, the Baroness von Richthofen, and despite the difference in their backgrounds (Lawrence was the son of a Nottinghamshire miner), the pair were a perfect match in terms of sexual compatibility and intellect. Frieda was a strong support for Lawrence in his artistic endeavours, including his battle against censorship and mis-understanding of his work, and even after his death continued the fight to have his work given its due recognition. The Lawrences were gypsies, constantly on the move, but they did make Taos their temporary home for a number of years and Frieda later moved there after Lawrence's death, marrying an Italian army officer, Angelo Ravagli, in 1950, who she first met 25 years earlier.

The first sojourn to Taos came at Mabel Dodge Luhan's invitation. In Frieda's own words, Mabel had written 'that [D.H. Lawrence] must know the Pueblo Indians, that the Indians say that the heart of the world beats there in New Mexico' (Lawrence 1934: 121). They had been in Australia before that, where Lawrence wrote *Kangaroo* (1923). The Lawrences were given a gift of a ranch in Taos, called Kiowa, but they wanted to pay Mabel for it, giving her an ori-ginal manuscript of *Sons and Lovers*. They lived there with Dorothy Brett (who they labelled 'The Brett'), and the three worked hard on the repairs, although Frieda had finally had enough when they visited Mexico (Lawrence 1934: 1490): 'The Brett came every day and I thought she was becoming too much part of our lives and I resented it ... [Lawrence] raved at me, said I was a jealous fool'.

It was a bucolic lifestyle; Frieda cooked, churned her own butter and looked after the animals, while Lawrence 'made cupboards and chairs and painted doors and windows' (Lawrence 1934: 145). Frieda explained what this meant to him:

> How he loved every minute of life at the ranch. The mornings, the squirrels, every flower that came in its turn, the big trees, chopping the wood, the chickens, making bread, all our hard work, and the people, and all assumed the radiance of new life.
>
> (p. 153)

He wrote prodigiously, but found it hard to write about what he saw: 'because though it is so open, so big, free, empty, and even aboriginal – still it has a sort of shutting-out quality, obstinate' (quoted in Lawrence 1934: 156). He did however write essays on the Indians, such as 'The Dance of the Sprouting Corn', which explored his fascination with 'the Indians' mysterious unity and the influence of the cosmos upon them' (Squires and Talbot 2002: 290). The Lawrences didn't visit Taos very often, however, preferring to be

> where one is alone with trees and mountains and chipmunks and desert, one gets something out of the air, something wild and untamed, cruel and proud, beautiful and sometimes evil – that is really America. But not the America of the whites.
>
> (quoted in Lawrence 1934: 168)

After his death in 1930 in France, Frieda came back to Kiowa ranch with Angelo and immediately became the subject of jealousy and local gossip. Brett felt that she was 'more truly his widow than Frieda' and 'Mabel and I shiver for Lorenzo [their nickname for Lawrence]' (Squires and Talbot 2002: 369). While she had indeed moved on with Angelo, Lawrence remained important in her life and she brought his ashes back to Taos to be buried at the ranch. Her pattern for many years thereafter was to leave during the harsh winters and return during the spring. In 1937, Frieda bought another ranch, Los Pinos, and her feuds with the other women ceased, as they all grew older and realised that these petty jealousies and squabbles were pointless. According to Squires and Talbot (2002: 420) 'Frieda and Brett were the lights of Taos, luring visitors with their fragrant memories of a bygone Europe'. Frieda died of a stroke in 1956, and was buried in Taos. Visitors today still look for associations with the Lawrences. In recognition of that interest, the D.H. Lawrence (Kiowa) ranch, owned by the University of New Mexico, is now open to the public for three days a week between July and October (Taos Community Foundation 2014).

Priest of Love (1981)

This story of D.H. Lawrence (Ian McKellen) and his wife Frieda (Janet Suzman) concentrates on the period when Lawrence leaves England to escape the persecution of censorship and the destruction of a thousand copies of his book *The Rainbow* for obscenity. The couple head to Taos in the United States, at the invitation of Mabel Dodge Luhan (Ava Gardner). Gardner is far too glamorous to play Mabel, with her severe bobbed haircut, and the part is badly written, with Mabel seemingly chuckling at any slight, great or small, thrown her way. It is difficult to believe that she was quite so good-humoured. She does however ask for trouble by immediately asking Lawrence when he arrives: 'And have you brought your disciples?' While we are not given much back-story, in reality, Lawrence did try to convince a group of kindred spirits to join him in New Mexico, a utopian vision which he labelled Rananim, but most people bailed on him (Squires and Talbot 2002). He brings forward the Hon. Dorothy Brett (Penelope Keith) as his sole acolyte. This is another badly written role; Brett comes across as a naive fool as well as obviously enamoured of Lawrence. It is hard to believe that a bohemian from Bloomsbury would be so ignorant of common sexual terminology ('Screwing?') even if she was sexually inexperienced ('You'll have to tell me what to do'). She takes up typing so she can help Lawrence with his manuscripts, and says 'I don't mean to interfere', but is clearly the third wheel in Frieda's eyes.

Mabel announces she is giving them a ranch, to which Lawrence takes exception: 'I don't like property, I don't like things, I don't like presents, I don't like patronage. And I don't *need* any of them'. They buy it off her, but it still rankles with them that Mabel made the offer. They clearly love life in New Mexico, with scenes of the couple riding and Lawrence's declaration: 'Something stood still in my soul and started to attend … a man could find religion here', but Mabel is a thorn in their side. They repair the old ranch and Lawrence is shown on the roof, affixing tiles. When Mabel's husband Tony arrives, Lawrence doesn't immediately react: 'I stayed on the roof because I thought you were somebody else'. Frieda pipes up: 'He thought you were Mabel!' Later at a party, Lawrence jeers at Mabel and the way she presents the Native American dancers to her guests: 'You take their civilisation and turn it into a circus! You pay them thirty pieces of silver and they go off to buy chewing gum'. Mabel's riposte is deadly: 'You take the thirty pieces of silver … you took my ranch'. Lawrence protests that they bought the ranch and proceeds to smash up the buffet table. The Lawrences leave with Brett and travel to Mexico. Here, we see the first signs of Lawrence's illness and his diagnosis with tuberculosis. He is given only two more years to live.

The scenes between Frieda and Lawrence show their passion for each other and earthy humour, as well as their healthy sex life. Frieda misses her children, however, and we are privy to scenes that show what she gave up to marry Lawrence. Yet she wouldn't change this, loving him the way she does. When Mabel offers herself as a bedmate for Lawrence ('I feel I can help him, I really do'), Frieda erupts in anger: 'I am the right woman for him and no one will take him away from me'. He pushes her away when he gets sick and she reacts by having an affair with their Italian landlord when he is in Capri with Brett. Lawrence appears in Brett's bedroom but is unable to perform. The implication is that he cannot stop thinking of Frieda. When he returns to her in Florence, there is a rapprochement and he starts writing again. It is to be his much admired, yet also maligned, masterpiece, *Lady Chatterley's Lover* (1928). It will use the 'f' word, which Lawrence argues needs to be taken out of the gutter – 'We writers, we're supposed to be brave'. He has the book privately printed in Florence.

We don't see the Lawrences return to Taos, although there are scenes with Mabel and Brett in New Mexico, receiving copies of *Lady Chatterley's Lover*, and poring over it. The book is seized in England and pronounced a 'landmark in evil' by *John Bull* magazine. An exhibition of Lawrence's paintings gets a similar reception from the authorities, who confiscate them. There is a scene with Herbert G. Muskett (Sir John Gielgud), the man who is trying to censor Lawrence, making a show of counting in front of each painting – either penises or bottoms, one is not sure which.

The last scenes in the film show Lawrence on his deathbed. We hear his voice saying: 'I shall always be a priest of love and a glad one'. Frieda realises that she will have to 'let him die'. There are no scenes showing what she does with the rest of her life, nor that she returns to Taos. We are left with the sense of a life wasted when Lawrence was at the very height of his writing powers. He was just 44.

Millicent Rogers

> It seems to me strange sometimes that I've only been in Taos fifteen months for I feel so much 'of it'. As if my people had been buried in it's [*sic*] grave-yards and my blood ties were in its earth. I feel so drawn to return when I'm away and so restless with the rest of the world because of it.
>
> (Millicent Rogers in a letter to Frieda Lawrence, 1949, quoted in Burns 2011: 286)

A Standard Oil heiress, Millicent Rogers suffered from ill-health all her life after a bout of rheumatic fever as a child, and living at high altitude in New Mexico didn't help (Burns 2011). She was always known as a woman of style and often made the pages of *Vogue* magazine, but her obsession with her looks meant that she ran up huge debts on clothes and jewellery throughout her life. She had so many Charles James ballgowns, starting as a young debutante, and then through-out her life, that she was able to provide 45 gowns to the Brooklyn Museum in 1948, for their 'Decade of Design' show. Her photographs show an immacu-lately groomed and coiffured blonde woman, with highly arched eyebrows and a slash of bright lipstick. She was careful with her figure, to best show off the clothes that she loved. She must have been a sensation on the streets of Santa Fe and Taos, as if Grace Kelly had just appeared in their midst (Burns 2011).

Rogers first visited Taos in 1947 in the wake of a break-up with the actor Clark Gable. She knew Mabel Dodge Luhan socially and they were introduced through her friends, the Adrians, but she kept her distance. The two fell out when Mabel accused Rogers of trying to steal her husband Tony (Burns 2011). Rogers focused on being a patron of local arts and was most friendly with Dorothy Brett out of the artistic coterie who had made their home in Taos. Like Mabel, she took an Indian lover, Tony Luhan's nephew, and was fascinated with their culture, assisting the Pueblo financially and popularising their clothing, jewellery and artefacts through her private collections. Her efforts seem to have been well received by the Pueblo Indians, judging by the numbers who turned up at her funeral in 1953. She was later buried at the cemetery near the Pueblo, 'her head toward Taos mountain' (Burns 2011: 328).

She bought an adobe home which she christened Turtlewalk, and set about expanding it to her exacting standards of style and comfort. It is still in the family. Not all the furnishings were local, although she was known for her collection of old Spanish doors and crucifixes, and painted her house in colours associated with the Indians, yellow and red. She had huge numbers of impressionist paintings on the walls, particularly Renoirs, which amazed her guests, and travelled with 'Manets, Monets, Renoirs and van Goghs – when she changed locales for a few months' (Burns 2011: 276). To gain a view of Taos Mountain from her bed, she simply had the room moved. Nothing was too much trouble, if it meant achieving perfection.

Her other great love was South-Western clothing, leading her to have the traditional skirts and jackets copied by her couturiers in more luxuriant but less authentic fabrics (Burns 2011). She made this look her own. In the late 1940s, the fashion editor of *Harper's Bazaar*, Diana Vreeland, saw Rogers 'wearing a chest full of turquoise and silver beads and a Navajo concho belt' (Burns 2011: 130) and was immediately captivated. Rogers eventually graced its pages, which gave the look wide publicity and the imprimatur of Vreeland's discerning eye. Rogers has played a central role in many fashion retrospectives, including those exhibitions staged by the Metropolitan Museum in New York, as an example of a fashion icon (Burns 2011). Even in the current era, modern designers such as Galliano pay tribute to her distinctive style in their collections.

A key element of her style was her Native American and Hispanic jewellery. She had always had a taste for the flamboyant, and often made her own jewellery as a hobby, which she gave to beaux like Gable (Burns 2011). It was natural that she would gravitate towards the spectacular pieces that she found in New Mexico, but the sheer volume she amassed is somewhat jaw-dropping, but perhaps characteristic of her obsession for beautiful things. Some of the thousands of pieces of jewellery she collected are now proudly displayed in the Millicent Rogers Museum in Taos, New Mexico, which was established three years after her death.

Dorothy Brett

I wish you could see this wonderful desert.... Today there is not a cloud in the sky... a lovely fresh wind is blowing and everything is misty and wonderful.... Soon I am going to paint.

(Letter from Dorothy Brett to Kathleen Cooke, 28 August 1934, quoted in Golden 1999: 63)

Dorothy Brett is lampooned in the biopic of Lawrence's life, *Priest of Love*, yet she was 'neither so dull nor so stupid as she liked to pretend' (Seymour 1992: 286). She overcame a number of adversities in her life, not least of which was deafness, causing her to carry an ear trumpet around with her (although there are suggestions that this was psychological – see Seymour 1992). The Brett children were neglected by their parents, with a nanny who beat them and a politician father (later Lord Esher) 'who was almost a stranger' to them (Nicholson 2002: 77). Brett was also sexually assaulted as a young girl, and this may have contributed to her shyness around men and crushes on women (Seymour 1992). She did however fall in love with D.H. Lawrence and while it was platonic on his side 'they became buddies, looking out for each other but at a measurable distance. They were comfortable and close without being intimate' (Squires and Talbot 2002: 294). Brett also had an affair with the literary editor John Middleton Murry, after the death of his wife, writer Katherine Mansfield, but this ended unhappily.

In 1910, Brett became a student of the Slade School of Art and painted all her life. Brett became one of the famous Bloomsbury Group during these student years, wearing trousers and bobbed hair (leading her to be labelled a 'crophead') at a time when this was considered scandalous in a young girl, and also frequented Lady Ottoline Morrell's Garsington, where many conscientious objectors spent the First World War, joined by assorted bohemians (Nicholson 2002; Seymour 1992). Her rejection of this intellectual and sophisticated urban milieu for the wilds of New Mexico was the turning point in her life. She essentially remained in the United States until she died, becoming a US citizen in 1938, although like the Lawrences, she travelled often.

She first came to Taos in 1924 with the Lawrences. There is evidence that she caused tensions in the Lawrence's marriage, with Frieda annoyed at her evident feelings for her husband and jealous of her friendship with Lawrence. After the Lawrences left Taos for good in 1925, Brett stayed on and lived alone, continuing with her painting, which gradually became to be recognised and attracted buyers. Yet there is evidence that the relationship repaired itself after D.H. Lawrence's death in 1930. Brett writes in 1934: 'We are extremely friendly all of us ... Mabel and Frieda and I ... strange in a way isn't it ... and yet out here where the life is so tough it is not strange' (Golden 1999: 64). She also became friends with the socialite Millicent Rogers and the pair were seen shopping for Native American artefacts in the markets and at the Pueblo (Burns 2011). They must have been an unusual looking pair – Millicent so elegant in her Native American inspired clothing and magnificent jewellery – while Brett often wore smocks, topped with a sombrero (Burns 2011) or dressed as a cowboy, with a 'knife in her boot' (Squires and Talbot 2002: 294).

During the period 1929–1935, Brett wrote a series of letters to a university student from Melbourne who was writing a thesis on Katherine Mansfield (Golden 1999). They give us a window into Brett's soul and show her as a contemplative and lonely personality who sadly didn't 'believe in being alone.... Sometimes it happens & it is good to get a perspective' yet 'the finest contact of all is marriage'. Lawrence is described as 'a very wonderful lovely man' and her loss at his death has turned her 'to stone'. New Mexico is clearly dear to her heart, 'I cannot tear myself away from it – from my four horses – the little Ranch – the singing dancing Indians'. She describes what she sees out her window to her young Australian correspondent, and brings alive the fascination that this completely foreign landscape and culture had for her:

> In the winter – which is now – I live in Taos in a seven windowed room – so that I can look all around the world. The sacred Pueblo Mountain with its head in a cloud – spotted with snow – a circle of snowy mountains frame the quiet desert & along the road go the Indians – on foot, on horseback – in wagons – shrouded in flaming blankets ... I need not more to see the world go by.

Brett has no desire to return home: 'The thought of England – Europe – hugging their glorious pasts – and looking frayed and feeble gives me the shudders'.

Taos: a cultural hub in the West

Both Taos and Santa Fe have built their tourism industries on their artistic heritage (Kemper 1979; Kimmel 1995; Rodríguez 1989; Rothman 1996). The railway brought these artists to New Mexico and they were attracted by its rusticity and the magnificent scenery (Rodríguez 1989). There was often a resistance to development as a result. For many of these artists, the local Native American and Hispanic populations were exotically attractive but interaction was limited to 'hiring them to sit as models for paintings and to perform domestic labor' (Rodríguez 1989: 82). Much of the work by people such as Mabel Dodge Luhan, while well intentioned, did nothing more than 'entrench Indian separateness' (Rodríguez 1989: 89). The Pueblo in Taos, continuously occupied since about AD 1200 (Kemper 1979) has been criticised as an example of *museumisation*, 'converted into a staged setting for the entertainment of tourists' (Rodríguez 1990: 544). The modern town of Taos retains its artistic heart and 'has one of the highest per capita artist components of any American community' (Kemper 1979: 94). The adobe dwellings are still a feature. Its altitude (7,000 feet) has helped to promote a thriving ski tourism industry and its hip vibe attracts celebrity residents such as the actress Julia Roberts.

For many years, attempts have been made at commodification of the local culture for tourists which has led to social tensions in Taos. For example, a summer fiesta was invented in the 1930s by a group of 'businessmen and artists ... for the explicit and unabashed purpose of attracting tourists' (Rodríguez 1997: 36). It overcame the perceived drawbacks of the traditional fiesta of San Geronimo held in September, which 'came two months late to capture the peak tourist season' (Rodríguez 1997: 36). Activities included a parade and a 'Billy the Kid episode' (Rodríguez 1997). In the 1960s, the San Geronimo fiesta was dumped. The summer fiesta has increasingly become less aimed at tourists and more Hispanicised, even though it is purely an 'invented tradition'. As Rodríguez (1997: 55) muses: 'That a tourist town contrived an event to lure customers seems less remarkable than the fact that locals would become enthusiastic proponents of its "authenticity"'. At the same time, the Taos plaza has been criticised for its *gentrification* into a 'kind of Southwest theme mall for tourists' (Rodríguez 1997: 47), with its souvenir shops, restaurants and galleries. It is no longer a true community space.

The lives of the women highlighted in this chapter and their association with Tao have not been forgotten. 2012 was declared the *Year of the Remarkable Women*. According to its project coordinator, it was:

> A year-long celebration honoring outstanding historic and contemporary women of Taos. The women portrayed shared their passions, accomplishments, advice, and the challenges they met in life. Taken together their stories provide a sampling of the breadth and depth of the remarkable women who call Taos home, who experience the physical, and sometimes ineffable, influence of the land and of the generations who have inhabited it.
>
> (Taos.org 2014)

Various events included an exhibition of Millicent Rogers' jewellery and sketches and another on 'Millicent Rogers & Her Circle' at the Millicent Rogers Museum. A film was also premiered titled *Remarkable Women of Taos: What's in the Water?* But is this feminine influence just limited to this outpost of the South-West? Most of the analysis in our book has by necessity been male-centric, reflecting the dominant trope of the West as a proving ground for manhood and the male hero. Yet as we have delved deeper into Western films and frontier narratives, we have been struck by the understatement of the role of women in shaping mythology. The women of Taos – Mabel, Georgia, Frieda, Millicent and Dorothy – gloriously eccentric and boldly creative – are an important part of the rich tapestry that constitutes the American West.

12 Little Bighorn

These battlesites are civil spaces where Americans of various ideological persua-
sions come, not always reverently, to compete for the ownership of powerful
national stories.

(Linenthal 1991: 1)

Like many Americans, I first learned about George Custer and the Battle of the
Little Bighorn not in school but at the movies. For me, a child of the Vietnam
War era, Custer was the deranged maniac of Little Big Man. For those of my
parents' generation, who grew up during World War II, Custer was the noble
hero played by Errol Flynn in They Died with Their Boots On.

(Philbrick 2010: xvii)

Introduction

Medicine Tail Coulee is a pivotal spot in one of the biggest mysteries in Western
mythology. Late in the afternoon of 25 June 1876, General George Armstrong
Custer paused in this grassy dry creek bed. Launching an attack on a large encampment of Sioux and Cheyenne, he had divided his Seventh Cavalry into three
groups. While Major Reno's column directly attacked the eastern end of the camp,
Custer led a flanking manoeuvre, aiming for a surprise attack at the rear. Skirting
along the heights of the valley, he came down the Medicine Tail Coulee to a point
where he might possibly ford the river. Instead he stopped for a short time and did
not cross. Possibly he encountered resistance and/or realised just how large the
camp was. He could have retraced his route, occupying a steep hill and waiting for
his reserve under Captain Benteen. However, rather than *eastwards*, he rode *westwards*, away from the other two columns. Why? What was he attempting to do?
We don't know – and can never know. Within a short time, Custer and every man
of his column were killed at the Battle of Little Bighorn.

Today, the site is protected and managed by the US National Parks Service
(NPS) as the Little Bighorn Battlefield National Monument. There is a small
visitor centre at the entrance and one winding road linking a series of interpretive panels. At Last Stand Hill, where Custer was finally overwhelmed, there are
monuments and gravestones to the fallen (Figure 12.1). However, apart from

these modest developments, the rest is undulating grassy hills. An isolated place in eastern Montana, there are few tourists. The visitor only has to walk a short distance away from the road to be completely alone and to imagine that this is what it really was like in 1876. Walking down to Medicine Tail Coulee, one can look at the landscape and easily see the choices that Custer had. It is a place to contemplate and speculate – why did he go West?

A difficult centenary

For all its fascination, this is a highly contested place. The centenary of the Battle of Little Bighorn was commemorated in 1976. Both in the lead-up and for a number of years later, the NPS was acutely aware of four contentious issues in effectively managing and interpreting this iconic site.

The first was with its name. At the time of the centenary, its official name was Custer Battlefield National Monument. However, many were uneasy with a name that gave such prominence to Custer. Though lionised as a hero for a long time, by the late twentieth century his reputation was quite tarnished and there were many who felt it inappropriate to honour his name. In 1868, he had led an unprovoked attack on a peaceful village on the Washita River, Oklahoma (Custer 1874) and this was what he was attempting to repeat at Little Bighorn. These concerns were debated for many years, until in 1991 the NPS decided to change

Figure 12.1 Monument and gravestones on Last Stand Hill (photo W. Frost).

the name of the site to one that was neutral and geographically focussed. This, the NPS argued, was in line with the naming of its other battlefield national monuments, particularly those from the Civil War. Nevertheless, great controversy arose with the change (Buchholtz 2005).

The second issue concerned interpretation. As with many other contested sites around the world, there were debates about what were the right stories to tell. As recounted by Robert Utley, a senior official of the NPS, philosophical views on interpreting Little Bighorn began to change after the centenary. At the commemoration, he:

> contested the speaker's platform with red power champion Russell Means. My speech which followed Means's incendiary rhetoric, was a plea to ... refrain from perverting history, the battlefield, and the anniversary in the service of modern political and social agendas.
>
> (Utley 1991: ix)

Means was an Ogala Lakota (Sioux). He had risen to prominence in the American Indian Movement which had gained much publicity through occupying iconic sites. Between 1969 and 1973, these included Alcatraz, the replica of the *Mayflower* in Boston Harbour, the Bureau of Indian Affairs Headquarters and Wounded Knee in South Dakota. Later he would have a career as an actor, his major films including *Last of the Mohicans* (1992) and *Pocahontas* (1995).

Accordingly, Utley represented the establishment and Means the marginalised attempting to have their story told as well. Utley occupied the high ground, backed by officialdom and resources, presenting his view as objective and historical. Means was characterised as a heretic, 'perverting history' to serve contemporary purposes (for more on this ongoing debate in heritage interpretation, see Frost and Laing 2013).

While the two views locked horns at the centenary, gradually there was a rapprochement. By 1991, Utley admitted that he and the NPS were wrong. Writing of dissonant viewpoints at US battlefield commemorations, Utley now felt that:

> such struggles are inevitable and should be anticipated. They can even be viewed as healthy symptoms of democracy ... promoting public discourse on fundamental issues. Second, in such struggles no single point of view should be allowed to prevail. The orthodox and the heretical should have equal access.
>
> (1991: x)

Reflecting this changing view, the 1991 Bill that changed its name also initiated a monument to the Native Americans who died in the battle. This commemorated both the defenders and the Crow who served as scouts for Custer. In addition, the white stone markers that had long signified individual soldiers were matched by red markers for individual Native Americans who fell in the battle (Figures 12.2 and 12.3).

Figure 12.2 White and Red markers for the fallen at Little Bighorn (photo W. Frost).

Figure 12.3 White and Red markers for the fallen at Little Bighorn (photo W. Frost).

The third issue was a growing realisation that the NPS visitor centre was in the wrong place. As early as 1986, staff began to voice the idea that what had been built in the past was back-to-front. The visitor centre, car park and entrance were all at the western end of the site. Custer and his troops had come from the east and the battle had progressively unfolded from that direction. The final stand occurred towards the west of the battlefield and this is what tourists first saw upon entering the site. If they continued eastwards, they essentially walked backwards through the chronology of the battle. Surely, staff argued, the tourist experience should follow Custer's attack, move westwards down the valley and finish at Last Stand Hill (Linenthal 1991). Modern interpretive panels follow this direction (Figure 12.4). Financial constraints have precluded such a radical realignment of the visitor facilities, though it remains a possibility in the future. Is this such a big problem? The idea of starting with a finale and then going back in time to explain what happened is common in cinema, as in for example *Sunset Boulevard* and *The Man who Shot Liberty Valance*. Last Stand Hill, with its monuments and grave markers, is the big attraction that tourists clamour to see and, perhaps for a proportion, it is all they want.

The fourth – and most heretical – was a reinterpretation of the battle by archaeologists, particularly Richard Fox. He argued that the pattern of shell casings and graves pointed to a rapid disintegration of Custer's force. Directly countering the heroic myth, he argued for a final panic:

Figure 12.4 Tourists and interpretive panels at Little Bighorn (photo W. Frost).

the end did not really come at Custer [Monument] Hill, the last stand of history, the swirling, desperate, gallant defense to the last man. It came more or less ignobly on the slopes beyond and in the tangled ravine underbrush [of Deep Ravine].

(Fox 1993: 216)

The Custer enigma

George Custer occupies a curious and contradictory place in the imagining of the West. Perhaps more than any other figure, interpretations of him have varied widely; from hero to madman, leader to martinet, self-serving to selfless patriot. Even today, this process continues, with the wars in Iraq and Afghanistan adding new dimensions to the myth. In 2006, Ernie LaPointe, Sitting Bull's great-grandson, visited noted Custer re-enactor Steve Alexander. LaPointe, a Vietnam veteran, commented to Alexander that 'Sitting Bull didn't dislike Custer ... he realized he was a military guy following orders' (quoted in Philbrick 2010: 305). Thirty years earlier, Custer's grand-nephew – also a serviceman – Colonel George A. Custer III, was pointedly not invited to the centenary. Within a generation, Custer has been reimagined as the *Universal Soldier*.

There was a strong linkage between geographical mobility and Custer's restless search for glory. He grew up in Monroe, Michigan, on the shores of Lake Erie and with Canada in sight. This was the old Western frontier of half a century and more previously. It was now tamed and Custer had to go east for opportunities. First it was West Point Military Academy in New York State. Then it was the Civil War battlefields, including Bull Run, Brandy Run and Gettysburg. He particularly distinguished himself at the last of these and at the age of 23 he was a general. It was during the war that Custer developed his distinctive dress style. Though cavalry were fast becoming anachronistic in modern warfare, officers on both sides looked romantically backwards 200 years to the elan and imagery of the Cavaliers of England's Civil War. Custer was from humble origins – and perhaps because of this, he readily embraced these aristocratic pretensions. At Gettysburg – his greatest triumph – he sported long blonde hair and a black velvet uniform with gold lace (Philbrick 2010).

However, with the end of the war, prospects for advancement disappeared. For a time he flirted with accepting a position fighting for the Mexican government under Benito Juárez against the French-backed Maximilian von Hapsburg. Eventually he joined the newly formed Seventh Cavalry, shifting to the western frontier. Here Custer was frustrated, his hopes for fame and celebrity rested on a Western European style war, not Western American guerilla style fighting. In this new environment he continued to affect an ostentatious style (Figure 12.5). Still with long hair and an impressive moustache, he wore white fringed-buckskins, creating an image of the experienced Indian-fighter.

The campaign of 1876 potentially represented the last chance for Custer. A dirty attempt to once again dispossess Native Americans of their land, there was the prospect of a decisive battle with Sitting Bull and the Sioux. The big

Figure 12.5 General George Armstrong Custer (photo Buffalo Bill Center of the West, Cody, Wyoming, USA; Vincent Mercaldo Collection, P.71.250).

fear driving Custer was that there would be no battle, but rather the Sioux and Cheyenne would scatter before his column. Accordingly, Custer's actions at Little Bighorn need to be seen in the light of his desire to attack as quickly as possible.

A vast encampment of Sioux, Cheyenne and other tribes had assembled on the Little Bighorn. Coming from the east, as one half of a pincer movement, Custer's original plan was to arrive before the infantry from the West and win glory through a decisive surprise dawn attack similar to the Washita. When he was spotted, he improvised. On the afternoon of 25 June, he split his force into three parts – something that has excited controversy ever since – in order to cut off any retreating forces. Where he miscalculated was in the size of the encampment. Instead of fleeing, the Sioux and Cheyenne counter-attack wiped out his entire column of 210 soldiers.

Coming just weeks before the centenary of the Declaration of Independence, news of such a large defeat shocked the nation. The centenary, with its associated International Centennial Exhibition in Philadelphia, was intended to glorify the Manifest Destiny of westward expansion. The expectation was that conflict with the Native Americans was essentially over (Custer 1874). Even then, public opinion was still for aggression. As the *Atlantic Monthly* observed of the Centennial Exhibition, 'the red man, as he appears in effigy and photograph in this collection, is a hideous demon, whose malign traits can hardly inspire any emotion softer than abhorrence' (quoted in Rydell 1984: 26). Custer was meant to cap the celebrations with a final subjugation of the last hostiles. That now had all gone wrong.

Following the battle, retribution was visited on the plains tribes, accelerating the processes of reservation, deculturation and assimilation. Paralleling this was memorialisation and valorisation of the Seventh Cavalry and Custer. A biography of Custer was rushed out by the fall of 1876. Written with the assistance of his wife Libbie Custer, it shifted all blame on to Major Marcus Reno, who had failed to move up to support Custer when he got into trouble. Libbie Custer would write three books on Custer's life and until her death in 1933 was a ceaseless upholder of his reputation.

The monument to Custer and his troops was erected in 1881. In 1890, a series of white marble headstones were erected, each naming the dead soldier and marking the spot where they were thought to have been killed (see Figure 12.2). Mistakenly, 252 markers were put in place, whereas only 210 died in the Last Stand. The cause of the confusion was that the extra markers were produced for those that died with Reno and Benteen, but were then placed around Custer (Fox 1993). A re-enactment was staged in 1909 and a grand commemoration of the fiftieth anniversary in 1926. Seventy thousand people were reputed to have attended, testament to the growing popularity of Western heritage after the First World War. At that event, riders representing the cavalry came from one direction and Native Americans from the other. They shook hands, observed a minute's silence and rode off in pairs (Linenthal 1991). Such symbolic reconciliatory rituals were influenced by the ongoing commemorations at Gettysburg – particularly the ceremonial handshake between Union and Confederate veterans over the stone wall on the crest of Cemetery Ridge.

And in this reimagining of the Custer myth, special prominence went to former cavalry scout and later theatrical impresario William 'Buffalo Bill' Cody.

Buffalo Bill becomes Custer

In 1869, William Cody returned home after scouting for the cavalry around Colorado. His wife Louisa was astonished to see that he now had long hair, a moustache and a small goatee beard. 'What on earth did you grow it for?', she demanded. Sheepishly he replied, 'Why, I had to ... It's the fashion out West now. You're not a regular scout unless you've got this sort of rigout' (quoted in Carter 2000: 122). Cody had scouted for Custer, though not as much as was later implied. Custer had adopted buckskins, the scouts his long hair. Two years later, Cody got to know Custer better; as both were recruited to accompany Grand Duke Alexis of Russia on a buffalo hunting expedition in Nebraska. The immense newspaper coverage of this event reinforced Custer's reputation and introduced readers to a new Western hero in Buffalo Bill. Grasping the opportunity, Cody headed East for a career in theatre.

With the 1876 launch of the military expedition against the Sioux, Cody closed his theatre run and returned to the West to scout for General Crook. A few days after the news of Custer's death had broken, Cody was involved in a skirmish with some Cheyenne. Charging to the front, Cody and a Cheyenne warrior, Yellow Hand, fired on each other. Cody killed Yellow Hand, scalped him and reputedly proclaimed 'First Scalp for Custer'. Reported widely in the newspapers, the fight was quickly exaggerated into a chivalric duel. The entrepreneurial Cody dashed off a new play – *The Red Right Hand; or Buffalo Bill's First Scalp for Custer* – and throughout 1876–1877 toured it across the country. At first, Cody exhibited Yellow Hand's scalp, war bonnet and weapons in shop windows of each town he played in. After he received complaints about such a grisly display, he shifted his trophies to the theatre lobbies. Cody was more than opportunistic, the evidence was that he carefully planned how to take advantage of his connections to Custer. On the morning of the fight with Yellow Hand, he dressed in a most peculiar costume. This was a Mexican *Vaquero* outfit, black velvet with red trimmings and silver buttons. It was one of his stage costumes. He knew there would be an attack and wanted to wear something memorable that he could later use in his plays (Carter 2000; Hutton 1992).

As Cody realised that a stage was too limiting for representing the West, he developed the idea of an outdoor Wild West show, something akin to the popular touring circuses of the time. This included displays of riding, sharpshooting (particularly Annie Oakley) and re-enactments. The latter focussed on Indian attacks, including on the Deadwood stagecoach, a settler's cabin and Cody's fight with Yellow Hand. For the 1885 season, he even persuaded Sitting Bull to perform. For the next 20 years, Cody toured the United States and Europe; becoming perhaps the most influential purveyor of the Western myth to mass urban markets (Murdoch 2001). Dressed in buckskins with long greying hair, Cody seemed a doppelganger for Custer and his show reinforced the legend of a hero's martyrdom.

Cinema and Custer

Films have reflected the changing interpretations of Custer and the Battle of Little Bighorn. With the boom in Westerns commencing in 1939, both Jack Warner and Sam Goldwyn saw Custer as a worthy subject for an heroic epic. Warner won through with an Errol Flynn production and Goldwyn (unfortunately) cancelled his version which would have had Walter Brennan as Custer! Following on from Flynn's swashbuckling performance, Hollywood representations of Custer began to change. In the second half of this chapter, we consider the five main film representations and how they grappled with changing interpretations over time.

They Died With Their Boots On (1941)

Errol Flynn portrayed the heroic Custer par excellence. His was a rebellious though noble Custer, drawing on Flynn's previous role as Robin Hood. Released on the eve of the Second World War, this film presented a reluctant hero who ultimately decides that duty must come before all else. It was a highly fictionalised account of Custer's story. Thoroughly romanticised, it reinforced the view of Custer as dashing and brave. Flynn, as always, gave a convincing performance of the extroverted hero. At 32 years of age – five years younger than Custer at his death – he was a worthy choice for a young hero. As in many of his films, Olivia de Havilland was the romantic lead as Custer's wife Libbie.

To make Custer a hero, Warner Brothers invented the plotline that Custer was actually a man of peace and was forced to give battle at Little Bighorn to expose endemic corruption within the government. This made no sense at all and ignored all the historical evidence that Custer actively sought battle – even exceeding his orders – with the aim that victory would make him a national hero. Nonetheless, while there were many blatant inaccuracies in this film, Hutton argues that:

> There is a veneer of truth – Custer was a dashing romantic soldier; he and Elizabeth did have a storybook marriage; the Sioux were a terribly wronged people; and the last stand was indeed the result of events set in motion by venal capitalists and inept, corrupt politicians.
>
> (1992: 503)

With the first half being a light-hearted romp, the second half moved towards tragedy. Intriguingly there were elements of *film noir*, which would become a very strong influence on Westerns later in the 1940s. Flynn's Custer is a two-fisted action man, but he is inexorably heading towards his doom. Further-more, his post Civil War world is dominated by corrupt politicians and shady carpet-baggers. Like pulp Western fiction writer Holly Martins (Joseph Cotton) in *The Third Man* (1949), Flynn's Custer is bewildered by the avarice and inhu-manity of his former military comrades.

Errol Flynn's Custer dominates the discourse about the meaning of Little Bighorn. His heroic portrayal is often used as the counterpoint to revisionists. Philbrick (2010) noted that whereas he grew up with *Little Big Man*, for his parents Flynn was Custer. Fraser decried the film as 'typical Hollywood dream-rubbish of the worst kind' (1988: 200). Joseph Medicine Crow, a Crow hired to work with the scriptwriters on the Flynn film, was sacked when he loudly stated that 'my grand-father always said Custer was very foolish' (quoted in Elliott 2007: 232). Over 20 years later, he would script the annual battle re-enactment. Others were more positive about the film, Hutton praised its style (while noting its inaccuracies). He observed that it 'is one of the few westerns to make the important connection between the Civil War and national expansion', and its 'greatest artistic triumph is in cutting to the essence of the American love affair with Custer' (1992: 501, 503). This was backed by Elliott, who argued that 'Flynn gets something essentially correct ... buoyant, capering cavalier, idealistic and flamboyant' (2007: 61).

Fort Apache (1948)

John Ford wanted to make a Custer movie, but he decided to change the histor-ical details in order to focus on the story elements he wanted to highlight. In *My Darling Clementine* he had created a completely fictional story around Wyatt Earp. In *Fort Apache* he did the same, going even further in changing names. Thus Custer became Colonel Owen Thursday (Henry Fonda), he was fighting the Apache not the Sioux and it was filmed in Monument Valley, which is neither Sioux nor Apache territory.

What Ford focussed on was Fonda as Custer/Thursday and his obsessive quest for fame. Thursday hates being sent West. For him, Fort Apache is a back-water where his career will rot. His disenchantment is expressed through his dis-taste for his officers and men. Captain York (John Wayne) particularly irritates him through constantly questioning his orders. Furthermore, Thursday has no time for the rituals and niceties of the fort and military society, aspects that Ford lovingly focusses upon throughout (Kitses 2004; Neale 1995; Pearson 1995).

Thursday sees that a spectacular victory is his only opportunity for returning East. Even though his orders are to make peace, he insults the Apache leader Cochise and sparks a battle. When York protests he is sent to the rear. Thursday has no respect for the Apache, he thinks of them as nothing more than savages and unworthy military opponents. Over-confident, he falls into an ambush and his command is massacred. In this sense Thursday is different to Custer, who knew the Sioux well and had a healthy respect for them. Nonetheless, like Thurs-day, Custer's difficulties at Little Bighorn were due to over-confidence and an obsession that victory would lead to promotion.

Fort Apache ends with a twist that greatly troubles some film historians (for example Kitses 2004). After the massacre, York has taken command of the regiment. Thursday is now a hero and jingoistic newspapermen gush about his exploits. York agrees, stating that 'no man died more gallantly' and 'he made it a command to be proud of'. Furthermore, York now dresses and talks like Thursday. It is an intriguing precursor to Ford's elegiac *The Man Who Shot Liberty Valance* (1962) and its sentiment that the Western legend is more valid than the truth.

Filmed just after the Second World War, there are clearly references to recent experiences with both rigid officers and deep comradeship in that conflict. Slotkin (1992) argued that Ford's Cavalry Trilogy combined Westerns with the post-war trend for combat films; focussing on the travails of a small unit on a dangerous mission in which they can only be successful in working together and trusting each other. In such combat films there is often a threat to unity – a vainglorious officer or disgruntled enlisted man – who must be overcome. In *Fort Apache* this is Thursday, but the trope reappears in many cavalry Westerns. For example, in *War Paint* (1953), a cavalry patrol led by Robert Stack moves through Death Valley. Stack's lieutenant is obsessed with completing the mission, but as his soldiers die off, the survivors become increasingly mutinous. The threat is not so much attack or the desert, but rather ill-discipline and disloyalty within the military.

Ford returned to Custer in *The Searchers* (1956). He filmed a sequence showing the aftermath of the attack at Washita, with a meeting between Custer (Peter Ortiz) and Ethan (John Wayne). The latter is disgusted with Custer's actions in attacking a peaceful village – and this allows Ford to again project his dislike of Custer. However, in the editing process Ford discarded this scene and the footage is now lost. Why did Ford remove it? Probably because it is out of kilter with the rest of the film, revealing Ethan's humanity far too early in the narrative.

Nearly 20 years after *Fort Apache*, Ford had seemingly mellowed as he commented:

> We've had a lot of people who were supposed to be great heroes, and you know damn well they weren't. But it was good for the country to have heroes to look up to. Like Custer – a great hero. Well he wasn't. Not that he was a stupid man – but he did a stupid job that day.
>
> (quoted in Bogdanovich 1967: 86)

Ford's Thursday is not Custer, but rather a fictional character drawn only partly from the real person. A generation later, a similar approach was taken very effectively. In *Apocalypse Now* (1979), the Cavalry is now an airborne unit and the war is in Vietnam. Colonel Bill Kilgore (Robert Duvall) is dynamic, sentimental and vainglorious. His bloody attack on a Vietnamese village draws to mind Custer's attack at Washita.

Custer of the West (1967)

The early to mid 1960s saw a trend to historical epics retelling heroic last stands. Starting with John Wayne's *The Alamo* (1960), others included *300 Spartans* (1962), *55 Days at Peking* (1963), *Zulu* (1964) and *Khartoum* (1966). All of these films included charismatic but flawed heroes, encounters with the *Other* and could be interpreted as allegories of American foreign policy during the Cold War (Slotkin 1992). Given their success, it was not surprising that film-makers were drawn to Custer and his Last Stand.

In 1963, Twentieth Century Fox commissioned a script and signed Fred Zinnemann, who directed *High Noon* (1952), *From Here to Eternity* (1953) and *A Man for All Seasons* (1966). The intention was an epic with an all-star cast, something along the lines of *The Longest Day* (1962). Charlton Heston was approached to play Custer, but declined, explaining: 'I don't see how you can make a serious film about a man who seems to have been not only egocentric, but muddleheaded' (quoted in Hutton 1992: 510). His refusal seems a great pity in hindsight. Heston specialised in the egocentric and muddleheaded, the obsessive and obstinate. The prospect of his playing such an enigmatic figure is one to savour. In writing this book, we had a number of discussions about who might have been an interesting Custer. Heston figured prominently; and of modern actors, we liked the idea of Leonardo DiCaprio.

Instead *Custer of the West* was made. It was shunned by critics and audiences. What particularly alienated them was that Custer was played by English actor Robert Shaw and it was filmed for budgetary reasons in Spain. It is not a bad film, but it is confused and what particularly did not work was the final battle scene.

The Last Stand is often represented as the outnumbered cavalry bunched together – back to back – and worn away by wave after wave of Sioux and Cheyenne. *Custer of the West* provided a variation of this. The Sioux and Cheyenne slowly ride around the soldiers, picking them off. In turn, the cavalry inflict heavy casualties on their attackers. This is an essential element of the myth of the Last Stand – that those who died heroically sold their lives dearly.

The full frontal attack is a common trope in Western cinema. Apart from Custer films, some other examples are worth noting. In *The Searchers* (1956), the Comanche throw away any element of surprise and then charge the Texas Rangers across a broad river, suffering high casualties. In *Yellowstone Kelly* (1959), the Sioux are fresh from defeating Custer when they attack a group of dispirited retreating soldiers. Lined up in formation, they wait, allowing the eponymous hero to rally the troops and form a defensive position. Only then do the Sioux launch a frontal attack, again with huge losses. In *Revolt at Fort Laramie* (1953), the Sioux wait until the soldiers have put their wagons in a circle and built barricades of boxes before attacking. Such bizarre military behaviour was repeatedly shown on the screen as film-makers believed audiences really enjoyed seeing Indians get killed.

The reality was very different. Custer himself described an attack on a cavalry wagon train. Forming a circle, they rode around the train. However, instead of providing easy pickings, the soldiers found that they were:

moving at such a rapid gait and in single file, [they] presented a most uncertain target. To add to this uncertainty, the savages availed themselves of their superior – almost marvellous – powers of hosemanship. Throwing themselves upon the sides of their well-trained ponies, they left no part of their persons exposed to the aim of the troopers … and in this posture they were able to aim the weapons either over or under the necks of their ponies.

(Custer 1874: 66)

George Catlin observed similar tactics amongst the Comanche:

a stratagem of war, learned and practiced by every young man in the tribe; by which he is able to drop his body upon the side of his horse … the instant he is passing, effectually screened from his enemies' weapons … he will hang whilst his horse is at fullest speed, carrying with him his bow and shield, and also his long lance of fourteen feet in length, all or either of which he will wield upon his enemy as he passes, rising and throwing his arrows over the horse's back, or with equal ease and success under the horse's neck.

(Catlin 1841: 327–328)

The evidence at Little Bighorn was that the Sioux and Cheyenne mainly fought on foot, slowly building up their numbers and using the cover of bushes and ravines to gradually infiltrate the cavalry skirmish lines. It is likely that Custer and his troops thought they were doing well until a final rush and close quarters fighting induced confusion and a breakdown of tactical cohesion (Fox 1993; Philbrick 2010). However, such a representation of the conflict has never made it on to the big screen.

Curiously, it is *Winchester 73* (1950) that comes closest to grappling with how Little Bighorn was fought. Set immediately after the battle, a troop of soldiers are surrounded by the Cheyenne. Inexperienced Eastern reinforcements, they look to cowboy Lin (James Stewart) for leadership. He tells them what he heard in a saloon the night before(!) – Custer was defeated because the army uses single shot carbines, whereas the Cheyenne have repeaters. As such, the first charges were weak, designed to draw the troops' fire. Then, when the soldiers were reloading, the main attack overwhelmed them. More than any other film, this draws together theories of the inadequacies of experience and weaponry. It also highlights that the Sioux and Cheyenne had repeating rifles, which Fox (1993) theorises would have had a demoralising effect on the cavalry.

Little Big Man (1970)

This was based on the very successful book of the same name by Thomas Berger. It tells the story of Jack Crabb, the sole survivor of the Battle of Little Bighorn. Orphaned after his wagon train is attacked by the Pawnee, Crabb is raised by the Cheyenne and periodically moves back and forth between White and Native American societies. Along the way, the everyman Crabb interacts with iconic real life figures such as Wild Bill Hickok and Custer (Laing and Frost 2012).

The film was notable for its sympathetic depiction of Cheyenne life and strongly appealed to the Woodstock generation. Stealing the film was Chief Dan George (a member of the Tsleil-Waututh band from Vancouver, BC). With great humour and dignity, he portrayed Lodge Skins, Crabb's adoptive grandfather and guide to Cheyenne culture and philosophy. His performance demonstrated the versatility and power of Native American actors and paved the way for others such as Will Sampson who starred in *One Flew Over the Cuckoo's Nest* (1975).

Director Arthur Penn crafted an intensely political critique of American militarism. This is particularly represented in the Washita attack, the film's most powerful scene, which draws strong parallels with the My Lai Massacre in Vietnam. Unfortunately, Penn went too far in caricaturing Custer as a madman along the lines of General Jack Ripper (Sterling Hayden) in *Dr Strangelove* (1962), even down to both obsessing about their bodily essences. As Hutton argued:

> Richard Mulligan's Custer is a preening buffoon who cannot be taken seriously ... failing entirely as menacing devil or a particularly dangerous opponent ... the great Indian victory at Little Bighorn is trivialized, for there can be no honour in defeating such a cowardly band of soldiers led by such a complete idiot.
>
> (1992: 515)

Son of the Morning Star (1991)

This was a big budget television movie. Made just after the success of *Dances with Wolves* (1990), it shared similar sentiments and style. Originally, Kevin Costner was to play Custer – a very strange casting choice – but he dropped out. Instead, Custer was played by Gary Cole, Libbie by Rosanna Arquette and Crazy Horse by Rodney A. Grant. Grant was an Omaha and had risen to prominence in *Dances with Wolves*. An effective feature of the production was the contrasting use of two female narrations, alternating between Libbie Custer (Arquette) and Cheyenne woman Kate Bighead (Buffy Sainte-Marie). A number of Native Americans present at the battle provided oral history accounts. Kate Bighead was interviewed in 1927 and her story was a major source for this film.

This was intentionally an *authentic* film version. There were no invented storylines or twists, rather it kept to the historical outline. Coming at a time when what happened was being questioned, particularly through archaeological techniques, it holds up very well. It does represent the fight as being characterised by rapid disintegration in the face of overwhelming odds, though there is little attention given to infiltration. Custer is not shown as the last survivor, as in many other versions. Its effectiveness is open to subjective debate, but its attempt to be historically accurate cannot be faulted. Cole tries hard, and at times is very effective. However, he is no Errol Flynn. This film might be the best representation of the battle, but even after over 70 years, Flynn remains the definitive Custer.

Cinema provides little assistance in understanding the mystery of Custer and the Little Bighorn. Instead, what we have are multiple narratives, influenced by different interpretations based on contemporary contexts. Depending on the film, Custer is either a hero or a fool, a soldier obeying orders or a maverick.

13 Stetsons and Daisy Dukes

California Gurls
We're unforgettable
Daisy Dukes, Bikinis on top.
(Katy Perry,
'California Gurls')

Like a Rhinestone Cowboy
Riding out on a horse in a star-spangled rodeo.
(Glen Campbell, 'Rhinestone Cowboy')

Introduction

The icons of Western clothing are instantly recognisable and a part of popular culture, as the song lyrics above attest. They are essentially beyond fashion, although periodically on trend approximately every seven years since the mid 1970s (George-Warren and Freedman 2001). Stetson hats, leather boots, large buckled belts, bandannas, chaps and denim are inextricably part of the mythology of the cowboy and the American West (George-Warren and Freedman 2001), and embody virtues such as 'a commitment to hard, honest labor, loyalty to a strenuous ethical and moral code, persistence in the face of hardship, rugged individualism and personal freedom' (Gray 2001: 7).

Indian clothing, involving suede, fringing and beading, is also a Western look, as is Mexican traditional clothing, including felt and appliqued Rio Grande jackets, the Chimayo coat, woven with various colours and featuring motifs such as arrows, diamond shapes, and stripes, and the fiesta dress (George-Warren and Freedman 2001). These are plunder from the *exotic*, creating new looks which are effective because of their unfamiliarity. This becomes less obvious once these styles become an accepted part of mainstream fashion. Adopting these fashions can therefore be a form of colonisation. It may also be used to define the distinctiveness (and superiority?) of non-indigenous fashion, by juxtaposing it with that of another culture, a demonstration or reinvention of *otherness* (Craik 1994).

In this chapter, we look at the origins of Western clothing, and its transition from everyday apparel to fashion item. It is often an illustration of the way that fashion borrows motifs from popular culture in the search for something new (Craik 1994; Cunningham and Voso Lab 1991b). This may also work in reverse, with popular culture appropriating themes and motifs from fashion (Cunningham and Voso Lab 1991b), in a cyclical process of derivation. In particular, we consider how film has been instrumental in either creating or reflecting *stereotypes* of the West, through the clothing worn by actors.

Adaptation and a contemporary twist to its heritage have always been part of Western clothing's appeal, a process of reconstitution and juxtaposition with other styles, known as *bricolage* (Craik 1994). In the 1950s, heiress Millicent Rogers took the Navajo blouse, voluminous squaw skirts, bold turquoise and silver Indian jewellery and moccasins, and popularised the South-Western style, while the Western shirt with snap fastenings, long sleeves and embroidery, made famous by designers Nudie Cohn and Nathan Turk, led to the Rhinestone Cowboy look. In more recent times, there are the ubiquitous 'Daisy Dukes', the briefest of denim shorts worn by Catherine Bach in *The Dukes of Hazzard* (1979–1985) and celebrated by Katy Perry in her hit song 'California Gurls' (2010), while jeans have become the wardrobe staple of youth all over the world, moving far beyond their working-class origins (Sullivan 2006).

We also focus on the nexus between Western clothing, gender and sexuality, including the ways in which it is used to invert sexual norms and traditions of both masculinity and femininity. Fashion studies have notoriously tended to overlook men's fashion (Craik 1994), yet in terms of Western clothing, one cannot discuss it without being cognisant of its link to notions of masculinity, including *myths* and *subversions* of masculinity (Horrocks 1995).

History of Western clothing

The diffusion of Western clothing from frontier to mainstream can be traced to a number of key influences – artworks later made into prints by the likes of A.F. Tait and Alfred Miller; newspaper articles and books, including the dime store novel; live performances such as Cody's Wild West Show and subsequently rodeos; mail-order catalogues; the growth of the dude ranch; Hollywood; and popular music. While all had their part to play in the acceptance of the Western look, we focus on cinema and some key fashion trendsetters.

The heroic frontiersman

The first distinctive clothing associated with the West was that of the trapper or frontiersman, who often wore shirts and trousers made of hide or buckskin, fringed shirts, jackets or leggings, woollen capes and moccasins. This was a style influenced by Native Americans, but was also practical, with buckskin more durable than wool for trousers. Books helped to make this style instantly recognisable, particularly illustrated versions of works by James Fenimore Cooper and Francis Parkman's *The Oregon Trail* (1847–1849), and 'the image [Parkman's] book created, that of the heroic frontiersman, enflamed the imaginations of thousands of readers, many of whom headed west in the late 1840s' (George-Warren and Freedman 2001: 14). Commercial production of this look in places like New Mexico was cleverly disguised as authentic gear made in situ. For example, Kit Carson's buckskin coats, with fringes and embroidery, may have had 'Hispanic origin ... and [been] machine sewn' (p. 14), based on a coat which is part of the Colorado Historical Society collection in Denver (George-Warren and Freedman 2001).

The cowboy

Cowboy clothing remains for most people the quintessence of the American West. The origin of this style was largely functional (Stall-Meadows 2011). Working cowboys wore a range of styles, depending on factors such as their location, tasks, practicality and affluence (Dary 1989; Murdoch 2001; Wilson 1991). Visiting town called for a modified look. Some were photographed in studios wearing items that were often not seen on working cowboys, such as pistols or chaps (Murdoch 2001; Wilson 1991, 1996). Some of these items may simply have been too expensive for these men to purchase on their limited wage, such as the leather vest, or were simply not needed in the conditions in which the men worked (Wilson 1996, 2001). These photographs were intended to be sent home to and impress family and friends (Wilson 1991) and may have served as a rite of passage.

By the time Owen Wister wrote *The Virginian* (1902), the look was largely settled, with Frederic Remington's illustrations depicting cowboys dressed 'virtually in a uniform and one that few cowboys actually wore' (Murdoch 2001: 72). Wister describes his hero, the Virginian, wearing hat, bandanna, gun-belt and boots:

> Lounging there at ease against the wall was a slim young giant, more beautiful than pictures. His broad, soft hat was pushed back; a loose-knotted, dull-scarlet handkerchief sagged from his throat; and one casual thumb was hooked in the cartridge-belt that slanted across his hips. He had plainly come many miles from somewhere across the vast horizon, as the dust upon him showed. His boots were white with it. His overalls were gray with it. The weather-beaten bloom of his face shone through it duskily, as the ripe peaches look upon their trees in a dry season. But no dinginess of travel or shabbiness of attire could tarnish the splendour that radiated from his youth and strength.
>
> (pp. 8–9)

The sight of the Virginian, set off by his clothing, makes school teacher Molly swoon:

The fringed leathern chaparreros, the cartridge belt, the flannel shirt, the knotted scarf at the neck, these things were now an old story to her. Since her arrival she had seen young men and old in plenty dressed thus. But worn by this man now standing by her door, they seemed to radiate romance.

(p. 83)

The effect his garb has had on Molly is not lost on her great-aunt. When looking at a photograph of the Virginian, she murmurs: 'My dear, you have fallen in love with his clothes' (p. 160). These accoutrements had also captured the imagination of the public who attended Buffalo Bill's Wild West show (Figure 13.1) and its many rivals (George-Warren and Freedman 2001), including some who would go on to be cowboys themselves (Murdoch 2001). Some of the performers ended up in films, such as Hoot Gibson, Hank Worden and Ben Johnson.

Mail-order catalogues were one source of this clothing, which 'appealed to the authentic cowboys and cowgirls as well as new consumers who were purchasing items for Western vacations or to emulate a Western lifestyle' (George-Warren and Freedman 2001: 39). Many cowboys however would buy their clothes and new boots when they came to town (Dary 1989; Murdoch 2001), rather than using catalogues. Sometimes the retailer came to where the men were, bringing a wagon of clothing to a round-up (Wilson 2001).

There are Spanish, Mexican and Native American cultural influences on cowboy clothing (Stall-Meadows 2011), which reflect the melting pot which was the American West. Some of this can be seen in the clothing worn by the cowboys in Buffalo Bill's Wild West show (Wilson 1996). Most items associated with the American cowboy were originally worn by the Mexican equivalent, the *vaquero*, back in the sixteenth century, except for the boots, which would have been too expensive and only worn by wealthy Spaniards (Dary 1989). The broad-brimmed hat may derive from the Mexican sombrero (Brandt 1989; Dary 1989; George-Warren and Freedman 2001). The cowboy version has a high crown, which protected the head from both sun and rain, and could be used as a form of water bucket for a cowboy's horse (Stall-Meadows 2011). It is often known as a *ten-gallon hat*, which may be linked to the Spanish word *gallón*, 'meaning braid (braiding around the brim)' (Stall-Meadows 2011: 46), and is said to have been invented by Buffalo Bill himself (Tompkins 1992). Certainly the hats worn by the men in his show often had exaggeratedly large brims, to allow them to stand out to audiences sitting in open air arenas (Wilson 2001). The most famous manufacturer of Western hats is still Stetson, named after the owner, John B. Stetson. They gained a symbolism through their colour. Black and white cowboy hats were often used in Hollywood westerns to distinguish the villains from the heroes (Gordon 1991; Wilson 2001).

Boots, often handmade in the early days, usually sported a pointed toe and high heel (Figure 13.2), to allow the cowboy to keep their feet in the stirrups (Wilson 2001), while the 'decorative stitching on the boot upper secured the lining and prevented the tops from sagging' (Stall-Meadows 2011: 47). They were also worn close fitting to assist horse riding, with a distinctive left and right

785 BROADWAY, N. Y.

Figure 13.1 Cabinet photograph with a group portrait of Buffalo Bill and eight Indian scouts. *c.*1886. L to R: (Pawnee) Brave Chief, Eagle Chief, Knife Chief, Young Chief, Buffalo Bill, (Sioux) American Horse, Rocky Bear, Flies Above, Long Wolf. Photographed by Anderson of New York (source: Buffalo Bill Center of the West, Cody, Wyoming, USA; P.69.1800).

Figure 13.2 Western boots in Tombstone (photo W. Frost).

foot, and were thus distinguished from the farmer's clumpy and interchangeable boots which had to mould to the feet through use (Hoy 1995). Their utility justified their cost, which in the late 1880s was about half the average cowboy's monthly wage (Dary 1989). *Chaps*, derived from the Hispanic word *chaparreras*, which was used to describe leather leggings, were worn to protect against thorny vegetation and brush (Figure 13.3). They were also made in bear hide or Angora wool, which provided additional warmth in the winter (George-Warren and Freedman 2001).

The Western *shirt* and *jeans* complete the outfit. Shirts were often made in checked or striped patterns, with laced or buttoned bib fronts and high cuffs (George-Warren and Freedman 2001). Cotton was generally the fabric of choice, although sometimes wool or flannel was preferred, to cope with the extremes of heat and cold (Dary 1989). Snap closures were later used in preference to buttons, to make it easier to unhook the shirt if it got caught on a bush or thorn (George-Warren and Freedman 2001). They were claimed to have been invented by Rodeo Ben (Wilson 2001), a European immigrant like Nudie Cohn and Nathan Turk, who also specialised in Spanish or Mexican-styled garments such as capes and bolero vests, and embroidered shirts with motifs such as flowers, birds, cacti and horses. Jack Weil was the other claimant to have invented snaps and used the slogan for his company Rockmount Ranch Wear – 'we put the snap in Western wear' (George-Warren and Freedman 2001: 128).

Figure 13.3 Chaps worn at Helldorado Days, Tombstone (photo W. Frost).

Levi Strauss brought denim, a hard-wearing cotton fabric, to the California goldfields in 1853, and the application of metal rivets to strengthen the areas of high stress (such as the pockets) made denim pants or jeans particularly suited to the work of a cowboy. However, they did not become commonplace until the 1920s or 1930s, with woollen pants largely used before that (George-Warren and Freedman 2001), complete with front vertical pockets to store things like knives or tobacco (Dary 1989). Pants were generally worn outside the boots, ostensibly because this was more practical, but also because it *looked better* (Dary 1989). Hollywood actors and dudes often wore them tucked in (Wilson 1996), presumably for the same aesthetic reason, to show off their highly decorated boots. While as originally worn, jeans were not a fashion item, but an example of 'serviceable, affordable clothing' (Gordon 1991: 31), many cowboys were conscious of their appearance.

Jeans took on a different meaning for a group of artists based around Santa Fe in the 1920s, who used them to deliver an *anti-fashion* message, as well as to identify with the 'ruggedness, the directness and the earthiness of the laborer, and were placing themselves as a part of the Western scene' (Gordon 1991: 32). The use of jeans in this way, to transgress social norms, is ironic, given that jeans were ultimately assimilated into mainstream fashion, becoming a fashion item in their own right.

The growth of dude ranches in the 1930s saw many guests wear jeans and then take this fashion back home, with Eastern stores now stocking the garments. Gordon (1991: 32) notes that 'this was perhaps the first instance where fashionable consumers were encouraged to take on the aura of a particular lifestyle by wearing jeans'. Jeans took on an aspirational quality, for men at any rate in this era, associated with ruggedness and manliness. Rodeo riders also popularised the wearing of jeans (George-Warren and Freedman 2001). In the 1950s, jeans became a uniform for teenagers, with films like *Rebel Without a Cause* (1955) highlighting their connection with anti-social and delinquent behaviour. They were also firmly associated with the TV and Hollywood cowboy, representing an escape into a 'still wild or "untamed" past where people did not have to fit into such carefully prescribed niches' (Gordon 1991: 33–34).

Hollywood also shaped the cowboy look, starting with cowboy heroes played by William S. Hart and Tom Mix. Mix was a dandy, wearing floral embroidered shirts and a white Stetson (George-Warren and Freedman 2001), a contrast to the more workaday clothing preferred by Hart. There was also the spangled and embroidered gear worn by the likes of the singing cowboys Roy Rogers and Gene Autry, whose influence is discussed later in this chapter. Actors like John Wayne, who adopted jeans in the Westerns (Hoy 1995), acted as *opinion leaders* (Cunningham and Voso Lab 1991b) and were later emulated by their fans (Schwer and Daneshvary 2011). He preferred authentic clothing, exemplified by the plain button bib-front shirt he wore in *The Searchers* (1956) and the cavalry shirt he wore in *Fort Apache* (1948), which looked lived-in and rumpled. Wayne's son Michael remembers how he would tie up his new jeans with rope off a pier and keep them submersed in the sea for several days, to make them look suitably worn-in (George-Warren and Freedman 2001). Hopalong Cassidy in his films made the dark shirt and pants and black Stetson famous, a look later adopted by the singer Johnny Cash, known as the Man in Black (LeBlanc 1991), and which would influence other musicians.

Some of these looks later found their way into advertising, such as the famous Marlboro Man advertisements between 1954 and 1999. He was often a cowboy, and helped to reposition the Marlboro brand as macho. Craik dubs the Marlboro Man as an example of the *New Man* – virile and active; strong and silent – which 'has been as much a reaction to the impact of feminism and changing opportunities for women as it has been a reassessment of masculinity itself' (1994: 197). Ironically, many of the actors who played the Marlboro Man later died of smoking-related diseases, exposed in the documentary *Death in the West* (1976).

The cowgirl

Women of the nineteenth-century frontier tended to wear prairie dresses of cotton with sun-bonnets, which were essentially no different from what they wore back East (Brandt 1989; George-Warren and Freedman 2001). Societal norms of what was 'proper dress' prevented many women from changing their style of dress to suit the conditions (Brandt 1989: 75). Those who worked on the ranches did not as a rule wear trousers until the 1920s, and even divided skirts or culottes were controversial, despite their utility for the female on horseback. While some women wore bloomers, they 'were an Eastern fad, not a Western style' (George-Warren and Freedman 2001: 28), although they gradually became more popular than divided skirts with the cowgirl stars of the rodeo (LeCompte 1993) They remained acceptable on the farms and ranches of the West, long after women in urban Eastern settings 'had abandoned it under social pressure' (Crane 2000: 120). This was an example of how ' "secluded" public spaces ... such as the American frontier' may enable the evolution of 'clothing styles that [are] unacceptable on city streets' (Crane 2000: 23) and a form of 'deviant clothing behavior' (Crane 2000: 120). Those cowgirls who went shopping in New York during the 1930s had to keep their brightly coloured Western clothes under wraps 'because local crowds would begin following them around town' (LeCompte 1993: 103).

The cowgirl look has evolved over time. Sharpshooter Annie Oakley wore lavish embroidered and fringed creations for Buffalo Bill's Wild West show (Figure 13.4). Images of her with hat and boots inspired the costumes that Hollywood designer Helen Rose (later to be famous for Grace Kelly's wedding dress) created for actress Betty Hutton in *Annie Get Your Gun* (1950). Although Oakley was a star, she 'did not set Western trends in fashion' (George-Warren and Freedman 2001: 22). Women joined the rodeo circuit and some enjoyed successful professional careers, transitioning from working on their family ranches (LeCompte 1993). Cowgirls at the rodeos wore divided skirts, jodhpurs and bloomers, worn with a bolero vest, boots and hat. Many made their own clothes (George-Warren and Freedman 2001).

Getting the right look: dude ranches and rodeos

Guests staying at dude ranches were encouraged to kit themselves out in style, either through mail-order catalogues or at local shops (George-Warren and Freedman 2001; Wilson 1996). Some ranches like Valley Ranch near Cody (Wyoming) had their own on-site store to outfit their guests (Wilson 1996, 2001). The dude ranch was a popular holiday spot, a trend which started as far back as the late nineteenth century, when *dudes* (the nickname for Easterners) would come out West to experience the cowboy life. Wearing the right clothes made the guests feel authentically Western (George-Warren and Freedman 2001) and marked a transition away from their everyday lives and into a fantasy world. For women, it was a place to wear trousers, which were rarely a part of female

Figure 13.4 Annie Oakley in a hat with a star on the brim and fringed dress (source: Buffalo Bill Center of the West, Cody, Wyoming, USA; P.69.69).

dress in American cities before the Second World War (Crane 2000). In the twenty-first century, these places are now simply known as ranches, but the clothing traditions still hold sway. At the Ranch at Rock Creek in Montana, the owner hires cowboys with college degrees, but who are garbed in Stetsons and chaps (Sherez 2014).

Clothing similar to that worn at dude ranches was worn both to watch and compete in rodeos, although the performers tended to be more flamboyant in

their approach (Wilson 2001). Buffalo Bill is also credited with the birth of
the professional American rodeo, starting with the 'contests in roping and
riding wild broncs, steers, and buffalo' that he organised for the July Fourth
Celebration in Nebraska in 1882 (LeCompte 1993: 6). Various towns hosted
these contests, often labelled as 'Frontier Days', 'to preserve and perpetuate
their heritage' (LeCompte 1993: 8), with winners receiving prizes in some
cases, leading to growing professionalism of the contests. Prominent examples were the Cheyenne Frontier Days and the Calgary Stampede. Women
were also part of both the Wild West shows and the rodeo circuit (Hoy 1995).
Given that 'many of the same stars who competed in frontier days also performed in Wild West shows, and both forms of western entertainment often
traveled with circuses, carnivals, and the like' (LeCompte 1993: 9), there was
a natural flamboyance to the clothing worn by participants. This was the
genesis for the styles worn by Hollywood's singing cowboys and country and
western singers.

The rhinestone cowboy

The distinction between clothing for show and work reached its heights in the
elaborately embroidered and rhinestone festooned Western clothing produced by
the likes of Nudie Cohn and Nathan Turk. Both were immigrants from Europe,
who came to America for a better life, and ironically played such a big part in
the development of Western clothing. Turk (or Teig as he was then) was born in
Poland in 1895 and came to New York as a teenager. Much of his inspiration
came from peasant embroideries he found depicted in his copy of *National Costumes of Austria, Hungary, Poland and Czechoslovakia* (George-Warren and
Freedman 2001). Hand-stitched arrowheads were applied to the edges of curved
pockets, creating the so-called *smile pockets*. He also inserted darts in the backs
of Western shirts, so that they tucked more neatly and securely into the pants
and belt. Turk's workmanship saw his clothes worn by the likes of movie stars
Gene Autry and Roy Rogers. Both were known for the distinctively decorative
clothing they wore as 'singing cowboys' in musical westerns of the 1930s and
1940s and on stage.

Nudie Cohn, born in Russia, sailed to America in 1913. His name Nutya
was misheard by the immigration officer, who gave him the name Nudie, and
it stuck (George-Warren and Freedman 2001). Nudie originally had a business
making costumes for the burlesque crowd, and this gave him a taste for
fringes, spangles, and above all, rhinestones. He dreamed of making clothes
for movie stars and musicians, and began making Western shirts. His first
break was making clothes for singer Tex Williams and his band, and he moved
on to the likes of Roy Rogers and his wife Dale Evans (Figures 8.4 and 8.5),
and many country and western singers. Nudie was a natural at self-promotion,
and drove a Pontiac car, and later a Cadillac, complete with steer horns,
around town. One of Nudie's cars now takes centre stage at the Lone Pine
Film Museum in California (Figure 13.5).

Figure 13.5 Nudie Cohn Cadillac, Lone Pine Film Museum (photo W. Frost).

Post-war trends

Many children in the 1940s and 1950s adopted Western wear for play, and this was often the result of what they watched on television. The networks enthusiastically embraced the Western narrative in the 1950s, exemplified by long-running television series such as *Wagon Train* (1957–1965), *Gunsmoke* (1955–1975) and *Bonanza* (1959–1973). Children had their own versions of what their parents watched, such as the Disneyland series *Davy Crockett: King of the Wild Frontier* (1955) and *Annie Oakley* (1955–1957). Davy Crockett's coonskin hat was a symbol of his identification with the outdoors, and became a popular item of boy's clothing, despite the fact that 'none of this was based on history, nor on legends, nor folktales (even the song was specially written for the TV series)' (Murdoch 2001: 29). *Annie Oakley* made the cowgirl look fashionable, both for women and little girls. Boys also donned cowboy hats and toy guns in holsters, to join their sisters in games of cowboys and Indians. This trend was not confined to the United States, with Australian children, for example, also enthusiastically adopting the garb and paraphernalia of the frontier, to enact myths that were equally powerful in the New World (McGrath 2001, 2007). They would have been exposed to the same television influences, as well as Westerns in the cinema. For girls, this allowed them the licence to engage in rough play, and as the sassy TV Annie, to act out the role of sheriff, complete with a badge

(McGrath 2007). Some children were able to access store-bought outfits, while others made do with home-made equivalents (McGrath 2001, 2007). Jennifer's uncle in the mid 1950s wore her father's Army slouch hat as a makeshift Stetson (Figure 13.6). The ubiquity of these play clothes or dress-ups was such that they became part of mainstream clothing for children (McGrath 2007). The movie *Toy Story* (1995) revived this look through the characters Woody and Jessie, and it is still a popular theme for children's parties, with birthday cards for boys in particular often displaying cowboy motifs. Jennifer's nephew wore a cowboy outfit for his second birthday party in 2009 (Figure 13.7). The concession to current political mores is that he doesn't carry a toy gun, unlike his great-uncle in the 1950s.

Figure 13.6 Ian Laing playing at cowboys in the mid 1950s (photo from the private collection of J. Laing).

Figure 13.7 Oscar Harvey at his cowboy-themed birthday party in 2009 (photo B.
    Harvey).

While Mexican and Native American influences are less prevalent in mainstream men's clothing, such motifs and elements have been adopted in a number
of feminine styles in the post-war period. Much of this influence can be traced to
the clothing worn in frontier regions close to the Mexican border, where many
Hispanics settled and some intermarried with the local Native Americans. For
example, female clothing adopted in Sonora between 1700 and 1848 reflected
the practicalities of living in a desert environment, but also a cross-fertilisation
of ethnic styles: 'Women wore short-sleeved blouses, sandals, and long
unbleached skirts imported from Hermosillo' (Haverluk 2003: 170).

The fiesta or squaw (*patio*) dress, with its flounced skirts, sometimes trimmed with wavy lines of rickrack braid, was inspired by Mexican and Native American traditional dress. The skirts were not ironed, but dried tied up in a bunch with string, to create the distinctive pleating (Burns 2011; George-Warren and Freedman 2001). It is sometimes referred to as *South-Western* dress (George-Warren and Freedman 2001) and is often identified with the Standard Oil heiress Millicent Rogers. We examine her life in New Mexico in Chapter 11, as one of a number of strong women who made the South-West their home in the twentieth century.

In the 1970s, the American WASP designer Ralph Lauren re-introduced the prairie look, epitomised by high necked frilled collar shirts for women and long cotton skirts, as well as Western shirts and fringed jackets. Many women adopted this romantic look, which was paralleled by the Victoriana craze epitomised by Laura Ashley in the UK. One of the more visible adherents in the early 1980s was the then Lady Diana Spencer, later Princess of Wales. She was photographed before her engagement to Prince Charles in this Sloane Ranger uniform, most memorably in a see-through floaty cotton skirt, and made the high-necked frilled white blouse the staple of female wardrobes the world over. Ralph Lauren has said that his Western collection of the 1970s was inspired by Gary Cooper in *The Plainsman* (1936) (George-Warren and Freedman 2001), but there are also traces of Millicent Rogers' South-Western look (Burns 2011). Like Cohn and Turk, Lauren (born Lifschitz), is another designer of European heritage who is drawn towards American Western style, and his stores are decorated to resemble a 'fantasy trading post' (George-Warren and Freedman 2001: 209).

Cinematic fashion trends

We consider two films, focusing on their influence on fashion trends, but also noting the similarity of their dominant narratives. Both encapsulate the view that in the West, a woman should not show off in public, and in particular, threaten to outshine a man. She must conform to a certain look, and her natural place is in the home.

Annie Get Your Gun (1950)

Buffalo Bill (Louis Calhern) has come to town, along with his troupe of entertainers. To get the publicity rolling for his show, he organises a shootoff in every town between Frank Butler (Howard Keel) and the best sharpshooter the town has to offer. Frank has no competition until he meets Annie Oakley (Betty Hutton), freckled, pigtailed, with clothes made of food sacks and in need of a good bath, but unerringly accurate with a gun. When she beats Frank in a shooting competition, Buffalo Bill offers Annie the opportunity to join his show, singing that *There's No Business Like Show Business*. Annie loves the idea of performing, but she has also fallen in love with Frank, so her decision is quickly made.

While her naivety and lack of sophistication are lampooned through songs like 'Doing What Comes Naturally' ('Folks are dumb where I come from'), Annie is quick on the uptake in terms of realising what it will take to win Frank's heart ('You Can't Get a Man with a Gun!'). Frank tells her before he knows of her prowess with a gun: 'You shouldn't be fooling around with a piece of junk like this. You could get hurt. You give this back to your pappy and get yourself a pair of knitting needles'. Annie doesn't conform to his ideal of femininity, as she is not the kind of girl 'you see in picture magazines ... sort of dainty, dimpled and rosy' ('The Girl That I Marry'). Others express the same view, with Buffalo Bill's off-sider explaining: 'Of course she looks terrible now, but we could dress her up!'

Annie's road to matrimony involves scrubbing her skin with lemon juice, to try to lighten her freckles, putting curlers in her hair, and learning to read. She is a frontier Cinderella and rejoices when Frank tells her: 'You're getting pinker and whiter every day'. While Frank says that he likes her 'to be ambitious. I want you to improve but it'll take some time', he is not talking about her shooting skills. When Buffalo Bill persuades Annie to 'dazzle' Frank by performing an outlandish stunt, clad in a red embroidered dress, with matching Western hat and white high-heeled boots, she thinks he will propose to her in his rapture, 'just like in a fairytale'.

Annie's dreams are shattered when Frank storms off, angry at the spotlight being moved onto her and telling her in a letter that she is 'too smart for me'. He later explodes: 'What a wife she'd be! Instead of staying home sewing, she'd be out shooting targets'. At first Annie is crestfallen ('I was going to be a lady for him and everything. I wish I'd never seen a gun!'), but later on she becomes incensed, singing 'Anything You Can Do, I Can Do Better'. At a shooting competition, Sitting Bull (J. Carrol Naish), who has made Annie his honorary daughter, doctors her gun so she loses to Frank. When she finds out, she is told by Sitting Bull: 'Keep missing, you win. Be second best. You get man with *this* gun'. Annie loses the competition and is swept back into Frank's arms. The end of the movie shows her all dressed in white, presumably now a bride. While she can perform with Frank, the billing is 'Butler and Oakley'. Annie remains in his shadow.

Urban Cowboy (1980)

Urban Cowboy reignited the craze for Western gear (Stall-Meadows 2011). It featured the bar Gilley's, in Pasadena, Texas (but moved to Houston in the movie), and described as 'three and half acres of concrete prairie!' by the uncle of John Travolta's character Bud. The clothes worn by the actors are based on those worn by regulars at Gilley's as well as descriptions of clothing in a 1979 article in *Esquire* magazine titled 'The Ballad of the Urban Cowboy: America's Search for True Grit' (George-Warren and Freedman 2001).

The wardrobe of Debra Winger's character Sissy includes tight jeans, a dark-brown Stetson, skimpy tops with shoestring straps, and a wedding ensemble that incorporates white cowboy boots, just like the ones that Betty Hutton wore as Annie Oakley. She is sexy in her nonchalance and lack of inhibitions. Sissy asks

Bud 'Are you a real cowboy?' to which he answers: 'That depends on what you think a real cowboy is!' Bud has undergone a transformation – when he arrives on his first night at Gilley's, he wears a white Stetson and has a beard. The next night, he switches to a black Stetson, is clean-shaven, and swaps his checked shirt for a solid navy Western shirt, complete with large belt buckle. Bud is shown in profile, almost comically handsome, and then dances with Sissy, an easy languorous two-step to the strains of 'Looking For Love in All the Wrong Places'. This could be Sissy's anthem.

Sissy constantly chooses men who treat her like dirt. Bud barks at her to 'Get me another beer!' and calls her a 'pig' for her housewifely skills: 'There's certain things a man wants from a wife'. He also doesn't 'want [her] showing off on that goddam bull!', referring to the mechanical bucking bronco, used to train rodeo riders, that Gilley's has introduced to bring in the crowds. When Sissy tells him that he is jealous because she rides the bull better, he hits her.

The next man she takes up with is no better; being more violent than Bud was towards her. Wes (Scott Glenn) is an ex-prisoner who Bud and Sissy have seen performing at the Huntsville Prison Rodeo while on their honeymoon. Bud marvels that 'these outlaws make good cowboys' as 'they don't give a shit if they get hurt'. When Sissy taunts him that she has 'got myself a real cowboy now', Bud retorts that 'I got myself a real lady'. He has taken up with a rich woman, Pam, who has a 'thing about cowboys. I like men with simple values. I like them independent, self-reliant, brave, strong, decent and open'. She toasts Bud: 'To cowboys. And all that implies'.

The soundtrack provides a background commentary to Bud's conduct, with the song 'Mama, Don't Let Your Babies Grow Up To Be Cowboys'. Bud likes the fact that Pam has apparently cleaned up his trailer – 'I just love a woman's touch around the house'. In fact it was Sissy who cleaned up, chastened by Bud's comments that she isn't a good homemaker. Bud eventually reconciles with Sissy after he has won the bucking bronco contest and Wes is exposed in his attempt to rob him of his cash prize. Bud finds out from Pam that it is Sissy who cleaned up his trailer. They end up together, but one wonders how long this relationship might last, given the respect Bud has shown to Sissy, and her need to stretch her wings in a male-dominated society.

As George-Warren and Freedman (2001: 184) note: 'those in the industry still talk about the Urban Cowboy years, with many of them crediting the movie, starring [Debra] Winger and John Travolta, for bringing them business like they had never experienced before'. It also rode on the success of Ralph Lauren's Western collection in 1978, and laid the ground for the resurgence in Western clothing across the globe (George-Warren and Freedman 2001). *Footloose* (1984) reinforced the trend with its feel-good tale of small-town Utah youngsters rebelling against a ban on dancing. Even toys adopted this trend. Western Barbie made her debut in 1981, clad in a white satin shirt and pants, fringed with black braid, white boots and a matching white cowboy hat on top of her long blonde bubble curls. She was designed to be able to wink when the back was pressed, which little girls loved, although 'many adults thought the heavy blue eyelids looked sleazy' (Dickey 1991: 26). This picks up on the association of female Western-style clothing as sexualised and sometimes *trashy*, a theme discussed later in this chapter.

Current trends

While the Western clothing craze sparked by *Urban Cowboy* didn't last, 'there was always the original customer to fall back on' (George-Warren and Freedman 2001: 190), who had worn this gear all their lives, regardless of fashion trends and styles (Figure 13.8). From time to time, trendsetters picked it up again. Princess Diana was photographed in the late 1980s wearing cowboy boots for the

Figure 13.8 The cowgirl look in a shop window in Roswell (photo W. Frost).

school run and at polo games (Graham and Blanchard 1998). Presidents of the United States routinely wore jeans during holidays or leisure, with Ronald Reagan in particular keen to emphasise his connections to the West, wearing jeans and a cowboy hat (Murdoch 2001), and George W. Bush photographed in jeans with a buckled belt when relaxing at his Texan ranch. Other films and television series that prompted a revival of the Western look include the Oscar-winning *Dances with Wolves* (1990) and the remake of *True Grit* (2010).

Jeans became a fashion staple worn by all ages and both sexes, and went upscale, thanks to designers such as Gloria Vanderbilt and Calvin Klein. They were no longer fashions of the street, and could be worn in most places and situations. Couture denim can still be seen in the form of cult brands such as 7 for All Mankind and True Religion, where they are less associated with a designer and more with a fashion label. Others preferred their jeans to look authentically worn-in and beaten-up. The fashion industry eventually realised that people would pay for the faded, prewashed look, and later even ripped jeans. It has been argued that this trend gives 'an illusion of experience' (Gordon 1991: 39), without the need to take part in the adventure or counter-culture that goes with it.

In the early part of the twenty-first century, the wearing of Western clothes by celebrities such as Prince William and his wife Catherine, the Duke and Duchess of Cambridge, on a visit to a rodeo on their royal tour of Canada in 2011, demonstrates its timeless quality. Catherine is also often photographed in skinny J. Brand jeans for less formal engagements, such as attending the London Olympics and, more recently, sailing in New Zealand on an official tour. The rodeo is still an influence on the purchase of Western clothing (Schwer and Daneshvary 2011). Western style remains a reliable theme for the pages of glossy fashion magazines, with the May 2014 issue of *Harper's Bazaar Australia* featuring a series of Western-inspired couture clothing under the banner of 'Go West!'

While Native American and Mexican-inspired clothing has ridden the waves of mainstream fashion, this does not mean that the cultures which engendered it are commensurately accepted. Haverluk (2003: 181) argues that, despite a widespread Hispanic cultural appropriation, illustrated by clothing but also by food and music, Hispanics still suffer 'economic and political marginalization'. Adoption of ethnic clothing could therefore be another form of colonialism.

Western clothing and identity

Clothing is often worn to denote identity, giving cues or signals to others as to who we are, who we *think* we are and who we would *like to be* (Craik 1994; McCracken 1990). This identity is therefore constructed, with clothing used to create 'simultaneously a set of habits and a space inhabited, a way of being in the world' (Craik 1994: 4), and may perform a *symbolic* function (Cunningham and Voso Lab 1991b; Wilson 1996). The wearing of Western clothing is an exemplar of this. We interviewed Wayne, who was wearing the full kit (hat, boots, Western shirt and vest) while travelling through New Mexico on vacation. He told us:

I'm a postman in Los Angeles. I deliver the mail and I'm just a postman. But, each year for my holidays I get dressed up like a cowboy and come to the West. I just hang around, drift from place to place. And I'm a cowboy ... I love Westerns. I've seen lots of movies. It's a look I love. Dressed like this, I'm a somebody. I'm a cowboy. Not a postman.

Gray (2001) argues that dressing as a working cowboy is a way of identifying with the values associating with these clothes – 'the virtues of the cowboy icon' (p. 7). Similarly, the flamboyant styles worn by performers, 'with their sequins and rhinestones and multiple layers of fringe, which some consider aberrations or even prostitutions of cowboy style, are in fact intensely personal expressions of the individualism of those who designed and wore them' (Gray 2001: 7). They play with the notion of masculine identity (see the discussion below), with their flashiness and bright colours 'that had once been restricted to women's dresses or the sparse fabric canvases provided by men's ties' (La Chapelle 2001: 8). In this way, they run counter to the examples of gay men examined by Johnson (2008), who often dress in an uber-masculine cowboy style at bars, 'playing dress-up' in the guise of a macho hero. Another paradox with the rhine-stone cowboy is the fact that many of the key designers who created these outfits, notably Nudie Cohn, Nathan Turk and Manuel Cuevas, were immigrants, and often incorporated their own cultural and ethnic traditions such as embroi-dery into their creations (George-Warren and Freedman 2001). While the origins of the clothing were working-class, the addition of glitz and the hefty price tags gave the wearer 'an aura of status and upward mobility' (La Chapelle 2001: 9), reflecting perhaps the aspirations of the designers themselves.

Playing at being a cowboy or frontiersman is nothing new. Theodore Roo-sevelt adopted Western dress when he moved to a ranch after the death of his wife and mother, sporting alligator-hide leggings and a bowie knife from Tiffany (George-Warren and Freedman 2001). President Calvin Coolidge in 1927 attended a July 4 celebration 'in a red shirt, blue bandanna, silver spurs – and chaps' (Murdoch 2001: 102), which was met with derision in some quarters (e.g. the *New York Times*) but was also a shrewd political move, linking himself with the mythical image of the West 'which called up instant memories of admired qualities' (Murdoch 2001: 103). Buffalo Bill saw his clothing as a costume (Tompkins 1992), and was performing the role of a frontier hero, even in his private life, through his ever-present Stetson. Some towns have a tradition of holding Western-themed events, where people are clad as various archetypes of the American West. Peñaloza (2000: 82) provides a case study of the National Western Stick Show and Rodeo, with 'stockmen in cowboy attire'. Clothing is used to invoke both the 'historical and mythical past' of this rural industry (p. 104). Tucson used to hold a Big Hat Day during the rodeo season, jointly organised by the local Lions club and the Rodeo Committee of the Tucson Chamber of Commerce. The sheriff would pretend to arrest people not wearing Western garb (George-Warren and Freedman 2001). The implication here is that those who don't wear Western clothing are not 'one of us'. Clothing here functions as a marker of place identity, rather than personal identity. Having what is seen as the appropriate gear sends the message that the wearer cares about and has a pride in the Western heritage of the destination.

The annual celebration of Helldorado Days in Tombstone allows the townsfolk and visitors to dress up as Western icons such as Wyatt Earp and take on roles that are inversions of their everyday life, such as saloon girls and sharp-shooters (see Chapter 5). The clothing adopted, particularly corsets and lace-up boots for the women (Figure 13.9), and the way it is worn with confidence, suggests a feeling of titillation in being perceived as non-conformist and outré, in what might be otherwise a conservative community. It also provides a link to the history or at least the perceived image of Tombstone as a rough and lawless town.

Figure 13.9 Typical saloon girl fashion worn at Helldorado Days, Tombstone (photo W. Frost).

Fashion designers also recognise that what they create, in homage to the American West, has a deeper meaning. The Italian designer Versace launched a Western-inspired collection in 1992–1993 and observed to *British Vogue*:

> The great Wild West revival we are experiencing probably depends on America's need to take possession of its roots again, while Europe feels a great attraction toward the refreshing Western myth – and toward a look that speaks of wild-open spaces in traditional ways. What is certain is that the Wild West re-revival isn't simply retro. It is a panacea for something that has been ailing us for a long time – the late twentieth century.
>
> (George-Warren and Freedman 2001: 208)

This suggests that Western clothing can be used to shape identity even when there is no personal connection to the heritage that spawned it. The connection is with the values or ethos that it represents, that have been largely absorbed through the books people read, and the films and television shows that they have watched.

Subverting and reinforcing norms: gender and sexuality

While Western clothing is firmly linked with a strongly masculine tradition, it is ironically often used to transcend or overturn norms of gender and sexuality. Sexualised or fetishized versions of the clothing are part of popular culture, such as the pink cowboy hat and leather chaps. The cowboy has long been venerated as a gay idol, and the homosocial relationships and latent homoeroticism in many Western films is discussed in Chapter 3 on John Wayne and Charlton Heston. Klein (1997) refers to the *queer frontier*, and an enduring image of *Midnight Cowboy* (1969) was Jon Voigt striding down a New York street, imagining himself a hit with the ladies, but instead appealing to gay men. The cowboy was one of the fantasy stereotypes adopted by the Village People when they formed in the mid 1970s and Johnson (2008) writes of a country-western gay bar in a metropolitan city of the United States where patrons dress in Western gear. This link is still pervasive in popular culture. A young man on the streets of Melbourne, wearing a Western shirt, Akubra hat, black jeans and boots, describes his style in a newspaper vox-pop as 'the Velvet Frontiersman. I look as if I drive cattle but I'm clearly soft-handed and effeminate' (Munro 2014: 8). Johnson (2008) attributes this popularity of the cowboy look with gay men to a desire to adopt 'hypermasculine qualities' in order to overcome prejudice: 'As they negotiate the double bind of being gay and male, many gay men retain the idealized sexual and gendered messages connected with the symbolic power, strength, and self-worth maintained in hegemonic masculinity' (p. 387). Johnson (2008: 400) labels this 'cowboy drag'. Some will tone this look down in different circumstances, for example to visit a bar which has a more trendy theme, by taking off their Stetson hat or even completely 'changing costume' (Johnson 2008: 397). This suggests that they use clothing to present a different side to themselves, including a different gendered identity.

For women, Western gear is generally associated with heterosexuality. The saloon girl is one example. In *Apocalypse Now* (1979), the Playboy Bunnies perform for the troops wearing skimpy Native American, cowgirl and cavalry soldier costumes. Another example is Daisy Duke, the white trash cousin in *The Dukes of Hazzard*, famous for her micro shorts created from jeans with the legs ripped off and a Western shirt knotted under her breasts, to expose her midriff. McGee (1983: 104) describes Daisy as an example of the traditional stereotype of the young Southern woman as 'earthy and sensible, breezily unpretentious, energetic and helpful'. And above all sexy. Jessica Simpson ramped up the costume in the movie version of *The Dukes of Hazzard* (2005), to provide more cleavage and make the shorts even briefer. The character of Sissy in *Urban Cowboy* is another case in point. One of the enduring images from the film is Debra Winger writhing on a mechanical bucking bronco in tight jeans and a cowboy hat, a simulated sexual act which drives her estranged husband Bud wild with jealousy.

Tight jeans in the 1980s were similarly sold using sexual allusions and imagery. The Calvin Klein campaign using model and actress Brooke Shields was notorious for its slogan – 'Nothing Comes Between Me and My Calvins' – generating outrage as Shields was only 15 at the time (Laing *et al.* 2014). Klein is reputed to have sold 125,000 pairs of jeans a week in 1979 (Gordon 1991) and contributed to the image of jeans as provocative and erotic, rather than simply casual wear.

Western clothing thus displays complex and sometimes contradictory messages, many of which are linked to those mythical values of individualism, toughness and independence traditionally associated with the West (Murdoch 2001; Schwer and Daneshvary 2011). These values are manifested in different ways or *stereotypes*, however, whether it be the urban cowboy, his sexy companion, or the velvet frontiersman. The symbolism of this clothing in terms of identity crosses gender, sexual and cultural boundaries and is easily understood. Cunningham and Voso Lab (1991b: 7) observe that 'using clothing in this short-hand convention communicates a wide range of ideas in a manner that words cannot, more quickly, and to a wider audience'. The messages that this clothing evokes are perennial, reflecting the desire that lies dormant in many of us for wide open spaces and a hero to look up to.

14 Travelling the Jurassic West

> The chief aim of interpretation is not instruction, but provocation.
> (Tilden 1957: 35)

Introduction

In the badlands of Montana, a group of people are digging. They pause to listen to their leader. Older than the others, he is dressed like a cowboy: jeans, a checked western shirt and a hat. He talks about long ago. Some of those listening snigger. The leader starts to get annoyed. Though they respect him, at times the others see him as a figure of fun. A young boy, aged about 10 or 12, pipes up. He does not see what is so scary about the story he is being told.

The leader focuses all his attention on the young boy. He is angry that he is being disrespected. 'Imagine you were there' he says directly to the boy:

> You enter a clearing and you see him. You keep still.... He'll lose you if you don't move.... But that's when the attack comes.... Not from the front, but the side.... He slashes you ... across the belly.

Now the boy is scared. And the others have stopped laughing and are listening intently. Given the Western location, the older man could be describing an Indian attack. Or possibly a grizzly bear. It is neither, he has gone farther back in time to imagine what the West was once like. He is talking about the Jurassic West.

This is one of the opening scenes of *Jurassic Park* (1993). The leader dressed like a cowboy is actually palaeontologist Dr Alan Grant (Sam Neill). The group he is putting in their place are his volunteers and graduate students. The attacker he is talking about is the velociraptor.

At the time this film was released, very few of the audience knew much about velociraptors. Dinosaurs have been a continuing area of fascination, especially for younger people, since the late nineteenth century. Natural history museums around the world contained gigantic skeleton replicas. Dinosaur films had long been popular, dating back to *The Lost World* (1925 and based on the novel by

Arthur Conan Doyle) and *King Kong* (1933, where Skull Island abounds in dino-
saurs). There had even been a dinosaur Western in *Valley of the Gwangi* (1969).
Distinguished by special effects from Ray Harryhausen, this loose remake of
King Kong featured cowboys capturing a tyrannosaurus in an isolated valley in
Mexico. These films meant that most people knew about tyrannosaurus,
triceratops and brontosaurus, but not velociraptor.

In writing the novel *Jurassic Park* (1990), Michael Crichton skilfully
included many of the latest theories about dinosaurs. While the central plot was
a hoary old story of dangerous animals escaping and threatening a small group
of people, what grabbed global attention was the presentation of a new vision of
what dinosaurs were like. These included both dinosaurs – such as velociraptors
– that were little known and new images of how old favourites probably looked
and moved.

These revolutionary theories included:

1   Dinosaurs were warm-blooded, more like birds than lizards.
2   They were much more agile than previously thought. Whereas films and
    museums had posed them as slothful with tails dragging along the ground,
    they were now seen as having tails and heads counterbalanced and level.
3   Some were quite small. The film included human-sized velociraptors and
    dilophosaurus, and the chicken-sized compys.
4   Some were highly intelligent. The carnivorous velociraptors were not only
    human-sized, but possibly just as intelligent as us.
5   Many dinosaurs had highly complex social arrangements, including being
    attentive parents. In the 1970s, palaeontologist Jack Horner had discovered
    fossilised eggs, nests and young in Montana. He named his new dinosaur
    maiasaurus, meaning good mother lizard.

The novel and film dramatically drew these new theories to the attention of the
public. Using a combination of puppets and the newly developed CGI (Com-
puter Graphics Imaging), director Steven Spielberg convincingly created cinematic dinosaurs. The film delivered a strong sense of *authenticity*; for viewers
this was what dinosaurs were actually like. The influence of the film was well
captured in the following quote from a recent scientific book on raptors. In its
introduction, it assumes its readers are familiar with *Jurassic Park*:

> No dinosaur has better captured the gothic side of human imagination than
> the cunning raptors depicted in the *Jurassic Park* movies. Rather than pre-
> senting us with slow, dull-witted lizards as in the early Hollywood classics
> such as Cooper and Schoedsack's *King Kong*, director Steven Spielberg's
> raptor's depicted dinosaurs in a new and disturbing image. With the power
> of hundreds of scientific experts restoring them, and embellished with the
> imaginations of Hollywood scriptwriters, the *Jurassic Park* raptors come
> across as fast, agile and highly intelligent predators.
>
> (Long and Schouten 2008: 21)

On the trail of dinosaurs in the West

In 1877, dinosaur fossils were discovered at Morrison, Colorado, just outside of Denver. That discovery is commemorated in the name of that town being applied to the Morrison Formation, a broad expanse of Jurassic sedimentary rocks which have become a productive source of fossils. In the late Jurassic period, this region was distinguished by a warm and humid climate, resulting in large rivers and an enormous shallow lake covering much of the West. Fossil finds are often associated with these rivers and the fertile lake shore. The Morrison Formation covers at least one million square kilometres, stretching from Alberta, Canada down into Texas. Fossils are found where there has been the geological uplift of the Rocky Mountains (such as at Morrison), or erosion. The latter has seen a strong connection between Badlands landscapes in Canada and the United States and rich fossil finds (Foster 2007).

Dinosaur museums and displays abound across the West. In Montana, funding from the state accommodation tax has led to the establishment of the Montana Dinosaur Trail. This co-operative marketing venture links 15 dinosaur museums, field stations and interpretive centres. Most Western states have at least one dinosaur tourist attraction. In this chapter, we will focus on two major sites: Dinosaur National Monument in Utah and the Siebel Dinosaur Complex at the Museum of the Rockies in Montana. The fieldwork that was undertaken at both of these sites was different from that at other places within this book. Reflecting the passionate interest of younger people in dinosaurs, these field visits were planned and led by Warwick's two children – Stephen and Alexander. Whereas a number of places connected to movies are viewed through a nostalgic lens, these dinosaur attractions are examined with the assistance of children of the twenty-first century.

Stephen Jay Gould's nightmare

In 1995, Stephen Jay Gould wrote an essay reflecting on the success of *Jurassic Park* and its implications for science and science education. He stressed that he enjoyed both the book and the film, though he was a bit disappointed that some of the science was incorrect. However, what he was really concerned about was the effect on museums and what they presented to visitors, particularly children. He noted that a number of natural history museums around the world had taken advantage of the opportunity presented by the film and had chosen to 'mount, at high and separate admission charges, special exhibits of colorful robotic dinosaurs that move and growl, but (so far as I have been able to judge) teach nothing of scientific value about these animals' (Gould 1995: 235).

Gould's nightmare vision was of dinosaur exhibits that were little more than theme parks with their animatronics suggesting Disneyland or the Rainforest Café chain. Entertainment and spectacle were privileged over education and understanding and little was done to encourage children to move beyond the blockbuster exhibition and explore other parts of the museum. Whilst not specifically cited by Gould, an example of such separation may be seen in the Natural History Museum in London. There, the prime attraction is an animatronic tyrannosaurus, a powerful photo opportunity encouraging visitors to hurry quickly past the displays of fossils (Figure 14.1).

Twenty years on, it is heartening to see that Gould seems to have got it wrong. The dinosaur museums of the American West are certainly strongly influenced by *Jurassic Park*, but they have not gone down the path of just basic animatronics. Instead, they have emphasised interpretation. The opportunity that *Jurassic Park* has provided them with is an expanded market dominated by children. Rather than just wanting thrills and spectacle, modern children are dinosaur savvy, knowing far more than their parents and with a seemingly insatiable desire to learn more.

Freeman Tilden and interpretation

The pioneering work on interpretation is by Freeman Tilden (1957), still highly influential today, particularly in the United States. Tilden has often been presented as a wise and experienced national parks ranger, developing his innovative ideas over decades of presenting guided tours, before finally writing them down. In such a mythologised image, he is a latter-day incarnation of John Muir.

Figure 14.1 Animatronic *Tyrannosaurus Rex* at Natural History Museum, London, UK (photo W. Frost).

The reality is unfortunately not that romantic. Tilden was an experienced newspaper journalist and fiction writer rather than a crusty park ranger. In 1941 he was hired by Conrad Wirth, director of the National Parks Service (NPS), to work on public relations and publicity. One particularly important task he had was to write a handbook that could be given to potential corporate sponsors and other stakeholders. As work proceeded on that, Tilden and Wirth began to develop a plan for an interpretation handbook. As that coalesced, Tilden realised that what was missing within current NPS practice was a basic philosophy to guide interpretation planning. Without such an intellectual foundation, there was a tendency to dismiss interpretation as lightweight entertainment for visitors and of little value (Craig 2007).

Tilden conceptualised interpretation as a service integral to both natural and cultural heritage. The NPS managed both types of sites – as in Yellowstone National Park (Chapter 9) and Little Bighorn Battlefield National Monument (Chapter 12). This service was provided by

> thousands of naturalists, historians, archaeologists, and other specialists ...
> engaged in the work of revealing, to such visitors as desire the service,
> something of the beauty and wonder, the inspiration and spiritual meaning
> that lie behind what the visitor can with his senses perceive.
>
> (Tilden 1957: 25)

More formally, he defined interpretation as 'an educational activity which aims to reveal meanings and relationships through the use of original objects, by first-hand experience, and by illustrative media, rather than simply to communicate factual information' (Tilden 1957: 33).

We find Tilden's first explanation more powerful and instructive than his second dictionary-style definition. The first better captures the notion of a profound experience, of the visitor getting something far better than they expected. However, we also experience a certain disappointment in reading Tilden's insightful work over half a century after it was written. Central to his premise was the idea that interpretation went beyond what the visitors could see by themselves. That is an idea that has often been lost in contemporary interpretation practice and rhetoric. The trend for minimising interpretation – most obvious in zoos, for example – is in direct contradiction of Tilden's argument. Furthermore, Tilden's warnings about the overuse of gadgetry, particularly that technology could never better a good human performance of interpretation, has now seemingly been forgotten by many interpretation developers.

Tilden's great success was in distilling a range of ideas into six core principles of interpretation. Such a set of numbered commandments were easy to remember for a wide variety of employees, volunteers and other stakeholders. Like their biblical equivalent, they had an authoritative status – set in stone they were both enduring and unchallengeable. Adapted for simplicity from Tilden (1957: 34–35), they were:

1   Interpretation must be related to the visitor as a person – either their personality or experience.
2   It must be based on and include factual information, but interpretation is not simply information.
3   It is an art and must be approached from a multi-disciplinary perspective.
4   'The chief aim of interpretation is not instruction, but provocation'.
5   It should aim to present a whole rather than a part.
6   Programmes for children should be separately developed and not be simply a dilution of the adult version.

In the 60-plus years since it was published, Tilden's work has been highly influential in heritage studies and practice. Whilst subject to modifications, its core tenets have not been challenged. Today, its legacy can be seen in the continued emphasis on story-telling and persuasive messaging in a wide range of heritage contexts. It certainly is regularly and widely applied at tourist attractions throughout the American West – even though (we would argue), there is a need to remain vigilant in ensuring its consistent and effective application. An unevenness in the usage of Tilden's principles is often apparent. The public governance of many heritage sites comes with many advantages, but also – unfortunately – with a strong tendency towards under-resourcing which results in deficiencies in the quality and maintenance of interpretation programmes.

The two case studies presented below provide interesting examples of how interpretive principles can be effectively applied. One, we would argue, is illustrative of world's best practice. Both are also valuable in demonstrating the changes and challenges that affect tourist attractions. In the heart of the West, they are examples of a new approach to imagining this region.

Museum of the Rockies, Bozeman, Montana

The Siebel Dinosaur Complex opened in 2007, financed by a US$2 million donation by businessman Thomas Siebel. From the outside, its architecture suggests a cinema multiplex, which is not really surprising, as similar to a cinema, such a museum occupies a contained space, cut off from the outdoors and natural light, in order to fully engage the imagination of visitors. Not all dinosaur museums follow such a path. The Utah Field House of Natural History State Park Museum at Vernal in Utah, for example, is dominated by full scale models in the open air.

Siebel's donation was conditional on securing palaeontologist Jack Horner as the curator. Horner was a consultant to *Jurassic Park* and the character of Alan Grant was partly based on him. Utilising Horner as curator was part of a strategy of linking the exhibition to the well-known film. Much of its interpretation makes specific reference to the *Jurassic Park* series and there is a strong emphasis on raptors.

Starting at the entrance, this museum is designed to provoke and challenge visitors and is an excellent example of the adoption of Tilden's principles of interpretation. In the forecourt of the museum, there is a full-size replica of a skeleton of a *Tyrannosaurus Rex* (Figure 14.2). It is posed in the modern style, head down, tail up and off the ground; unlike the animatronic robot at the Natural History Museum (Figure 14.1). This modern interpretation of posture was popularised in *Jurassic Park*.

The next display, after the entry doors, is in stark contrast. Much smaller, it depicts what appears to be a modern waterfowl. It is curious that such a mundane exhibit is placed in what would normally be such a prominent position. The interpretive panel discloses that while this looks like a modern bird, it is indeed prehistoric and suggests that the visitor look closer for how it differs from its modern descendant. It takes a while, it just looks like a normal bird. Finally, the revelation comes. This is a prehistoric bird which evolved with a row of teeth on its beak.

Moving further in, a series of interpretive panels explain that this museum subscribes to a number of new and controversial theories about dinosaurs. It warns that these contest conventional views and that the aim is to convince visitors to revise their views on dinosaurs. One panel provides a detailed explanation of how scientists develop hypotheses, test them and accordingly evolve new theories. It emphasises that such processes often lead to disagreement amongst scientists in a field and that their perspectives are subjective.

Figure 14.2 Tyrannosaurus Rex at the entrance to the Museum of the Rockies. Note the posture and how it contrasts to the replica in Figure 14.1 (photo W. Frost).

'Nothing in the biological sciences', it states, 'can be said to be absolutely true, though if enough scientists agree their consensus may be viewed as truth'. It is a bold and audacious position for a science museum to take. Again, in line with Tilden, the interpretation designers have sought to engage through provocation.

The next panel moves straight to the big, contested theory, proclaiming that *Dinosaurs Are the Ancestors of Birds!* Eight shared characteristics of birds and dinosaurs are listed. Drawing on the previous panels about hypotheses, theory and consensus, this panel concludes:

> Birds share more characteristics with *Dromaeosaurid* and *Troodontid* dinosaurs (a group named *Deinonychosauria*), than with any other group of animals. Therefore we can hypothesize that birds evolved from this group of dinosaurs. This means that birds are actually a group of reptiles, rather than a distinct group unto themselves. Birds are living dinosaurs. Until someone can demonstrate that another group of animals shares more characteristics with birds than do dinosaurs, the theory is considered to be strong, and therefore, scientifically true ... BIRDS ARE AVIAN DINOSAURS – BIRDS ARE LIVING DINOSAURS!

This interpretation gives special meaning to the two entrance displays. The toothed waterbird in the foyer is as much a dinosaur as the tyrannosaurus outside. The tyrannosaurus, bipedal and more dynamically posed than in the past, suggests a bird, albeit a giant. As we move into the main exhibition hall, more bird/dinosaurs are revealed and the interpretive narrative continues.

Two dinosaur discoveries from Montana are given prominence in the main hall. They are deliberately placed before the more well-known tyrannosaurus and triceratops. The first is maiasauria, discovered by Jack Horner near Choteau in the foothills of the Rockies. Maiasauria was a duck-billed dinosaur and its name means 'good mother lizard'. What was found was a nest, with eggs and young. Importantly, the young were older than hatchlings. They were in the nest being protected and fed in the manner of many modern birds.

The second is deinonychus, discovered near Billings on the Yellowstone River in central Montana. These were predators similar to velociraptor – which hail from Mongolia – though larger. It is this dig that is recreated at the beginning of *Jurassic Park*. When Spielberg made *Jurassic Park*, he conflated the two, keeping the name velociraptor, but making them larger. The display at the Museum of the Rockies draws heavily on *Jurassic Park* to interpret deinonychus. In particular, exhibits demonstrating their hunting are linked to the film (Figure 14.3). Even the changes made for the film are used to explain certain features. Most significantly, the interpretation hypothesises that they were probably feathered and possibly brightly coloured (Figure 14.4). However, while Spielberg considered portraying them this way, he ultimately decided that viewers might find this hard to accept and instead opted to have them more conventionally dun-coloured and without feathers.

Figure 14.3 Display of *Deinonychus* hunting (photo W. Frost).

Figure 14.4 Display highlighting plumage of *Deinonychus*. Note differences to how *Velociraptors* are imagined in *Jurassic Park* (photo W. Frost).

Dinosaur National Monument, Utah

Discovered in 1909, the fossils here are tightly concentrated in a small area. This is most likely the result of flash floods drowning large numbers of dinosaurs and then depositing their remains together when the waters receded (Foster 2007). In the 1950s, proposals to flood the area for a new reservoir led to a counter strategy to develop visitor facilities and encourage tourists to this remote part of Utah. At that time, the NPS had embarked on Mission 66, an ambitious plan to fund a series of visitor centres in the ten years leading up to the fiftieth anniversary of the service in 1966.

Mission 66 was self-consciously modernistic. Prior to this strategy, NPS buildings tended towards the rustic, a distinctive rough stone and timber look, best exemplified in national parks like Yellowstone and Glacier. In contrast Mission 66 buildings emphasised glass and concrete, evoking the imagery of the space race and post-war World Fairs. At Dinosaur National Monument, the geology of the site provided the opportunity for an extraordinary interpretive design. Built over and around a sloping fossil bed, it allowed tourists to look down on palaeontologists at work on the 'Dinosaur Quarry'. So close together were the fossils, that as they were removed, new ones were uncovered. The state-of-the-art facility offered a view of the greatest concentration of dinosaur bones in the United States and the chance to watch science at work.

That was the plan. However, almost immediately after its opening in 1958, problems began to appear. The centre was built on unstable shale, as it shifted, the building began to crack. For nearly 50 years, the NPS operated successfully with ongoing repairs, but the risk continued to grow. The collapse of some glass panels was the catalyst and, following an occupational health and safety review, the building closed in 2006.

Across the United States, NPS operations are centred on visitor centres. This is where interpretation is delivered. In many cases, it is where entry fees are collected. Indeed, in smaller NPS sites, if the visitor centre is closed for staffing reasons, then there is no entry fee to the property. With its iconic visitor centre closed and its future uncertain, the NPS faced difficult choices about how to operate at Dinosaur National Monument.

The site was visited in 2008. At that stage, a small temporary visitor centre had been constructed, accompanied by a portable building for the concessionaire to sell souvenirs. In lieu of the normal visitor centre experience, all entry fees were waived. Furthermore, the temporary centre was a few kilometres from the now derelict visitor centre, which, due to its unsafe condition, visitors were discouraged from venturing anywhere near (Figure 14.5).

Inside the temporary centre, a helpful park ranger chatted with visitors. This was quite a different experience from the normal NPS mode of operation, which was usually mainly focussed on ensuring that visitors were paying the entrance fee. Indeed, it was a fascinating case of de-commodification. With the monetary imperative removed, the ranger had a very different relationship with the visitors. They were no longer customers. He was no longer an ersastz sales clerk,

Figure 14.5 Dinosaur National Monument Visitors Centre, closed in 2006 due to its dangerous condition (photo W. Frost).

but instead came out from behind the counter, mingling with visitors and talking with them about the small number of fossil displays.

With limited displays and an iconic building off-limits, the park ranger faced major challenges in dealing with visitors. While some were satisfied with a quick visit, others perhaps wanted more, especially after a long drive to such an isolated location. The juggling act he was forced to perform was to quickly read the visitor and judge their expectations and capabilities.

For those he judged to be both adventurous and interested, he suggested a walk along a trail to visit a fossil in situ. A map was provided, on which he drew in an X to mark the spot to aim for. This treasure map came with qualifications. Were the visitors up to walking a few kilometres through the Utah desert? It was hot, did they have water? Did they look like they could read a map and cope with being away from their car? Did they understand there were no trail markers, signs or NPS staff out there? This risk assessment had to be done quickly and unlike more established NPS properties, encouraging tourists to take this option was a temporary expedient.

The trail wound through the rocky hills (Figure 14.6). Like much of the West, it seemed vaguely familiar from numerous films. Arid and difficult, it was conversely attractive and comforting. For the Frost children, however, it was not a landscape about cowboys or films; it was a place rich in fossils. Along the trail, small fossils, particularly shells, were in abundance. Stops were frequent, but driving us on was the X on the map.

Climbing higher on a narrow rock ledge, we reached our goal. In the rockface at chest height was the thigh bone of a stegasaurus (Figure 14.7). It was two metres long. In most museums, dinosaur fossils are small and it is often hard to imagine where they fit. Museums have large reconstructions, but the visitor knows they are made of plaster and wire. Here, outside of a museum, in a rocky desert with no other person seen since leaving the car park, was a real fossil much larger than we had ever imagined.

This experience was an interesting counterpoint to our visit to the Museum of the Rockies. Both were equally exciting and profound, peak experiences for those interested in dinosaurs. The Museum of the Rockies was exceptionally curated, a world-class exemplar of Tilden's principles of interpretation. Dinosaur National Monument gained its impact from being authentically in a spectacular wilderness. Like the Grand Canyon, Yellowstone and Monument Valley, it was one of the great wonders of nature in the West, that had to be visited and experienced.

Figure 14.6 Walking trail through Dinosaur National Monument (photo W. Frost).

Figure 14.7 Fossil of a stegasaurus thigh bone (photo S. Frost).

15 Las Cruces Spaceport

> Space, the final frontier. These are the voyages of the starship Enterprise. Its 5-year mission: to explore strange new worlds, to seek out new life and new civilisations, to boldly go where no man has gone before.
>
> (Captain Kirk, played by William Shatner, opening narration of *Star Trek*, 1966–1969)

Introduction

The West is closely associated with another frontier – that of *outer space*. It is the site for a range of installations that have now become tourist attractions. New Mexico, for example, juxtaposes a cowboy heritage with a reputation as the space capital of America. It contains the Very Large Array and White Sands National Monument. The planned spaceport at Las Cruces will facilitate the growth of space tourism, such as Richard Branson's Virgin Galactic packages, although the recent crash during a test-flight of the vehicles may make potential tourists think more soberly about these experiences. In addition, Roswell in New Mexico is famous for its links with UFOs, commemorated in its annual festival and UFO museum. Yet the connection between outer space and the West goes beyond this.

We also consider in this chapter how the Western myth has often helped to shape or feed into the science fiction genre, with examples including *Lost in Space*, *Star Trek*, *Star Wars* and the most recent and overt hyper-reality of *Cowboys and Aliens*. This is part of the paradox of the West – while it is intrinsically linked to America, it can be applied to other frontiers and provides a familiar underpinning to stories of hardship, exploration and adventure.

Space: the final frontier

The 'discovery of new territory' is one of the 'long-enduring story lines or tropes' (Adler 1989: 1375) and underpins our fascination with frontiers. They are 'places of possibility, an open future, and uncertain outcomes' (Hains 2002: 5). Turner (1962 [1893]: 3) saw the frontier in its geographical context as 'the hither edge of free land' but also in social terms as 'the outer edge of the wave ... the meeting point between savagery and civilization'. He further characterised the American frontier as an example of boundless opportunity before pronouncing it *closed* in the sense of a historical movement and as a metaphor for what Simpson (1999: 130) calls 'the drying up of the wellspring of American values and culture'. By contrast, MacCannell (1999: 186) points out the tourist frontier is symbolically eternal, in that 'the tourists themselves believe that [the frontier] has no end, that there is always some new frontier'.

Our perception of what constitutes a travel frontier has necessarily expanded over recent years, as human beings push into previously exotic and remote locations, 'in what would [once] have been thought of as the unlikeliest of places' (Urry 2002: 142). As the frontiers of this world contract due to the pressure of population and development, the space frontier takes on greater significance, as perhaps the last testing ground for virtues such as self-reliance and initiative (Belk and Costa 1998; Terrie 1990). Comparisons are thus often made between space exploration and the opening up of the West. There are the same wide open spaces, which are undeveloped and wild. Astronaut Michael Collins, one of three men on the historic Apollo 11 flight, refers to space as 'the only physical frontier we have left' (Collins 1974: 467), and former US President George H.W. Bush declared in 1990, when announcing initiatives related to space exploration: 'And just as Jefferson sent Lewis and Clark to open the continent, our commitment to the Moon/Mars initiative will open the Universe'.

Not all proponents of space exploration and travel however agree with the analogy between space and a frontier, with Kim Stanley Robinson, author of the best-selling *Mars Trilogy*, describing it as 'false advertising' (Berinstein 2002: 9), due to the fact that human beings need artificial crutches such as spacecraft and supplies of oxygen before they can explore space on their own, preventing true independent existence. Others criticise the frontier concept as an American construct, with negative connotations of dominance, conquest or imperialism (Berinstein 2002; Husbands 1981). The fact that there are no permanent colonies in space is another argument used by Robinson for not regarding it as a frontier, although it may only be a matter of time before this is a reality (Laing and Frost 2014).

The space Western

The crossover between narratives about outer space and the American West and prevalence of intertextuality is not a recent phenomenon. According to Pfitzer (1995):

> The connections between western 'flight' and aeronautic 'flight' had already been anticipated by dime novelists, some of whom found it easy enough to transform western cowboys into space cowboys, high-noon gunfights into celestial shootouts, and frontier expansion into the politics of space ownership on the high frontier.

Even earlier, is Edgar Rice Burroughs' novel *A Princess of Mars* (1917), recently made into the film *John Carter* (2012). The hero is an American Civil War veteran who is prospecting for gold in Arizona and trying to hide from the Apache, when he is transported to the planet Mars. Burroughs had been stationed in Arizona as a soldier, and was a great fan of Wister's *The Virginian* (1902). He brings many of the familiar elements of the Western to his story of warlike tribes on Mars, with John Carter musing that some of the Martians resembled 'a band of the red Indians of my own Earth'. Director George Lucas was a keen fan of the John Carter books (Gordon 1978) and like Burroughs, incorporates an amalgam of space and Western frontier mythology in his *Star Wars* series of films.

The *Star Trek* series has similarly been noted for its frontier themes, which are 'linked to westward expansion and Manifest Destiny' (Geraghty 2005: 192). Its founder Gene Rodenberry described it as 'Wagon Train to the stars' (Curtis 1980: 599), referencing the television series (1957–1965), characterised by different plots and guest stars each week. Like *Star Wars*, it has a dedicated and sometimes obsessive fan base (Kozinets 2001; Shefrin 2004), and thus enjoys a great deal of cultural power as a result (Geraghty 2005), reinforcing myths about American society and presenting them to a new generation/audience. The plots were often based on the *American monomyth* – that version of Campbell's hero journey that has been particularly associated with the Western (Geraghty 2005; Jewett and Lawrence 1977). It involves a hero who comes to a community that is threatened by evil and is the only one who can defeat this and restore order. Once the community has been saved from this calamity, the hero can no longer remain and must continue their journey. This is the plot of *Shane* and *The Searchers*.

Moon Zero Two (1969) was billed as the first Moon Western, and features a futuristic tourist industry which handles regular flights to the Moon and Mars, and a permanent presence on the Moon, complete with a saloon bar. Mining is one of the local industries, like many a Western town. The tourist as the Other is a theme running through the film, extending to the local population as well as temporary visitors. 'We are all foreigners here. Perhaps we should never have come' says Captain Kemp (James Olson). The landscape is majestic, but forbidding, rather like the Western frontier ('I suppose bleak is as good a way to describe it'). A few years later, the film *Westworld* (1973) showed tourists in a Western theme park of the future being attacked when the gunslinger robot runs amok (Yul Brynner, wearing his all-black outfit from *The Magnificent Seven*). There are also many Western references in the long-running television series *Doctor Who*, including the recent episode 'A Town Called Mercy' (2012), set in the nineteenth-century American West but filmed in Spain, where a cyborg gunslinger wearing a Stetson is hunting down an alien who is hiding in the town jail.

It was also inevitable that children's television would build on these links in the 1950s and 1960s, given the interest in both space and cowboys. In *Lost in Space* (1965–1968), the Robinson family meet an astronaut called Jimmy Hapgood (Warren Oates) in the episode titled 'Welcome Stranger' (1965). A regular in Peckinpah Westerns, Oates talks like an old-timer, with comments like 'You're as lost as a wood tick on a bald mountain'. In a subsequent episode, 'West of Mars'

(1966), Doctor Smith meets his evil doppelganger, an outlaw clad in black called Zeno. The doppelganger was also a familiar device used in *Star Trek* to highlight 'human duality' (Geraghty 2005: 194). There is even a sheriff character, known as the enforcer, who is hunting him down. It is no coincidence that the two main characters in the animated film *Toy Story* (1995) are a cowboy doll, Woody (Tom Hanks), and an astronaut doll, Buzz Lightyear (Tim Allen).

Probably the most obvious example of the blurring between the sci-fi movie and the American West is the iconic *Star Wars* (1977), which was always intended by its director, George Lucas, to be a space Western. It can best be understood as a pastiche which borrows from and weaves together a number of myths and genres, including the Arthurian legend, fairytales, the hero's journey and the Saturday afternoon matinee (Collins 1977; Gordon 1978). Roth (1985: 184) labels this *cultural vraisemblance*, where a film corresponds 'to collectively held conceptions of the world' and common experiences or backgrounds.

Andrew Fenady, who produced *Chisum* (1970), was clear about the role that movies such as *Star Wars* played in the wake of the demise of the Western: 'The Western got absorbed. *Star Wars* was like a Borden Chase western, with two uneasy friends, except with rockets and spaceships instead of horses and wagons. Setting it in space worked' (quoted in Eyman 2014: 569). It was a commercial hit and spawned a number of sequels as well as prequels (Shefrin 2004). Interestingly, in the early twenty-first century, both genres are thriving and popular, and can even be overtly juxtaposed, illustrated by *Cowboys and Aliens* (2011).

Star Wars (1977)

Star Wars has been described both as a *space opera* and a *space Western*. There is a formula at play – boy rescues girl from peril and defeats the villain, saving the day (Gordon, 1978). Luke Skywalker (Mark Hamill) is a young farmboy who lives with his aunt and uncle on the planet Tatooine. The farm might easily be 'a Kansas homestead in the 1800s' (Collins 1977: 6) and the focus on making the desert bloom is reminiscent of the myth of the American frontier as a Garden of Eden. Luke dreams of becoming a space pilot and living a more adventure-filled life. His fantasy comes true, but not perhaps in the way he wished for. Luke comes home to discover his farm on fire and his aunt and uncle murdered. It is a scene reminiscent of Ethan and Marty discovering the aftermath of the Comanche raid in *The Searchers* (Gordon 1978; Roth 1985).

Imperial forces are to blame, but they have made it look like the work of the Sand people. Obi Wan Kenobi (Alec Guinness), a Jedi knight, can tell this raid has been staged, as he knows that it does not carry the traditional hallmarks of the Sand people. This type of subterfuge is often utilised in Western films, where Native Americans are blamed for crimes which they did not commit, as a way to spread unrest or encourage counter-attacks. Like many a Western hero, Luke seeks to avenge the death of his family (Collins 1977). The irony, of course, is that the mastermind behind the massacre is Luke's *father* – Darth Vader.

Luke and Obi Wan meet up with Han Solo (Harrison Ford) in the Cantina, a space saloon. They are trying to catch a ride on his spaceship, the Millennium Falcon. As Roth (1985: 181) observes, 'the saloon is the locus of evil' in the Western and often a place of temptation. The Cantina is crammed full of sinister types and the bartender tells Skywalker 'We don't serve those types in here', indicating the droids, C3PO and R2D2. Skywalker is drinking at the bar, minding his own business, when an alien picks a fight with him, boasting: 'We're wanted men. I have the death sentence on twelve systems'. When he refuses to back down, Obi Wan powers up his light sabre and slices off the alien's arm. Solo is the equivalent of the gunslinger who is quick on the draw, taking everyone by surprise. Obi Wan later fights with Darth Vader, a version of the gunfight with lasers, and the showdown finishes with Obi Wan's death. It is left to Luke to seek revenge, cutting off Darth Vader's hand in *Return of the Jedi* (1983).

Solo wears a vest, reminiscent of a cowboy, and carries his laser gun in a holster, using it 'with all the skill of Wyatt Earp in a number of shoot-outs' (Collins 1977: 6). He has a sidekick, Chewbacca, a furry Wookie, a creature which Lucas described in an interview in *Rolling Stone* magazine in 1977 as 'like the Indians ... like noble savages' (Gordon 1978: 318). He is the hired gun, who snarls at Princess Leia (Carrie Fisher): 'I expect to be well paid. I'm in it for the money'. Leia is feisty and can use a gun, like a space-age Calamity Jane (Collins 1977). There are those who are paid to kill Solo, with Greedo, Jabba the Hutt's henchman, telling Solo: 'Jabba put a price on your head so large, every bounty hunter will be looking for you'. After a fight in the Cantina, a space saloon, ending in Greedo's murder, Solo slings the bartender a coin, with the comment: 'Sorry about the mess'.

Star Wars generally adopts the Western convention that the heroes (Luke Skywalker, Princess Leia) wear white and the villains/outlaws (Darth Vader) wear black (Curtis 1980; Tiffin 1999), although the Imperial storm-troopers are a contradiction in their white uniforms. This perhaps acknowledges the less clear-cut distinction between good and evil seen in Adult Westerns, such as *Shane* and the fact that there are examples of the genre where the nexus between the colour of clothing and morality is reversed (e.g. *Johnny Guitar*). Han Solo wears a mixture of colours, reflecting his ambiguous status as both hero and anti-hero.

Space Cowboys (2000)

If John Wayne had still been alive at the turn of the twenty-first century, this might have been a film designed for him. Four ageing pilots, Frank (Clint Eastwood), Hawk (Tommy Lee Jones), Jerry (Donald Sutherland) and Tank (James Garner) are asked to go into space to fix a satellite which they designed 40 years earlier. It is going off course and may crash into Earth. The men had been trained as astronauts but never made it into space. When they reach the satellite, they find out the truth – it is armed with nuclear missiles. One of the astronauts,

Hawk, who is dying from cancer, volunteers for a suicide mission – pushing the satellite manually away from Earth and aiming it at the Moon. The film uses the well-known trope of the rescue of Earth and the human race from impending nuclear doom.

Three of the four lead actors were heavily identified with the American West. Eastwood was the star of a number of iconic Westerns and had won an Oscar for *Unforgiven* (1992). Garner was Bret Maverick in the television series *Maverick* (1957–1962) and had played Wyatt Earp in *Hour of the Gun* (1967). Tommy Lee Jones' work includes *Lonesome Dove* (1989), *No Country for Old Men* (2007) and *The Homesman* (2014). While Canadian Sutherland had appeared in a Western – *Dan Candy's Law* (1974) – he was better known for Second World War caper films, such as *The Dirty Dozen* (1967) and *Kelly's Heroes* (1970). He had originally been offered the role of Wyatt Earp in the episode of *Doctor Who* titled 'The Gunfighters' in 1966, which was subsequently played by John Alderson.

The cowboy associations of these would-be astronauts reflect the image set by the original Project Mercury astronauts in 1959. All hailed from small-town America (Schefter 1999) and four were born in the West – Gus Grissom in Mitchell, Indiana, Scott Carpenter in Boulder, Colorado, Gordon Cooper in Shawnee, Oklahoma and Deke Slayton in Sparta, Wisconsin. Profiles in *Life* magazine and their own achievements fed the heroic myth of the test pilot turned astronaut, personified in Tom Wolfe's *The Right Stuff* (1959).

Cowboys and Aliens (2011)

Stories of alien abduction in the twentieth and twenty-first centuries have been likened to captivity narratives involving Native Americans in the nineteenth century. Sturma (2002: 318) observes that 'Although captive narratives have been most evident in the United States, they appear to be a common feature of many frontier communities' and tap into primal fears associated with the Other. Alien abduction accounts often refer to some sort of examination and punishment, which is consistent with captivity narratives (see Slotkin 1973). Both can be seen as a manifestation of deeper anxieties involving safety and identity (Sturma 2002). The plot of *Cowboys and Aliens* plays on this anxiety, with human victims grabbed by long tentacles dangled from a spaceship, like a cow being lassooed on the prairie, before being experimented on.

The film was based on a 2006 graphic novel of the same name; an example of the modern predilection for mash-ups across genres such as Jane Austen and zombies. Like many current-day Westerns (*Paul, Brokeback Mountain, Silverado*), it was largely filmed in New Mexico, notably around Abiquiu, where artist Georgia O'Keeffe had her ranch, and the expansive skies and rugged mesas and buttes form an impressive backdrop for the special effects. A number of tourist maps have been created of New Mexico filming locations (www.new-mexico.org/true-film/), as well as a Film Trails brochure created by the New Mexico Tourism Department.

The action takes place in the town of Absolution, a gold mining town dominated by wealthy rancher Colonel Dolarhyde (Harrison Ford). The aliens also want the gold to power their technology, which is a convenient but not very plausible plot device. This is an old-fashioned fight over resources. Jake Lonergan (Daniel Craig), an outlaw, helps to rescue the abducted townsfolk and in doing so is redeemed. Sheriff Taggart (Keith Carradine) allows him to leave town. Like *Shane*, Jake cannot stay in a place where his past will return to haunt him.

Roswell

It is a drive of 135 kilometres from Fort Sumner to Roswell and there are no towns in between, only a treeless rolling prairie to the west of the Pecos River. Every now and again, there are gates for various ranches, though no buildings can be seen. It is a powerful and evocative landscape, highly attractive through its desolation. Entering Roswell, the contrast to Fort Sumner is striking. Whereas the latter seems in decline, Roswell is booming and the outskirts are marked by new hotels, shopping malls and restaurants. This is a tourist destination that is blossoming. The cause is visible downtown. Whereas many Western towns have countered the decline of the main street through the creation of historic precincts, Roswell's is dominated by 1950s architecture. It is a tourism zone, but the theme is not cowboys and outlaws, but rather aliens and UFOs. The connection between Roswell and outer space possibly led to it being chosen by the Red Bull team in 2012 as the site for hosting Felix Baumgartner's 24-mile jump from a balloon (Laing and Frost 2014). The publicity however emphasised Roswell's moderate climate, possibly nervous about making the link too overt.

The UFO story is told in the Roswell UFO Museum and Research Center. Housed in a former art deco cinema, it is the centre of tourist activity (Figure 15.1). In 1947, the local newspaper reported a US military press release that a UFO had crashed outside of town (Figure 15.2). Within a day, the story had been retracted. It was not a UFO, the military stated, but rather a weather balloon that had crashed and been misidentified. Nonetheless, the story refused to go away. Ongoing allegations of a cover-up became part of popular culture folklore.

In 1996, a small festival themed on UFOs was held. Attracting only about 1,000 people, it was conceived as a rehearsal of a bigger event to commemorate the fiftieth anniversary. It was that event that grabbed global attention, pulling in 450 journalists who wrote over 1,000 articles. Attendance was around 50,000 people, equivalent to the size of the town (Paradis 2002). The combination of films, television and a festival boosted Roswell's tourism industry. Rather than being a fairly nondescript medium sized town, it became an internationally recognised brand.

In his excellent study of the festival and its impacts, Paradis argued that 'the newly discovered UFO theme became an important component not just of Roswell's local economy, but of the entire state of New Mexico.... By 1999 the UFO theme had invaded nearly all promotional materials and informational products' (2002: 34). Like Tombstone (Chapter 5) and Lone Pine (Chapter 8), Roswell has achieved tourism success through complementary developments of

Figure 15.1 Exterior of Roswell UFO Museum (photo W. Frost).

Figure 15.2 Replica newspaper used for *Roswell*, Roswell UFO Museum (photo W. Frost).

a festival and museums. The contrast with nearby Fort Sumner (Chapter 6) and its lack of success is striking.

The Roswell UFO Museum is compact, well laid-out and curated. Near the entrance are a series of interpretive displays tracing the story of the crash. Government denials of a conspiracy are featured and heavily critiqued. It is well done, with an emphasis on witness statements and an avoidance of heavy-handed preachiness. Towards the back of the museum there are a number of dioramas and illustrations of what the crash site may have looked like. Pride of place goes to a full size mock-up of a flying saucer and aliens (Figure 15.3). At regular intervals light flash, smoke bellows and the animatronic beings move. As this occurs, visitors cluster around taking photographs.

In the second half of the museum, the emphasis is more on popular culture interpretations of the story. The largest exhibit is of the alien autopsy scene from the television movie *Roswell* (1994), utilising various props donated by that film's producers. Outside, the surrounding shops and cafés also heavily feature a similar interpretation. Images of slender green men with large eyes and no ears are everywhere, particularly dominating a wide array of souvenirs. Not to be outdone, the local McDonald's is in the shape of a flying saucer (Figure 15.4).

In a park just next to the McDonald's sits a statue that provides a different vision of Roswell's cultural heritage. Dedicated in 1999, it is of cattleman John S. Chisum (Figure 15.5). Closely linked with Billy the Kid, he has been portrayed in films as both hero (*Chisum*, 1970) and villain (*Pat Garrett and Billy the Kid*,

Figure 15.3 Life-sized model of UFO and aliens, Roswell UFO Museum (photo W. Frost).

Figure 15.4 Roswell McDonald's takes on the appearance of a flying saucer (photo W. Frost).

Figure 15.5 Statue of John Chisum, Roswell (photo W. Frost).

1973). As Paradis (2002) found, there are many locals who are not happy with the emphasis on UFOs. Their view is that Roswell should focus on its cowboy past. The statue of Chisum recognises this, though he is greatly outnumbered by alien representations.

In the 1990s, Roswell became a hot story in film and television. This included the films *Independence Day* (1996) and *Men in Black* (1997) and the television productions *Roswell* (1994), *Roswell High* (1999–2002) and *Taken* (2002). Filmed but not set in New Mexico, *Paul* (2011) also references the *Roswell Incident* and thus illustrates the ongoing fascination with UFOs and aliens, albeit depicted in a humorous way. It was released the same year as *Cowboys and Aliens* (2011), another spoof on the West as a point of contact with outer space.

Paul (2011)

Graeme (Simon Pegg) and Clive (Nick Frost) are two English geeks in heaven at Comic Con in San Diego, complete with Princess Leia wannabees. They are about to head off on a road trip of 'America's most famous UFO hotspots'. This film is thus a male *buddy* movie, as well as a road movie (see Chapter 4). Graeme and Clive tell the waiter delivering their room service at their hotel all about their itinerary: 'We're going to Area 51 and the Black Mailbox in Nevada, then down to Camp Verde, then to Apache Junction and then on down to Roswell, New Mexico, for the site of the famous crash of '47'. Clive pipes up 'Stop it! It's an alleged site!' to which Graeme replies: 'Why would they admit there was a crash if the crash happened somewhere else?' When the waiter looks bemused, Graeme asks: 'Do you believe in aliens?' The Hispanic looking waiter becomes anxious: 'What do you mean "aliens"?' Clive and Graeme quickly change the subject. Of course, Clive and Graeme are also aliens. As urban Englishmen, they wander through a foreign world, generating suspicion and hostility from the locals.

Their first stop in their RV is Area 51, Nevada, where they pose beside an alien-themed motel and diner. Their waitress is Jane Lynch (Coach Sue Sylvester from *Glee*) and she makes sure they get their 'Aliens on Board' sticker as they leave. At the Black Mailbox, a car passes them and crashes off the side of the road. This is supposed to be an area well known for UFO sightings and the road that leads there (State Route 375) was renamed the Extraterrestrial Highway by the state of Nevada in 1996. The mailbox marks the road towards Area 51, a US Air Force facility which is the subject of conspiracies and rumours about secret military projects. Paul, a CGI alien (Seth Rogen), emerges from the car. He looks like the stereotypical bug-eyed, large-domed alien, and explains this later as deliberate, saying that human beings have been 'drip fed images of my face' over 60 years, so that they won't go to pieces when faced with the real thing. He needs Clive and Graeme's help to escape the clutches of the government, and they take him along, with Graeme removing the 'Alien on Board' sticker.

The film is essentially made for a fan audience, with popular culture references and clues littered throughout, which the dedicated space nerd will instantly understand. For example, the boss of the government goons chasing them is revealed to be Sigourney Weaver, Ripley from *Alien* (1979). When they enter a bar, the country and western band is playing the theme music used in the Cantina scene from *Star Wars*. Steven Spielberg is referenced by Paul when he mentions a phone call to assist the director with the development of *E.T: The Extra-Terrestrial* (1982). The other subtle homage to Spielberg occurs when Paul is taken to a small town and the local movie theatre is showing *Duel*, his 1971 movie about a road trip from hell, as well as *Easy Rider* (1969).

The final scene where Paul is rescued by a spacecraft was filmed at the Devils Tower in Wyoming, which was famously used in *Close Encounters of the Third Kind* (1977). It is a popular destination for fans of that film (Riley *et al.* 1998) as well as a magnet for climbers, although there have been concerns raised by Native Americans about the cultural sensitivities of using a sacred site for climbing, leading the National Park Service to place a voluntary ban on climbing for the month of June each year in its Climbing Management Plan (Dustin *et al.* 2002). This has resulted in an average 85 per cent reduction in climbing for that month (NPS 2013).

New Mexico: the space capital of America

The US space industry has its roots in the development of rockets and nuclear capability during the Second World War (Schefter 1999), much of which took place at White Sands, New Mexico. White Sands, with its snow-white dunes composed of gypsum, has been a national monument since 1933. The monument is surrounded by areas that have been used for military operations such as White Sands Missile Range, taking advantage of the vast expanses and lack of development.

Trinity Site on the White Sands Missile Range (Figure 15.6) marks the place where the first nuclear weapon was tested in 1945. This landmark is now only open to the public once a year. The Americans took the German V-2 rocket technology (Figure 15.7) and the expertise of their scientists such as Wernher von Braun and developed the Redstone missile and later the multistage Jupiter rocket. The aim behind some of this development was to beat the Soviet Union into space (Schefter 1999). The Soviets won that race, with the Sputnik satellite and later the first human being in space, Yuri Gagarin, but ceded to the United States in sending the first human being to the Moon.

White Sands was also used for astronaut training in landing the Space Shuttle (Figure 15.8) and was one of the designated Shuttle landing sites, when a scheduled landing at Cape Canaveral was deemed too dangerous. There is a free on-site Museum which covers the history of White Sands, along with an outdoor missile park (Figure 15.9), showing examples of rockets that were fired and tested at the facility.

New Mexico is also known for its radio telescopes and observatories, such as the Very Large Array (Figure 15.10), which is a series of 27 radio antennas or dishes spread out across the desert near Socorro. This facility was used in the film *Contact* (1997). Based on a book of the same name by Carl Sagan, it features a scientist, Dr Ellie Arroway (Jodie Foster) who receives messages from space and interacts with aliens. This character was said to have been based on

Figure 15.6 Visitors to Trinity Site memorial, White Sands, New Mexico (photo J. Laing).

the real-life female scientist Dr Jill Tarter, who researches in the area of SETI –
the search for extra-terrestrial intelligence – looking for evidence of activities by
intelligent life such as 'large-scale astroengineering projects, generation/harness-
ing of power, interstellar/interplanetary travels, wars [and] information
exchange' (Tarter 2004: 398). It should be noted however that the Very Large
Array has never been used for SETI experiments.

Spaceport America

A focus for future space tourism in New Mexico will be the town of Las Cruces,
the site of Spaceport America. Visitors to the region can take a bus tour of the
site (Spaceport America 2013). According to Christine Anderson, the head of
the New Mexico Spaceport Authority, space tourists will eventually depart on
sub-orbital flights from the facility, and current activities taking place include
various launches and rocket tests, as well as photo shoots and movie promotions.
Las Cruces has a strong Hispanic heritage, with Old Mesilla an attraction for
visitors. The state of New Mexico however is hoping that space tourism will be
the primary attraction to the region, as evidenced by its decision in 2006 to fund
'the world's first purpose built spaceport' (Spaceport America 2014a). Much of
this was premised on the presence of Virgin Galactic and its WhiteKnightTwo

Figure 15.7 V-2 rocket launch site, White Sands, New Mexico (photo J. Laing).

Figure 15.8 Shuttle Training Aircraft, White Sands, New Mexico (photo J. Laing).

and SpaceShipTwo, with the company 'pledging to pay over $50 million in rent over a 20 year period and generating over $200 million in revenue from passenger flights' (Spaceport America 2014a). Recent tragic events however will push flights on these vehicles further into the future, as a recent press release makes brutally clear:

> The scramble to get everything ready for the launch of the world's first commercial flights from Spaceport America came to a screeching halt nearly a month ago when Virgin Galactic's spaceship broke up over the California desert during a test flight. There was heartbreak, but now the New Mexico Spaceport Authority is scrambling again. This time, the focus is on drawing more tenants to the nearly quarter-billion-dollar spaceport and maintaining support among state lawmakers.
>
> (Spaceport America 2014b)

Virgin Galactic has been the most high-profile member of the space tourism industry to date, thanks to its charismatic CEO, Sir Richard Branson, and the publicity surrounding the celebrity guests who had bought a ticket into space with the company (Laing and Frost 2014). It was using the technology developed

Figure 15.9 Missile Park, White Sands, New Mexico (photo J. Laing).

Figure 15.10 Very Large Array, Socorro, New Mexico (photo J. Laing).

by Burt Rutan's Scaled Composites, which won the Ansari X-Prize, offered to the first non-government organisation that could fly three people into space and back (defined as 100 kilometres vertically from the surface of the Earth), with its *SpaceShip One* and an airborne launcher, the *White Knight*. With its 'anchor tenant' grounded for the foreseeable future, Spaceport America is looking to other companies such as Elon Musk's SpaceX, which is testing a reusable rocket at the site.

The crash of the Virgin Galactic test flight is a reminder of the nascent development of the industry and the risks attached to this type of tourism. The interest shown by the likes of Angelina Jolie and Brad Pitt in the venture should not cloud these facts. Space travel is not for the faint-hearted, making the parallels with travel throughout the American West even starker. Like all frontiers, there are dangers, which help to create authentic and visceral experiences and add to the appeal of the journey, but make the return perilous and uncertain.

16 Once upon a time

There are only two stories. A man goes on a journey or a stranger comes to town.

(attributed to Leo Tolstoy)

Introduction

In this concluding chapter, we consider two pairs of films. One pair is from the early 1950s and heralded the *Adult Western*, which became so popular in the period. The other pair are recent films, over 50 years later. These are indicative of how the mythology of the West is interpreted in our modern times. All may be seen as *game-changers*, being influential in altering how both audiences and other film-makers perceived the Western narrative. As throughout this book, our choices here are subjective. We present these four not as the best nor as our favourites, but rather as representative of changing perspectives and attempts to reinvent the Western to attract new audiences.

In considering these films, we return to some of the theories about film and media induced tourism that we considered in the opening chapter. In particular, we are interested in the ongoing debate regarding what it is about certain films that generates tourism flows. In the context of the Western, the destination is clearly a wide range of areas of the American West. However, this raises questions of the specificity of locations. Does a film draw tourists specifically to the landscape featured in a film? Or, is the landscape more generic? Is scenery even the prime motivator, or are issues of character, story and authenticity more important?

The 1950s and the Adult Western

The development of the Adult Western is usually explained as a reaction to the rapid spread of television. As cinema attendances fell, film-makers responded by adding adult themes and situations that could not be shown on television. This is, however, only part of the story. The Second World War had a strong influence on American society, changing tastes and attitudes. Actors and film-makers such as James Stewart, Sam Peckinpah, Sterling Hayden, Henry Fonda and Kirk Douglas had seen military service and it changed their outlooks. Contemporary issues such as the McCarthy witch-hunts, the Cold War and conflicts in Asia all had their influences and were often represented allegorically in these new Westerns.

Winchester '73 (1950)

This starts like a typical Jimmy Stewart film of the 1940s. He's Lin McAdams, a cowboy just arrived in Dodge City. As in *Mr Smith goes to Washington* (1939), *It's a Wonderful Life* (1946) and *Harvey* (1950), he talks slowly, is well meaning and perhaps a bit innocent. Coming to the aid of dance hall girl Lola (Shelley Winters), he tangles with the sheriff (Will Geer). To his horror, he realises that he's picked a fight with Wyatt Earp and quickly has to back down.

And then it all changes when he runs into Dutch Henry Brown (Stephen McNally) in a saloon. There's history between the two. Except that Wyatt Earp enforces a 'no guns in town' policy, they would immediately shoot it out. Earp muses on what could make two men hate each other so.

The story now digresses to the Winchester '73 rifle. An exceptional, one in a million weapon, it is the prize in a target shooting competition to celebrate the 1876 Centennial. Lin beats Dutch Henry for it, who then steals it off him. The film now follows the story of the rifle as it keeps changing hands. Prized for its perfection, it also functions as a curse. Those who gain it through wrongdoing will quickly die.

Dutch Henry loses it in a poker game to a gun-runner. Following the recent defeat of Custer, the Southern Cheyenne have gone on the warpath. Their chief, Little Bear (Rock Hudson) kills the gun-runner who has tried to cheat him. In turn, Little Bear is killed when he attacks a cavalry troop. One of the soldiers (Tony Curtis) finds the rifle on the battlefield. Knowing that it will be taken off him by an officer, he gives it to Steve, who is Lola's fiancé.

Steve has become involved in a plan to rob a bank in Tascosa. The leader of the outlaws is the notorious Waco Johnny Dean (Dan Duryea). Desiring both the rifle and Lola, he kills Steve. Steve's task was to recruit another top gun. That's Dutch Henry. And close on his trail is Lin. As the bank robbery plays out, Lin kills Waco Johnny and finally Dutch Henry.

This is *film noir* transferred to the West. Rather than the girl, it's the Winchester '73 that's the femme fatale that men lust after. Five of the characters that possess it are shot – the irony is that the perfect weapon provides them with no defence.

For James Stewart, *Winchester '73* was the opportunity to reinvent himself. Just turned 40, he was starting to get too old for his typical boyish roles. Furthermore, audience tastes were changing, moving away from light romantic comedies. Strategically, Stewart negotiated a two-picture deal. He would reprise his successful stage role in *Harvey*, but also undertake a Western. Audiences and the press were surprised. Stewart's small-town persona had been a standard in films since the 1930s. Up to this stage he had made 37 films. Only one – *Destry Rides Again* (1939) – was a Western and that was a comedy. *Winchester '73* not only placed Stewart in a different genre, but created a new persona. Outwardly he was still the same bemused slow-talking likeable character, but lurking just below the surface was an uncontrollable rage and desire for revenge. It was the perfect role to define a new type of hero for Adult Westerns (Eliot 2006; Kitses 2004).

Screenwriter Borden Chase noted with pleasure that in the previews there were sniggers and laughter when Stewart's name fronted the opening credits. All that changed as the action unfolded. When Stewart flies into a frenzy to beat up Waco Johnny Dean, there were gasps of horror from the audience. Chase knew they had a hit (Eliot 2006). Stewart would make four more movies with Anthony Mann. All were Westerns with strong *film noir* themes of revenge and violent heroes. *The Man From Laramie* (1955), for example, is pure *noir*. Stewart plays an undercover investigator trying to find out who staged a robbery. It could easily have been set in contemporary Los Angeles rather than nineteenth-century New Mexico. Stewart made 40 films from 1950 onwards. Eighteen, or nearly half were Westerns. As well as working with Mann, he made three with John Ford and he also utilised his new style in three classic pictures with Alfred Hitchcock.

Throughout this second career (and particularly in Westerns), Stewart played a different type of hero. Ambiguous and conflicted, his characters have a duality, an outward good-natured demeanour hiding an inner rage or secret. Furthermore, both heroes and villains share similar characteristics and personalities, making them difficult to distinguish (Loy 2004). Others quickly copied this new *Adult Western* hero. John Wayne in *The Searchers* (1956), Randolph Scott in *Ride Lonesome* (1958), Gary Cooper in *Man of the West* (1958) and Gregory Peck in *The Bravados* (1958) all epitomised these dark heroes on a quest. These were deeply psychological films, as Slotkin described them, they had a:

> Highly stylized *film noir* atmosphere with which the action is invested – deep shadows claustrophobic settings, and grim and hostile landscapes embodying a dim view of human nature and human possibilities ... the revenger Western gives us a landscape that mirrors the hero's introvert psychology. Often it is a desert landscape ... social authority and support are lacking; he must rely on himself, and perhaps one other person, for the fulfilment of his obsessive quest and/or redemption.
>
> (1992: 381–382)

Mann's use of scenery and location is interesting. The first act takes place in Dodge City. This was filmed on a set in Hollywood. It's deliberately both old-fashioned and suggestive of television. Indeed the interplay between naive Lin and paternalistic Wyatt Earp could have fitted perfectly into the standard half hour Western television episode of the period. Then, once Dodge City is left behind, all of that changes. Filmed on location in New Mexico, the scenery is open and authentic, whereas the Dodge City set was claustrophobic and fake. Lin's quest now involves a dangerous journey through magnificent country, tracking Dutch Henry to Tascosa. That town, which once had pretensions of being another Dodge City, has failed, with the railway instead running through nearby Amarillo. Whereas Dodge City was prosperous, Tascosa is represented as mean and decaying, a perfect setting for a *noir* Western.

The 400-kilometre journey from Dodge City to Tascosa is through a wasteland populated by dark and dangerous characters. On the one hand there are 'good people' – a recurring motif in Mann's work – Lin's friend High-Spade, the soldiers and Lola. However, they all have burdens or deficiencies which increase the danger. High-Spade tries to keep Lin sane, to redirect him back to a better life. He is the 'brother' that Lin has lost, but in being so loyal, he risks death. The soldiers are green troops, thrown against the Cheyenne with inadequate weaponary and training. Like Custer's troops, they look like being massacred. Lola is the *good* bad girl, wanting to settle down, she errs in hooking up with Steve. As a saloon girl, she attracts Waco Johnny Dean, who kills Steve to get her and the rifle.

Against them are a host of villains: the Cheyenne on the warpath, a mendacious gun-runner and two sets of outlaws. Lin must get past all of these obstacles on his journey to Tascosa. It is, symbolically, a last journey, likely to result in his death. Tascosa is dying, by the time this film was made it was seen as a ghost town. Lin is on a *katabasis*, a journey through the land of the dead. He ends his quest by killing his brother, Dutch Henry, but redeems himself by protecting his friends.

High Noon (1952)

Frank Miller has been released from prison. He has sworn to kill Marshall Will Kane who put him there five years ago. He is on the noon train to Hadleyville, where three of his gang wait to greet him. Meanwhile, Kane (Gary Cooper) has just married Amy Fowler (Grace Kelly). She is a Quaker. At her urging, he has agreed to retire as a lawman. The news that Miller is coming throws their wedding reception into a panic. Initially, he opts to flee, but then decides he must stay and fight. Otherwise, he reasons, he will always be looking over his shoulder and worrying about the vengeful outlaw.

Kane's wedding day quickly becomes a nightmare. Amy walks out on him. She became a Quaker after seeing her lawmen father and brother killed. She won't stay if he fights. She will catch the same train out that is bringing Miller in. Then Kane finds that his three best friends (Thomas Mitchell, Lon Chaney and Harry Morgan) all desert him. Likewise, the judge leaves town and his deputies quit. He faces Miller's gang alone. Rather than a main street showdown, there is running battle through streets and building, with the outnumbered Kane sniping at his enemies. When the gunfire starts, Amy returns and helps her husband – both are still dressed in their wedding outfits. With all the villains dead, Kane stares at the townspeople as they come out of their hiding places. Disgusted, he throws his marshall's badge into the dirt and rides away with Amy.

High Noon is a stylistic masterpiece. Its makers wanted a film that looked completely different to anything before. Opting for black and white, they chose a realistic documentary style. Minimal make-up was used. They wanted Cooper (just turned 50) to look old and haggard. The faces of the characters are shown in close-up, a technique that would be taken up and perfected by Sergio Leone. Everyone is dirty and sweating. Once the shooting starts, the town is represented as a claustrophobic wasteland, the tall buildings and narrow streets mimicking canyons. Kane keeps on the move, scared that he will be boxed in, the town-scape providing 'a sense of menace, of being unable to escape' (Calder 1974: 99). The viewer is reminded of the street-fighting of the Second World War, less than a decade earlier. The railroad, symbol of progress, is the harbinger of doom. Death comes not on a horse, but as a passenger on a train. Kane is often glancing at clocks, calculating that his time is running out. The train whistle signifies that it is high noon and time for the showdown. One key innovation is the use of a song throughout. 'Do Not Forsake Me Oh My Darling', sung by Tex Ritter, constantly reminds us of the two contrasting things going through Kane's mind. These are, first, that his wife has left him and, second, he does not want to live as a coward. That the townspeople will not support him is particularly shocking.

High Noon can be directly contrasted with *Abilene Town*, made only six years earlier. In that film, the marshall is Randolph Scott. He successfully recruits the farmers and storekeepers to help him chase off the troublemakers and accordingly he gets the girl and lives happily ever after. The film-makers of *High Noon* looked at that story and posed the question: what would happen if the marshall found that no support was forthcoming from his friends?

The casting was also a triumph. Like James Stewart, Cooper's popularity had been declining. He was looking to a Western for a boost in his career. Grace Kelly was at the beginning of her career, this was her first major role. The use of Thomas Mitchell was disconcerting. Normally, he was cast as a wise supporter of the hero. He had, for example, won the Oscar for Doc Boone in *Stagecoach*. It is a shock when Kane (and the audience) realise that he has deserted him. To put it into a modern context, it would be akin to having Morgan Freeman suddenly revealed to be the villain. Lee Van Cleef, in his first film, stands out as one of Miller's gang. He convinced director Fred Zinnemann that his character should have no dialogue. Even though he is silent, he steals every scene with his malevolent brooding presence.

Above all, *High Noon* is supremely effective as an allegory. Released at the height of the McCarthyist witch-hunts, it echoes writer Carl Foreman's personal story of being shunned by those he thought his friends. Accordingly, the citizens of Hadleyville represent those of the United States, moral cowards running from danger. The use of Westerns as vehicles for modern issues was not new. There was a history with Westerns of 'infusing its narratives with social/political sub-texts without alienating large groups of its potential audience' (Coyne 1997: 3). This subterfuge was aided by having Westerns set in the past, thus disguising their contemporary commentary. In this case, for many conservatives *High Noon* was too obvious. John Wayne, in particular, was highly critical and made *Rio Bravo* (1959) as a response.

However, *High Noon* is open to multiple interpretations depending on one's convictions (Costello 2005; Coyne 1997; Graham 1979; Hughes 2008).

Bill Clinton declared it his favourite film, 'a shrewd choice', both connecting him to a 'conservative heartland' that loved Westerns and emphasising his liberalism (Coyne 1997: 2). Gary Cooper was a noted conservative, so it was intriguing that he took the part and had no regrets. Countering the anti-McCarthyist interpretation, the film may also be seen as linking Kane to the United States, standing alone in the fight against communism, while its allies opt for isolationism (Graham 1979). Costello (2005) argues that there is a dichotomy between writer Foreman's allegory and the vision of the individual standing up for his convictions intended by Zinnemann and Cooper. Furthermore, Graham (1979) noted that the film was still extremely popular, even amongst viewers who have no knowledge of these 1950s issues. He argued that the appeal of the story is in a lone lawman at odds with a hypocritical or uncaring community. As such, this subtext has universal appeal and application. The longevity, appeal and influence of the film has been widely discussed (Costello 2005; Coyne 1997). Such is its place in popular culture, that it is notable in the high-rating television series *Big Bang Theory* (2007–), the romantic pairing is between a lanky Texan called Cooper (Jim Parsons) and Amy Fowler (Mayim Bialik).

Both films were released at a time when Americans were becoming more mobile and leisured. Post-war prosperity was epitomised by car holidays. Westerns provided a framework. This was matched by an interstate highway building programme championed by President Dwight Eisenhower, raised in Abilene and who as a young officer in the First World War had commanded a military convoy that drove across the United States. More a publicity stunt than a strategic necessity, this spearheaded a long campaign for improved road access in the West.

Part of each film was shot on Hollywood backlots. Some of these were starting to be opened up to what we now see as film-induced tourists. Anticipating Disneyland (1955), actor/stuntman Ray Corrigan opened Corriganville, just north of Los Angeles, in 1949 (Rothel 1991). His business plan was twofold. The Western sets and surrounding rocky countryside was available for hire for film and television productions, such as *Fort Apache* (1948) and *Rin Tin Tin* (1954–1959). Indeed, IMDb.com lists 355 productions for Corriganville. The other half of the operation was opening as a Western theme park, attracting at its peak 10,000–20,000 visitors per weekend (Rothel 1991).

A similar venture developed at Old Tucson in Arizona. Built in 1939 as a movie set, in 1959 it also opened as a theme park and for a long time was claimed as Arizona's second most visited tourist attraction behind the Grand Canyon (Rothel 1991). IMDb.com records 216 productions made here. *Winchester '73* used it for Tascosa. For the journey from Dodge City to Tascosa, the countryside around the Santa Rita Mountains south of Tucson was used and this area has remained popular with both tourists and film-makers.

Whilst *High Noon* was mainly filmed on backlots, some footage was shot in California's Central Valley. The original intention was to film near Gallup in New Mexico, but the budget could not afford this (Hughes 2008). Instead, the train footage was undertaken at Warnerville using the Sierra Railroad. At this time it was undertaking the transition from steam to diesel, but its operators realised that there was a revenue stream in keeping some rolling stock for hire to Hollywood. IMDb.com records 130 productions filmed at the Sierra Railroad. Today, it is operated by California State Parks as 1897 Railtown State Historic Park and provides steam-train rides and is still used for films (Frost 2008; Figure 16.1).

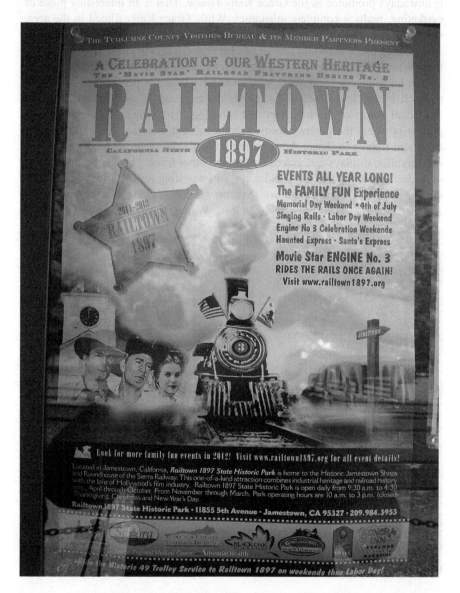

Figure 16.1 Sierra Railroad, used in *High Noon* and still operating as a tourist attraction (photo W. Frost).

Grace Kelly's role in *High Noon* still attracts tourist interest. While she was filming the railroad scenes, she stayed at the Sonora Hotel. Recently restored, the hotel operators have retained the suite she occupied, complete with 1950s style trappings. Nearby is Colombia State Historic Park. An old gold mining town, it was preserved and opened in 1945 as a living history museum. *High Noon* used it for one scene. This utilised the Wilson House (Figure 16.2), which is nowadays promoted as the Grace Kelly House. That is an interesting piece of marketing, really a complete misnomer. While Grace Kelly filmed in the area, she was not involved in the footage shot at Colombia. Instead it is Gary Cooper who goes to the house to try and recruit his friend Sam Fuller (Harry Morgan) to help. When Kane knocks on the door, Sam hides, refusing to answer.

The locations for *High Noon* raise interesting issues of perceptions of authenticity. It is not the landscape that draws the attention of modern-day fans, but individual sites tied to characters and sub-plots. The railway is integral to the plot. It is where the outlaws wait for Miller and it is where Amy changes her mind and returns for Kane. Visitors can still ride the steam locomotive and see memorabilia, displays and videos on this and other films. The nearby main street of Jamestown looks like the backlot set, an interesting reversal. DeLyser (1999) noted a similar effect at Bodie, with visitors seeing it as akin to a set and believing that movies were filmed here. Indeed, Warwick was told by a California

Figure 16.2 Wilson House, Columbia State Historic Park, incorrectly promoted as Grace Kelly's House (photo W. Frost).

State Parks official that Clint Eastwood made films there. It looks like the set for *Pale Rider* (1985) or *Unforgiven* (1992), but it was not. No films were made there. There is an interesting intertextuality at work. Hollywood sets were partly based on real towns and restored historic towns sometimes look like film sets.

The attention on Grace Kelly is particularly interesting. She is an exemplar of how some actors become a strong focus for fans, so that the *places of imagination* become associated with their personal life rather than films. Accordingly, the search for the authentic is linked to the person. This raises issues of *parasocial interaction* (Kim 2012); the fans want to be in places where Grace Kelly was. The operators of the Sonora Hotel react to this, promoting that this was not only where she stayed, but that her suite is available for hire. The invention of the Grace Kelly House is intriguing. Nowhere in the film is there any reference to where she lives. The Wilson House looks appropriate, it was used in the film, Grace Kelly was in the area filming; so it becomes easy to conflate all of this to provide a site attractive to tourists.

The twenty-first-century Western

At the beginning of the 1970s, interest in the Western began to rapidly wane. A range of reasons for this have been suggested, including the growth of science fiction and other genres, anti-war sentiment, growing urbanisation and urbanity and a decline in quality. The low point occurred in the 1980s. A revival came in the form of two films which won the best-picture Oscars, a rarity for Westerns even in the glory days of the 1950s and 1960s. These were *Dances with Wolves* (1990) and *Unforgiven* (1992). Since then Hollywood has returned to the Western. While not at anything like the levels of the past, a steady stream of Westerns continue to be successful.

With these modern Westerns, two key features are notable. The first is that they are conscious and respectful of previous Westerns. Their makers include references to past films, partly to claim authenticity and partly in recognition that their audiences are knowledgeable of the tropes and narratives of the Western. The second feature is that these new Westerns also take account of modern concerns, such as international conflicts, a declining US economy, the rise of fundamentalism and law and order issues. There is, of course, nothing new about this. Hollywood did the same in the 1930s, 1940s, 1950s and 1960s. The use of Western for allegory and modern reflection continues to be a constant.

Open Range (2003)

Boss Spearman (Robert Duvall) is an itinerant free grazer on the open range. Rancher Baxter (Michael Gambon) tries to chase him off and one of Spearman's outfit is killed and another badly wounded. Spearman and his offsider Charlie (Kevin Costner) come to town to have it out with Baxter and the corrupt marshall. It is a very simple plot. It is the common narrative of many Westerns, the hero fighting back against powerful interests that want to force him back. What counts here is the style, dialogue, characters and their relationships. As Howard Hawks observed of *El Dorado* (1967), 'no story ... just character' (quoted in Eyman 2014: 423).

Boss provides the moral centre. Straightforward, determined and with a strong sense of fairness, this is the sort of crusty role that John Wayne filled in films of the 1960s and 1970s. In contrast, Charlie is quieter and happy to play the secondary role. However, as the danger increases, it becomes clear that Charlie has a back-story. He is quick to anger and has nightmares. When they catch four cowboys sent to frighten them off, Charlie wants to kill them and Boss only calms him down with great difficulty. Finally, Charlie tells his story. Trained as a sharpshooter in the Civil War, he came West to be a hired gun. He quit ten years ago and has worked as a cowhand since. Here there are shades of *Shane* and the alternative story of Billy the Kid (see Chapters 6 and 7).

This is a story that dates back at least as far as Owen Wister's novel *The Virginian* (1902). On the frontier, a community is gradually growing, but is hampered by lawlessness. The hero – whether Charlie, the Virginian or numerous other examples – can use violence to rid the community of the threat. However, once violence is unleashed with rage and savagery (well exemplified in *Open Range*), how can the hero settle down within that now peaceful community? Such a paradox pre-dates the Western and can be seen throughout mythology (Campbell 1949), a heritage that many film-makers were well aware of.

Open Range reverses many of the conventions of previous Westerns. Unlike *High Noon*, the townspeople eventually decide that they too must make a stand and rid themselves of the corrupt marshall and hired guns. A romance develops between Charlie and Sue (Annette Bening). At first, he believes that she is the doctor's wife. Accordingly, the audience is privy to a developing illicit attraction, raising similarities with *Hondo* (where the hero kills the husband), *The Searchers* (the wife is killed) and *Shane* (the hero must leave). However, late in the film it is revealed that Charlie is mistaken, Sue is the doctor's sister. Now their love blossoms, but is darkened by the impending showdown. The common trope of Westerns is that she must try to convince Charlie not to fight (as in *The Virginian*, *High Noon* and *Gunfight at the OK Corral*). As Tompkins (1992) argues, this is a disturbing convention in Westerns. The hero must prove his masculinity by rejecting feminine notions of peace, tolerance and civilization.

Instead of following convention, *Open Range* chooses a different path. Sue does not try to stop Charlie, but reassures him of her support. This is symbolised by her giving him a locket with her photograph inside – recalling similar keepsakes for soldiers going off to the Civil War. That Sue and the townspeople support Boss and Charlie implies that they also share the responsibility for the gunfight. This allows the two cowboys the opportunity for redemption. Unlike so many other Westerns, the heroes will stay and settle down in this community.

Director Costner assumes that the audience are familiar with past Westerns. Murdoch argues that Western films are a *consistent fantasy* and that 'more than any other genre, the Western operates within conventions and these conventions are not the framework but the genre's essence' (2001: ix). Chief amongst these conventions, Murdoch argues, is conflict involving the lone hero. Costner certainly recognises this. While including new twists and interpretations, he fundamentally follows a familiar narrative. This is what John Ford did with *Stagecoach* in 1939 (see Chapter 1) and is likely to keep being repeated in the future.

The film is graced by spectacular scenery. The open range is rich and green, cut by broad rivers and framed by snow-capped mountains. It suggests Wyoming or Montana. However, it was not shot in the United States, but rather in Canada, specifically Alberta, in the Bow River Valley between Calgary and the Rockies. Similarly, recent Westerns such as *Unforgiven* (1992), *Shanghai Noon* (2000) and *The Assassination of Jesse James by the Coward Robert Ford* (2007) were also shot in Alberta. These are *runaway productions*, set in the United States, but filmed elsewhere for budgetary reasons (Frost 2009).

The most famous runaway productions were the Spaghetti Westerns of the 1960s and 1970s (see Chapter 2). These influenced others to try and duplicate the model. *The Drifting Avenger* (1968) was a Japanese production filmed in Tamworth Australia. It starred Ken Takakura, famous for the 1960s cult television series *The Samurai*. Appropriately, while dressed snappily as a gunslinger, he also wielded his samurai sword. A more recent example comes from New Zealand (and we thank Lloyd Carpenter of Lincoln University for bringing it to our attention). This is *Good for Nothing* (2011), promoted as a *Pavlova Western*. Its locations included Old West Town Mellonsfolly (a Western-themed attraction) and a mining site at Bannockburn suggestive of Monument Valley (Figure 16.3).

Figure 16.3 Bannockburn Sluicings Historic Reserve, used in the Pavlova Western *Good for Nothing* (photo W. Frost).

Canada first started attracting Western film productions with *McCabe & Mrs Miller* (1971). Much of this was filmed in a park on the outskirts of Vancouver. In the 1990s there was a big increase in television production based at Lions Gate Studios in Vancouver and this spilled over into cinema. In the case of British Columbia, its film office is housed within its tourist commission and there are certain synergies in attracting both tourists and film production companies. Apart from major films, Canada has also specialised in TV movie remakes of classics, such as *High Noon* (2000), *The Virginian* (2000) and *Angel and the Bad Man* (2009).

The big question is how does this *locational dissonance* affect tourism? If we look at examples of historical films like *Braveheart*, the evidence is that tourists flow to Scotland where it was set, rather than Ireland where it was filmed. Even though a Braveheart Trail has been constructed and marketed in County Wicklow, the small number of tourists it draws is well below Scotland (Frost 2009). The success of *Lord of the Rings* in encouraging tourism to New Zealand is qualified by those films being fantasy and Middle Earth being fictional. Accordingly, there is no alternative destination and so tourists are drawn to find authentic experiences where the film was shot (Buchmann *et al.* 2010; Butler 2011; Karl *et al.* 2007).

Does this apply to the West? There is a long history of using California as a cheap stand-in. This includes places like Lone Pine and Jamestown and the various studio ranches and backlots around Hollywood (Frost 2009; Rothel 1991). Sometimes this results in absurdity. For example, in *Montana* (1950), Errol Flynn attempts to explain his accent. Though born in Montana, he has grown up in Australia, but he has missed the rugged mountain scenery and has now decided to come home. All perfectly sensible. Except the film is not shot in Montana, there is no backdrop of towering mountains. Instead, it has been shot in the Central Valley, a region that looks a lot like Australia, complete with eucalyptus trees.

It is an area that requires further research, but it appears that tourists seek the places portrayed in Westerns rather than the locations where they were shot. There are, however, two exceptions. The first is those instances where tourist attractions have been developed, such as the Lone Pine Film History Museum, Old Tucson and the Sierra Railroad at Jamestown. The second is that some iconic landscapes have been used for a variety of locations, but the audience knows that such liberties are being taken. Monument Valley, often standing in for Texas or New Mexico, is a case in point.

Meek's Cutoff (2010)

On the Oregon Trail in 1845, three families decide to take a short cut. Their guide is the Mountain Man Meek (Bruce Greenwood). Gradually they realise that Meek is a garrulous blowhard who is lost. Their's has become a castaway narrative (Laing and Frost 2014). Shot around Burns in the remote south-eastern corner of Oregon, the landscape is arid, featureless and treeless. Caught in the rain shadow of the Cascade Mountains, these pioneers forlornly keep hoping for a glimpse of distant mountains to guide them.

They capture a lone Indian (Rod Rondeaux). Meek identifies him as a Paiute (though the closing credits state that he speaks Nez Perce). Emily (Michelle Williams) and her husband believe that the Indian can guide them towards water. Meek disagrees. The Indian could be leading them to safety, or they could be walking into a trap.

As with *Open Range*, it is a slight plot. There are shades of *Stagecoach*, with an array of different characters thrown together in a dangerous situation. An enigmatic ending provides no resolution. As a Western, this is a very different film. There is little action and no twists. As with *Once Upon a Time in the West*, it is a rare instance of a Western with a female lead. Even then, the blonde Williams is deglamorised, with brown hair and through much of the film her face is hidden under an enormous bonnet. Greenwood is similarly unrecognisable under a prodigious beard. Continuing the playing against type, though Rondeaux is one of the modern Western's top riders and stuntmen, here he is on foot.

What distinguishes this film is its look. The landscape dominates; endless and potentially menacing. Many scenes are without dialogue, as the pioneers trudge determinedly through the striking environment. Complementing this otherworldly backdrop, great attention has been paid to the authenticity of costume and equipment. The women nearly always keep their heads covered – and faces partly obscured – with enormous 1840s bonnets. Such distinctive visuals compensate for the lack of action and a resolution.

Some concluding remarks

It is now 75 years after *Stagecoach* and the 1939 boom in A Westerns. While we are not aware of any ceremonies to mark the anniversary, it is one that should be recognised and commemorated. Media – particularly, but not limited to, film – has created the myth of the West. As convincingly argued by some, that myth says something about the national pysche and identity of Americans (Murdoch 2001; Slotkin 1992). However, we also need to realise that the West is not just part of America's cultural heritage. Across the world, its imagery and narratives are beloved and consumed by many. There is something about the West that attracts and fascinates and that is just as strong in Germany, Britain, Australia or Thailand.

Indeed, it is striking that the West is transportable to other places and cultures. The filming of Spaghetti Westerns in Almeira, Spain has resulted in the development of attractions based on film sets. In Thailand, there are a range of Western-themed attractions and festivals, particularly based on Thai interest in dressing up as cowboys. This may be conceptualised as *conspicuous consumption*, developing in a period when jeans and other Western apparel were expensive (Cohen 2008). In New Orleans, Black *crews* parade wearing elaborate Native American costumes. For these Mardi Gras Indians, this combines *conspicuous display* with the construction of an identity that revels in being different

(Beeton 2015). In Lewes, England, the annual Guy Fawkes Night Parade features a similar appropriation of Native American costume. Watched by crowds of up to 50,000 spectators, the procession of the Commercial Square Bonfire Society features participants dressed in beaded buckskins, moccasins and elaborate feathered headdresses. Originating in the nineteenth century, this tradition is reputed to have been started by locals returning home after working on railroad construction in the West. Interestingly, this costuming is explained as recognition of the oppression of Native Americans (Sharpe 2005).

This outsider's view of the West is a feature that deserves further research. Apart from the interest of foreign tourists and audiences, it is noteworthy that many key players in Western films were born overseas. A number of actors famous for playing Indians, for example, were foreign-born and seemingly chosen for their Otherness. These included Henry Brandon (Germany), Michael Pate (Australia) and Iron Eyes Cody (Italy). Errol Flynn was an Australian. His regular co-star, Olivia De Havilland, was born in Japan of British parents. Robert Shaw, who also played Custer, was English. Yul Brynner was from Siberia. Glenn Ford was from Canada. So was director Allan Dwan. Maureen O'Hara was Irish. Dimitri Tiomkin, who composed the music for many Westerns and won two Oscars for *High Noon*, was from the Ukraine. Most tellingly, a range of directors were from overseas. These included Fred Zinnemann (Austria), Michael Curtiz (Hungary), Sergio Leone (Italy) and John Farrow (Australia). This involvement of outsiders suggests that the evolution of the Western myth has been influenced by more than a home-grown perspective.

A wide range of Western actors and directors were from the East. Regular villains Henry Silva, Eli Wallach and Jack Palance were city-dwellers who did not know how to ride horses or shoot pistols until they were cast in Westerns. John Ford was from Maine. Randolph Scott from North Carolina. Burt Lancaster, Kirk Douglas, Jack Nicholson, Lee Marvin and John Carradine were New Yorkers. Thomas Mitchell and Lee Van Cleef hailed from New Jersey. James Stewart came from Pennsylvania and Alan Hale from Washington, DC. Out of the mid-West came Howard Hawks, John Sturges, John Wayne, Roy Rogers, Dean Martin, Budd Boetticher, Steve McQueen, Paul Newman, Charlton Heston and Gail Russell. All of them came West searching for opportunities and became adept at providing the illusion that they were authentically Westerners. Director John Sturges, for example, was from Illinois, but justified the authenticity of his vision of Wyatt Earp in *Gunfight at the OK Corral*, by saying 'I'm a westerner myself' (quoted in Hughes 2008: 91).

When we started writing this book, we already had a strong interest in the West and had viewed a wide range of films. However, as we made progress, we slowly began to realise that some of our views were being challenged. In concluding, we want to highlight two areas that deserve further research if we are to better understand the dynamics and impacts of the Western myth.

The first is the role of women. Conventional thinking is that females were either ignored or marginalised in Westerns (Coyne 1997). That was what we expected to find. Instead, we have shifted towards the views of others

(Hausladen 2003; Howe 2005), that many Westerns portrayed women strongly and positively. What we see is a continuum of representation of their influence. In a few films like *Johnny Guitar, Meek's Cutoff* and those with Barbara Stanwyck or Jane Russell, the female character is the most important and dynamic. At the other end of the scale, there are some Westerns in which women are completely absent, for example *The Good, the Bad and the Ugly*. However, in the majority, women play an important role. In many cases they are matched against a strong man of few words, but who is also a repressed man who cannot articulate his feelings and emotions. The female role complements this, allowing a release or softening, even if this is only shown in a subtle way (Howe 2005). A few examples are worth noting: Gail Russell in *Angel and the Badman* and *Seven Men From Now*; Grace Kelly in *High Noon*; Jean Arthur in *Shane*; Angie Dickinson in *Rio Bravo* and Annette Bening in *Open Range*. It is also notable that in a smaller number of films, the female takes this role, but fails to transform the man. Examples of this are Rhonda Fleming in *Gunfight at the OK Corral*; Senta Berger in *Major Dundee* and Joan Hackett in *Will Penny*. While these are all secondary roles, these parts are integral to the plots of these movies.

Costuming is important in signifying the woman's role. In some cases the female lead wears working clothes, demonstrating that they are the ones who are making homes, farms and communities. Examples of this include Jean Arthur in *Shane*, Geraldine Page in *Hondo* and Michelle Williams in *Meek's Cutoff*. In contrast, there are female characters whose costume demonstrates different types of strength and resilience. Joan Crawford dresses like a man in *Johnny Guitar* and there are others in which the heroine on occasions dresses like a man, raising issues of gender confusion (Kelm 2009). In contrast, Jane Russell (*Montana Belle*), Rhonda Fleming (*Gunfight at the OK Corral*), Angie Dickinson (*Rio Bravo*) and Dana Delaney (*Tombstone*) wear rich, glamorous and provocative outfits. This latter grouping highlights the sexualisation of Western costumes, greatly in evidence in the modern West at events like Tombstone's Helldorado Days. Furthermore, male characters in Western films also sport colourful clothing, sometimes signifying that they are flash villains (Lee Marvin in *The Man Who Shot Liberty Valance*; Zachary Scott in *Colt .45*) and sometimes to claim higher status (as in the various Wyatt Earp films).

The second area of reconsideration is not so positive. As we viewed more and more films, we became increasingly despondent with the portrayal of Native Americans. The films of the 1940s and 1950s took two approaches to Native Americans. They were either a savage threat (as for example in *Stagecoach*), or there was a focus on attempts at peace. The latter film usually had a lone White hero attempting to prevent the Sioux or Apache going on the warpath. Pitted against the hero was a corrupt villain, usually an Indian agent. While these films had worthy intentions, the Native American chief was always played by a White actor, with dark make-up and a pidgin vocabulary. Such movies were often allegorical, highlighting either corruption or America's reluctant role as world policeman (Slotkin 1992).

It was not until the late 1960s that Native American actors became more prominent. Films like *Little Big Man* and *Dances with Wolves* were particularly successful with this approach, though they still had White leads in Dustin Hoffman and Kevin Costner respectively. Yet, despite audience engagement with these narratives, twenty-first century films have gone backwards. Very few recent Westerns have any references to Native Americans. Of those that do, Johnny Depp plays Tonto in *The Lone Ranger* (2013) and Maori actor Temeura Morrison plays an Apache in *Renegade* (2004).

What we found particularly surprising was how few Westerns feature Native Americans. This deficiency seemed consistent over the decades. Explanations are challenging. Barr (1996) argued that many films focussed on law and order in towns and had little place for Native Americans. He found that the *savage other* was represented by outlaws and corrupt officials, banks and railways. These were also the standard villains in many contemporary dramas. Utilising these conventions left little place for Native Americans. Such a view was echoed by Sergio Leone, who chose not to feature Native Americans in any of his films. He justified this by arguing that he was interested primarily in the outlaw and revenge dynamics (Frayling 2005).

And yet tourists are very interested in Native Americans. Particularly foreign tourists. Pitchford (2008) found very different patterns for visitors to Native American heritage centres. Whereas the average American stayed for about 45 minutes, German tourists were highly engaged, with some staying for two full days. For our study of explorer travellers (Laing and Frost 2014), we interviewed Jack (pseudonym), a German adventurer and film-maker. He told us of his childhood in Germany, where:

> My dad was always an Indian lover and a travel lover ... we had Wild West movies and the Indians always were the losers ... they were always the baddies and my dad was always on the other side, which I couldn't understand as a young boy ... it started like that, I think, I mean he implanted it in my system and so I was very interested, very thrilled about expeditions ... not with mountains and stuff like that, always with tribes.

Here we see a disconnection between movies and tourism. In films, Native Americans are marginalised and potentially this is becoming even more so in recent times. In contrast, tourism in the West often has a focus on Native Americans. Monument Valley, as detailed in Chapter 2, is a Navajo Tribal Park, successfully owned and operated by the local Navajo. For tourists, their guides at Monument Valley are Native Americans. Similarly, Grand Canyon West has been developed as a tourist attraction by the Hopi. While the Little Bighorn Battlefield is managed by the NPS, tourist services are provided at the park border by the Crow Agency Trading Post. And throughout the West, a multitude of stores provide Native American art, jewellery, clothing and souvenirs for tourists (Figure 16.4).

Figure 16.4 Native American themed clothing and souvenirs, Santa Fe (photo J. Laing).

The West is an instructive exemplar of a *place of the imagination* (Reijnders 2009, 2011). It exists in two realms: it is both a real place and one collectively constructed in our imaginations. It can be consumed in a cinema, at home on the television, even increasingly on one of a variety of mobile devices. And then, based on that engagement and consumption, it can be explored and experienced through travel.

The West is now a tourist zone. Indeed, it has been one for quite a long time (Pomeroy 1957). The economies of many states, towns and regions are based on tourism. As in many parts of the world, tourism has surpassed other industries in adding value, even though that might not always be acknowledged. The cowboy is an icon of the West, but there is much much more employment in tourism, hospitality and events than in the cattle industry. Las Vegas, Santa Fe and Denver stand out as tourist destinations. Lone Pine, Jamestown, Bisbee and Tombstone are much smaller, though tourism is just as important to their local economies.

Like all cultural heritage tourism, that of the West is heavily mediated. Though based on history, it is romanticised and fetishised. Through film and other media, the West remains a fascinating and attractive fairy tale, but it is a fairy tale that the fan can visit and experience.

References

Adler, J. (1989) 'Travel as performed art', *American Journal of Sociology*, 94(6), 1366–1391.

Bain, A. (2014) 'Road warriors: Our next great highway', *The Age*, 31 May, 19.

Bapis, E.M. (2006) '*Easy Rider* (1969): Landscaping the modern Western', in D.A. Carmichael (ed.), *The Landscape of Hollywood Westerns: Ecocriticism in an American Film Genre* (pp. 157–181), Salt Lake City: University of Utah Press.

Barr, C. (1996) 'Dodge City', in I. Cameron and D. Pye (eds), *The Book of Westerns* (pp. 181–188), New York: Continuum.

Basinger, J. (2007) *The Star Machine*, New York: Knopf.

Beeton, S. (2004) 'Rural tourism in Australia – has the gaze altered? Tracking rural images through film and tourism promotion', *International Journal of Tourism Research*, 6, 125–135.

Beeton, S. (2005) *Film-Induced Tourism*, Clevedon: Channel View.

Beeton, S. (2010) 'The advance of film tourism', *Tourism and Hospitality Planning & Development*, 7(1), 1–6.

Beeton, S. (2015) 'Mardi Gras Indians: Rituals of resistance and resilience in changing times', in J. Laing and W. Frost (eds), *Rituals and Traditional Events in a Modern World* (pp. 186–205), London and New York: Routledge.

Belk, R. and Costa, J.A. (1998) 'The mountain man myth: A contemporary consuming fantasy', *The Journal of Consumer Research*, 25(3), 218–240.

Berinstein, P. (2002) *Making Space Happen: Private Space Ventures and the Visionaries behind them*, Medford: Plexus Publishing.

Bignell, J. (1996) 'Method Westerns: *The Left-Handed Gun* and *One-Eyed Jacks*', in I. Cameron and D. Pye (eds), *The Book of Westerns* (pp. 99–110), New York: Continuum.

Blake, M.F. (2007) *Hollywood and the O.K. Corral*, Jefferson: McFarland.

Bogdanovich, P. (1967) *John Ford*, revised 1978 edition, Berkeley: University of California Press.

Bogdanovich, P. (1975) *Picture Shows: Peter Bogdanovich on the Movies*, London: Allen & Unwin.

Bogdanovich, P. (1978) *John Ford*, Berkeley: University of California Press, revised and enlarged edition.

Brandt, B.M. (1989) 'Arizona clothing: A frontier perspective', *Dress*, 15(1), 65–78.

Brown, G.P. (1988) 'Observations on the use of symbolic interactionism in leisure, recreation and tourism', *Annals of Tourism Research*, 15(4), 550–554.

Buchholtz, D. (2005) 'Cultural politics or critical public history? Battling on the Little Big Horn', *Journal of Tourism and Cultural Change*, 3, 18–35.

Buhler Lynes, B. (2004) 'Georgia O'Keeffe and New Mexico: A sense of place', in B. Buhler Lynes, L. Poling-Kempes and F.W. Turner (eds), *Georgia O'Keeffe and New Mexico: A Sense of Place* (pp. 11–58), Princeton and Oxford: Princeton University Press and Santa Fe: Georgia O'Keeffe Museum.

Buchmann, A., Moore, K. and Fisher, D. (2010) 'Experiencing film tourism: Authenticity and fellowship', *Annals of Tourism Research*, 37(1), 229–248.

Burns, C. (2011) *Searching for Beauty: The Life of Millicent Rogers*, New York: St Martin's Press.

Burroughs, E.R. (1917) *A Princess of Mars*, 2007 edition, London: Penguin.

Butler, R. (2011) 'It's only make believe: The implications of fictional and authentic locations in films', *Worldwide Hospitality and Tourism Themes*, 3(2), 91–101.

Byrne, J. (1995) *A Genius for Living: A Biography of Frieda Lawrence*, London: Bloomsbury.

Calder, J. (1974) *There Must be a Lone Ranger: The Myth and Reality of the American Wild West*, London: Hamish Hamilton.

Campbell, J. (1949) *The Hero with a Thousand Faces*, 1993 reprint, London: Fontana Press.

Carl, D., Kindon, S. and Smith, K. (2007) 'Tourists' experiences on film locations: New Zealand as "Middle Earth"', *Tourism Geographies*, 9(1), 49–63.

Carter, R.A. (2000) *Buffalo Bill Cody: The Man behind the Legend*, New York: Wiley.

Catlin, G. (1841) *North American Indians*, 1989 reprint, New York: Viking.

Caton, K. and Santos, C.A. (2007) 'Heritage tourism on Route 66: Deconstructing nostalgia', *Journal of Travel Research*, 45(4), 371–386.

Clauss, J. (1999) 'Descent into Hell: Mythic paradigms in *The Searchers*', *Journal of Popular Film and Television*, 27(3), 2–17.

Clay, J. and Jones, R. (2008) 'Migrating to riches? The evidence of the California Gold Rush', *Journal of Economic History*, 68(4), 997–1027.

Cohan, S. and Hark, I.R. (1997) 'Introduction', in S. Cohan and I. Ray Hark (eds), *The Road Movie Book* (pp. 1–14), New York: Routledge.

Cohen, E. (2008) *Explorations in Thai Tourism: Collected Case Studies*, Bingley: Emerald.

Cohen, S. (2010) 'Chasing a myth? Searching for "self" through lifestyle travel', *Tourist Studies*, 10(2), 117–133.

Cole, S. (2000) '"Macho Man": Clones and the development of a masculine stereotype', *Fashion Theory*, 4(2), 125–140.

Collins, M. (1974) *Carrying the Fire: An Astronaut's Journeys*, New York: Farrar, Straus & Giroux.

Collins, R.G. (1977) '*Star Wars*: The pastiche of myth and the yearning for a past future', *The Journal of Popular Culture*, 11(1), 1–10.

Collison, F. (2014) 'The Grand Canyon Railway', in M.V. Conlin and G.R. Bird (eds), *Railway Heritage and Tourism: Global Perspectives* (pp. 166–189), Bristol: Channel View.

Connell, J. (2012) 'Film tourism: Evolution, progress and prospects', *Tourism Management*, 33(5), 1007–1029.

Corrigan, T. (1991) *A Cinema Without Walls: Movies and Culture after Vietnam*, New Brunswick: Rutgers University Press.

Costello, M.J. (2005) 'Rewriting *High Noon*: Transformations in American popular and political culture during the Cold War, 1952–1968', in P.C. Rollins and J.E. O'Connor (eds), *Hollywood's West: The American Frontier in Film, Television, and History* (pp. 175–197), Lexington: University of Kentucky Press.

Cowie, P. (2004) *John Ford and the American West*, New York: Abrams.

Coyne, M. (1997) *The Crowded Prairie: American National Identity in the Hollywood Western*, New York and London: Taurus.

Craig, B. (2007) 'Introduction to the Fourth Edition', in F. Tilden, *Interpreting Our Heritage*, 4th edition, 1st pub. 1957, Chapel Hill.

Craik, J. (1994) *The Face of Fashion: Cultural Studies in Fashion*, London and New York: Routledge.

Crane, D. (2000) *Fashion and its Social Agendas: Class, Gender and Identity in Clothing*, London and Chicago: University of Chicago Press.

Cresswell, T. (1993) 'Mobility as resistance: A geographical reading of Kerouac's "On the Road"', *Transactions of the Institute of British Geographers*, 18(2), 249–262.

Crichton, M. (1990) *Jurassic Park*, 1993 reprint, London: Arrow.

Crowther, B. (1986) *Charlton Heston: The Epic Presence*, London: Columbus.

Cumbow, R. (2008) *The Films of Sergio Leone*, Lanham: Scarecrow, revised and enlarged edition.

Cunningham, P.A. and Voso Lab, S. (1991a) 'Introduction', in P.A. Cunningham and S. Voso Lab (eds), *Dress and Popular Culture* (pp. 1–4), Bowling Green: Bowling Green State University Popular Press.

Cunningham, P.A. and Voso Lab, S. (1991b) 'Understanding dress and popular culture', in P.A. Cunningham and S. Voso Lab (eds), *Dress and Popular Culture* (pp. 5–18), Bowling Green: Bowling Green State University Popular Press.

Curtin, P.A. (2008) 'Fred Harvey Company public relations and publicity (1876–1933)', *Journal of Communication Management*, 12(4), 359–373.

Curtin, P. (2011) 'Discourses of American Indian racial identity in the public relations materials of the Fred Harvey Company: 1902–1936', *Journal of Public Relations Research*, 23(4), 368–396.

Curtis, J.M. (1980) 'From *American Graffiti* to *Star Wars*', *The Journal of Popular Culture*, 13(4), 590–601.

Custer, G.A. (1874) *My Life on the Plains*, 1963 reprint, London: Folio Society.

Cutright, P. (1985) *Theodore Roosevelt: The Making of a Conservationist*, Urbana: University of Illinois Press.

Dary, D. (1989) *Cowboy Culture: A Saga of Five Centuries*, Lawrence: University Press of Kansas.

Davis, J.S. and Morais, D.B. (2004) 'Factions and enclaves: Small towns and socially unsustainable tourism development', *Journal of Travel Research*, 43, 3–10.

Davis, R.L. (1998) *Duke: The Life and Image of John Wayne*, Norman: University of Oklahoma Press.

DeLyser, D. (1999) 'Authenticity on the ground: Engaging the past in a California Ghost Town', *Annals of the Association of American Geographers*, 89(4), 602–632.

DeLyser, D. (2003) '"Good, by God, We're Going to Bodie!" Ghost towns and the American West', in G.J. Hausladen (ed.), *Western Places, American Myths: How We Think about the West* (pp. 273–295), Reno and Las Vegas: University of Nevada Press.

Dibb, M. (1996) 'A time and a place: Budd Boetticher and the Western', in I. Cameron and D. Pye (eds), *The Book of Westerns* (pp. 161–166), New York: Continuum.

Dickey, S.J. (1991) '"We girls can do anything – right Barbie!" A survey of Barbie doll fashions', in P.A. Cunningham and S. Voso Lab (eds), *Dress and Popular Culture* (pp. 19–30), Bowling Green: Bowling Green State University Popular Press.

Dilsaver, L. (2003) 'National significance: Representation of the West in the national park system', in G.J. Hausladen (ed.), *Western Places, American Myths: How We Think about the West* (pp. 111–132), Reno and Las Vegas: University of Nevada Press.

Donovan, T. (1974) '"Oh, What a Beautiful Mornin'"': The musical, *Oklahoma!* and the popular mind in 1943', *The Journal of Popular Culture*, VIII(3), 477–488.

Donovan, T. (1978) '*Annie Get Your Gun*: A last celebration of nationalism', *The Journal of Popular Culture*, XII(3), 531–539.

Dustin, D.L., Schneider, I.E., McAvoy, L.H. and Frakt, A.N. (2002) 'Cross-cultural claims on Devils Tower National Monument: A case study', *Leisure Sciences*, 24(1), 79–88.

Eagan, D. (2010) *America's Film Legacy: The Authoritative Guide to the Landmark Movies in the National Film Registry*, New York and London: Continuum.

Eckstein, A.M. (2004) 'Introduction: Main critical issues in *The Searchers*', in A.M. Eckstein and P. Lehman (eds), *The Searchers: Essays and Reflections on John Ford's Classic Western* (pp. 1–45), Detroit: Wayne State University Press.

Eisler, B. (1991) *O'Keeffe and Stieglitz: An American Romance*, 1992 edition, New York and London: Penguin.

Eliot, M. (2006) *Jimmy Stewart: A Biography*, New York: Harmony.

Elliott, M. (2007) *Custerology: The Enduring Legacy of the Indian Wars and George Armstrong Custer*, Chicago and London: Chicago University Press.

Eppinga, J. (2010) *Tombstone*, Charleston: Arcadia.

Eyman, S. (1999) *Print the Legend: The Life and Times of John Ford*, Baltimore: Johns Hopkins Press.

Eyman, S. (2014) *John Wayne: The Life and Legend*, New York: Simon & Schuster.

Falassi, A. (1987) 'Festival: Definition and morphology' in A. Falassi (ed.), *Time Out of Time: Essays on the Festival* (pp. 1–10), Albuquerque: University of New Mexico Press.

Falconer, R. (2005) *Hell in Contemporary Literature: Western Descent Narratives since 1945*, Edinburgh: Edinburgh University Press.

Fiske, J. (1989) *Understanding Popular Culture*, Boston: Unwin Hyman.

Flannery, T. (2001) *The Eternal Frontier: An Ecological History of North America and its Peoples*, Melbourne: Text.

Flora, J.M. (1996) 'Shane (novel and film) at century's end', *Journal of American Culture*, 19(1), 51–55.

Forsdick, C. (2005) *Travel in Twentieth Century French and Francophone Cultures: The Persistence of Diversity*, Oxford: Oxford University Press.

Foster, J. (2007) *Jurassic West: The Dinosaurs of the Morrison Formation and their World*, Bloomington and Indianapolis: Indiana University Press.

Fox, R.A. (1993) *Archaeology, History, and Custer's Last Battle: The Little Big Horn Reexamined*, Norman and London: University of Oklahoma Press.

Fradkin, P.L. (2002) *Stagecoach: Wells Fargo and the American West*, New York: Free Press.

Frankeberger, R. and Garrison, J. (2002) 'From rustic romanticism to modernism, and beyond: Architectural resources in the national parks', *Forum Journal* (Summer), 8–21.

Frankel, G. (2013) *The Searchers: The Making of an American Legend*, New York: Bloomsbury.

Fraser, G.M. (1988) *The Hollywood History of the World*, London: Michael Joseph.

Frayling, C. (2005) *Once Upon a Time in Italy: The Westerns of Sergio Leone*, New York: Abrams.

Freedman, C. (2007) 'Post-hetero sexuality: John Wayne and the construction of American masculinity', *Film International*, 25, 16–26.

Friedrich, O. (1986) *City of Nets: A Portrait of Hollywood in the 1940s*, New York: Harper & Row.

Frost, W. (2006) '*Braveheart*-ed *Ned Kelly*: Historic films, heritage tourism and destination image', *Tourism Management*, 27(2), 247–254.

Frost, W. (2008) 'Projecting an image: Film-induced festivals in the American West', *Event Management*, 12(2), 95–104.

Frost, W. (2009) 'From backlot to runaway production: Exploring location and authenticity in film-induced tourism', *Tourism Review International*, 13(2), 85–92.

Frost, W. (2010) 'Life-changing experiences: Film and tourists in the Australian Outback', *Annals of Tourism Research*, 37(3), 707–726.

Frost, W. (forthcoming) 'Challenges in story-based interpretation for Gold Rush heritage and visitors', in L. Carpenter and L. Fraser (eds), *Rushing for Gold*, Dunedin: University of Otago Press.

Frost, W. and Hall, C.M. (2009) 'Reinterpreting the creation myth: Yellowstone National Park', in W. Frost and C.M. Hall (eds), *Tourism and National Parks: International Perspectives on Development, Histories and Change* (pp. 16–29), London and New York: Routledge.

Frost, W. and Laing, J. (2011) *Strategic Management of Festivals and Events*, 1st edition, South Melbourne: Cengage Learning.

Frost, W. and Laing, J. (2012) 'Travel as hell: Exploring the *katabatic* structure of travel fiction', *Literature and Aesthetics*, 22(1), 215–233.

Frost, W. and Laing, J. (2013) *Commemorative Events: Memory, Identities, Conflict*, London and New York: Routledge.

Frost, W. and Laing, J. (2014) 'The magic of steam trains and travel in children's stories', in M.V. Conlin and G.R. Bird (eds), *Railway Heritage and Tourism: Past, Present and Future* (pp. 42–54), Bristol: Channel View.

Frost, W. and Laing, J. (2015) 'Gender, subversion and ritual: Helldorado Days, Tombstone, Arizona', in J. Laing and W. Frost (eds), *Rituals and Traditional Events in a Modern World* (pp. 206–220), London and New York: Routledge.

Garber, M. (2013) *Bisexuality and the Eroticism of Everyday Life*, New York: Routledge.

Gardner, M.L. (2011) *To Hell on a Fast Horse: Billy the Kid and Pat Garrett and the Epic Chase to Justice in the Old West*, New York: Morrow.

George-Warren, H. and Freedman, M. (2001) *How the West Was Worn*, New York: Harry N. Abrams.

Georgia O'Keeffe Museum (2014) *Museum History*, www.okeeffemuseum.org/history.html (accessed 10 November 2014).

Geraghty, L. (2005) 'Creating and comparing myth in twentieth-century science fiction: *Star Trek* and *Star Wars*', *Literature/Film Quarterly*, 33(3), 191–200.

Glueck, G. (1987) 'Friend of O'Keeffe Glad Fight's Over', *New York Times*, 1 August, www.nytimes.com/1987/08/01/arts/friend-of-o-keeffe-glad-fight-s-over.html (accessed 10 October 2014).

Golden, J. (1999) 'Letters from Dorothy Brett, 1929 to 1935', *English Language Notes*, 37(2), 51–67.

Gorbman, C. (2007) 'Hearing *Thelma & Louise*: Active reading of the hybrid pop score', in B. Cook (ed.), *Thelma & Louise Live! The Cultural Aftermath of an American Film* (pp. 65–90), Austin: University of Texas Press.

Gordon, A. (1978) '*Star Wars*: A myth for our time', *Literature/Film Quarterly*, 6(4), 314–326.

Gordon, B. (1991) 'American denim: Blue jeans and their multiple layers of meaning', in P.A. Cunningham and S. Voso Lab (eds), *Dress and Popular Culture* (pp. 31–45), Bowling Green: Bowling Green State University Popular Press.

Gould, S.J. (1995) *Dinosaurs in a Haystack: Reflections in Natural History*, New York: Harmony.

Graham, D. (1979) 'High Noon', in W.T. Pilkington and D. Graham (eds) *Western Movies* (pp. 51–62), Albuquerque: University of New Mexico Press.

Graham, T. and Blanchard, T. (1998) *Dressing Diana*, Princeton: Benford Books.

Gray, J.L. (2001) 'Preface', in H. George-Warren and M. Freedman (eds) *How the West Was Worn* (p. 7), New York: Harry N. Abrams.

Gregg, R.W. (1999) 'The ten best films about international relations', *World Policy Journal*, 16(2), 129–134.

Hains, B. (2002) *The Ice and the Inland: Mawson, Flynn, and the Myth of the Frontier*, Melbourne: Melbourne University Press.

Hauser, K. (2004) 'A garment in the dock; or, how the FBI illuminated the prehistory of a pair of denim jeans', *Journal of Material Culture*, 9(3), 293–313.

Hausladen, G.J. (2003) 'Where the cowboy rides away: Mythic places for Western film', in G.J. Hausladen (ed.), *Western Places, American Myths: How We Think about the West* (pp. 296–318), Reno and Las Vegas: University of Nevada Press.

Haverluk, T.W. (2003) 'Mex-America: From margin to mainstream', in G.J. Hausladen (ed.), *Western Places, American Myths: How We Think about the West* (pp. 166–183), Reno and Las Vegas: University of Nevada Press.

Helldorado Inc (2012) *Official Publication: Helldorado 83rd Anniversary Celebration*, Tombstone: Helldorado Inc.

Henriksson, M. (2014) *Route 66: A Route to America's Landscape, History and Culture*, Lubbock: Texas Tech University Press.

Heston, C. (1979) *Charlton Heston. The Actor's Life: Journals 1956–1976*, 1980 edition, Harmondsworth and New York: Penguin.

Heston, C. (1995) *Charlton Heston: In the Arena*, London: HarperCollins.

Hitt, J. (1990) *The American West from Fiction (1823–1976) into Film (1909–1986)*, Jefferson: McFarland.

Hoberman, J. (2003) *The Dream Life: Movies, Media and the Mythology of the Sixties*, New York: The New Press.

Hobsbawm, E.J. (1969) *Bandits*, London: Weidenfeld & Nicolson.

Hocker Rushing, J. (1983) 'The rhetoric of the American western myth', *Communication Monographs*, 50(1), 14–32.

Hocker Rushing, J. and Frentz, T.S. (1978) 'The rhetoric of "rocky": A social value model of criticism', *Western Journal of Speech Communication*, 42(2), 63–72.

Holland, D. (1990) *On Location at Lone Pine: A Pictorial Guide to One of Hollywood's Favorite Movie Locations for 70 Years*, Granada Hills: Holland House

Holtan, O.I. (1970) 'The agrarian myth in *Midnight Cowboy, Alice's Restaurant, Easy Rider* and *Medium Cool*', *The Journal of Popular Culture*, IV (1), 273–285.

Holtsmark, E.B. (2001) 'The *katabasis* theme in modern cinema', in M.M. Winkler (ed.), *Classical Myth and Culture in the Cinema* (pp. 23–50), Oxford and New York: Oxford University Press.

Horrocks, R. (1995) *Male Myths and Icons: Masculinity in Popular Culture*, London: Macmillan.

Howard, C. (2012) 'Horizons of possibilities: the *Telos* of contemporary Himalayan travel', *Literature & Aesthetics*, 22(1), 131–155.

Howe, W. (2005) 'Almost angels, almost feminists: Women in *The Professionals*', in P.C. Rollins and J.E. O'Connor (eds), *Hollywood's West: The American Frontier in Film, Television, and History* (pp. 198–217), Lexington: University of Kentucky Press.

Hoy, J. (1995) *Cowboys and Kansas: Stories from the Tallgrass Prairie*, Norman and London: University of Oklahoma Press.

Hughes, H. (2008) *Stagecoach to Tombstone: The Filmgoers' Guide to the Great Westerns*, London and New York: I.B. Tauris.

Husbands, W. (1981) 'Centres, peripheries, tourism and socio-cultural development', *Ontario Geography*, 17, 37–60.

Hutton, P.A. (1992) 'Correct in every detail: General Custer in Hollywood', in P.A. Hutton (ed.), *The Custer Reader* (pp. 488–524), Lincoln: University of Nebraska Press.

Ireland, B. (2003) 'American highways: Recurring images and themes of the road genre', *The Journal of American Culture*, 26(4), 474–484.

Jewell, B. and McKinnon, S. (2008) 'Movie tourism: A new form of cultural landscape?', *Journal of Travel & Tourism Marketing*, 24(2), 153–182.

Jewett, R. and Lawrence, J.S. (1977) *The American Monomyth*, Garden City: Anchor Press.

Johnson, C.W. (2008) '"Don't call him a cowboy": Masculinity, cowboy drag, and a costume change', *Journal of Leisure Research*, 40(3), 385–403.

Kelm, M.-E. (2009) 'Manly contests: Rodeo masculinities at the Calgary Stampede', *Canadian Historical Review*, 90(4), 711–751.

Kemper, R.V. (1979) 'Tourism in Taos and Patzcuaro: A comparison of two approaches to regional development', *Annals of Tourism Research*, 6(1), 91–110.

Kerouac, J. (1957) *On the Road*, 2008 edition, London: Penguin.

Kim, S. (2012) 'Audience involvement and film tourism experiences: Emotional places, emotional experiences', *Tourism Management*, 33(2), 387–396.

Kim, H. and Richardson, S. (2003) 'Motion picture impacts on destination images', *Annals of Tourism Research*, 30(1), 216–237.

Kimmel, J.R. (1995) 'Art and tourism in Santa Fe, New Mexico', *Journal of Travel Research*, 33, 28–30.

Kinsey, J. (2006) *Thomas Moran's West: Chromolithography, High Art, and Popular Taste*, Lawrence: University of Kansas Press.

Kipling, R. (1899) *From Sea to Sea and other Sketches: Letters of Travel Vol. 2*, 1922 edition, London: Macmillan.

Kitses, J. (2004) *Horizons West: Directing the Western from John Ford to Clint Eastwood*, London: British Film Institute.

Klein, K.L. (1993) 'Frontier products: Tourism, consumerism, and the Southwestern public lands, 1890–1990', *Pacific Historical Review*, 62(1), 39–71.

Klein, K.L. (1997) *Frontiers of Historical Imagination: Narrating the European Conquest of Native America, 1890–1990*, 1999 edition, Berkeley and Los Angeles: University of California Press.

Klinger, B. (1997) 'The road to dystopia: Landscaping the nation in *Easy Rider*', in S. Cohan and I.R. Hark (eds), *The Road Movie Book* (pp. 179–203), London and New York: Routledge.

Knight, S. (2003) *Robin Hood: A Mythic Biography*, Ithaca: Cornell University Press.

Kohlberg, L. and Gilligan, C. (1971) 'The adolescent as a philosopher: The discovery of the self in a postconventional world', *Daedalus*, 100(4), 1051–1086.

Kooistra, P. (1989) *Criminals as Heroes: Structure, Power & Identity*, Bowling Green: Bowling Green State University Press.

Kozinets, R.V. (2001) 'Utopian enterprise: Articulating the meanings of Star Trek's culture of consumption', *Journal of Consumer Re*search, 28, 67–88.

Krim, A. (1998) '"Get your Kicks on Route 66": A song map of postwar migration', *Journal of Cultural Geography*, 18(1), 49–60.

Laderman, D. (2002) *Driving Visions: Exploring the Road Movie*, Austin: University of Texas Press.

La Chapelle, P. (2001) 'All that glitters: Country music, taste and the politics of the Rhinestone "Nudie" suit', *Dress*, 28(1), 3–12.

Laing, J. and Frost, W. (2012) *Books and Travel: Inspiration, Quests and Transforma-tion*, Bristol: Channel View.

Laing, J. and Frost, W. (2014) *Explorer Travellers and Adventure Tourism*, Bristol: Channel View.

Laing, J., Frost, W. and Williams, K. (2014) 'Très chic: Setting a research agenda for fashion and design events', in K. Williams, J. Laing and W. Frost (eds), *Fashion, Design and Events* (pp. 191–205), Abingdon: Routledge.

Langford, N. (1871) 'The wonders of Yellowstone', *Scribner's Monthly*, 2(1), 1–17 and 2(2), 113–128.

Langford, N. (1905) *The Discovery of Yellowstone Park: Journal of the Washburn Expe-dition 1870*, 1972 reprint, Lincoln: University of Nebraska Press.

Lawrence, D.H. (1913) *Sons and Lovers*, 1990 edition, Harmondsworth: Penguin.

Lawrence, D.H. (1920) *Women in Love*, 1988 edition, New York: Chelsea House.

Lawrence, D.H. (1923) *Kangaroo*, 1989 edition, Sydney: Collins Australia.

Lawrence, D.H. (1924) 'Just back from the snake dance – tired out', *Laughing Horse*, (September), 26–29.

Lawrence, D.H. (1928) *Lady Chatterley's Lover*, 2006 edition, London: Penguin.

Lawrence, F. (1934) *'Not I, But the Wind…'*, New York: The Viking Press.

Lawrence, J.S. (2005) 'The Lone Ranger: Adult legacies of a juvenile Western', in P.C. Rollins and J.E. O'Connor (eds.), *Hollywood's West: The American Frontier in Film, Television, and History* (pp. 81–96), Lexington: University of Kentucky Press.

LeBlanc, A. (1991) 'All part of the act: A hundred years of costume in Anglo-American popular music', in P.A. Cunningham and S. Voso Lab (eds), *Dress and Popular Culture* (pp. 61–73), Bowling Green: Bowling Green State University Popular Press.

Leclercq, J. (1886) *Yellowstone Land of Wonders: Promenade in North America's National Park*, 2013 reprint, Lincoln: University of Nebraska Press.

LeCompte, M.-L. (1993) *Cowgirls of the Rodeo: Pioneer Professional Athletes*, Urbana and Chicago: University of Illinois Press.

Leigh Brown, P. (1997) 'The muse of Taos, stirring still', *New York Times*, 16 January, www.nytimes.com/1997/01/16/garden/the-muse-of-taos-stirring-still.html (accessed 5 November 2014).

Leith, D. (2002) 'Growing up with Westerns: Masculinity and *The Man from Laramie*', *Changing English*, 9(2), 133–145.

Limerick, P.N., Milner, C. and Rankin, C.E. (eds) (1991) *Trails: Toward a New Western History*, Lawrence: University of Kansas Press.

Linenthal, E.T. (1991) *Sacred Ground: Americans and their Battlefields*, Urbana and Chicago: University of Illinois Press.

Long, J. and Schouten, P. (2008) *Feathered Dinosaurs: The Origins of Birds*, Melbourne: CSIRO.

Lowenthal, D. (1998) *The Heritage Crusade and the Spoils of History*, Cambridge: Cam-bridge University Press.

Loy, R.P. (2004) *Westerns in a Changing America 1955–2000*, Jefferson: McFarland.

Luhr, W. (2004) 'John Wayne and *The Searchers*', in A.M. Eckstein and P. Lehman (eds), *The Searchers: Essays and Reflections on John Ford's Classic Western* (pp. 75–92), Detroit: Wayne State University Press.

Mabel Dodge Luhan House (2014) *The Mabel Dodge Luhan House Historic Inn and Workshops*, www.mabeldodgeluhan.com/ (accessed 30 November 2014).

McBride, J. (2001) *Searching for John Ford: A Life*, New York: St Martin's Press.

MacCannell, D. (1999) *The Tourist: A New Theory of the Leisure Class*, Berkeley and Los Angeles: University of California Press.

McCracken, G. (1990) *Culture and Consumption: New Approaches to the Symbolic Character of Consumer Goods and Activities*, Bloomington and Indianapolis; Indiana University Press.

McDonough, K.A. (2005) '*Wee Willie Winkie* goes West: The influence of the British Empire genre on Ford's Cavalry genre', in P.C. Rollins and J.E. O'Connor (eds), *Hollywood's West: The American Frontier in Film, Television, and History* (pp. 99–114), Lexington: University of Kentucky Press.

McGee, M.G. (1983) 'Prime time Dixie: Television's view of a "simple" South', *Journal of American Culture*, 6(3), 100–109.

McGhee, R.D. (1988) 'John Wayne: Hero with a thousand faces', *Literature/Film Quarterly*, 16(1), 10–21.

McGivern, C. (2000) *John Wayne: A Giant Shadow*, Bracknell: Sammon Publishing.

McGrath, A. (2001) 'Playing colonial: Cowgirls, cowboys and Indians in Australia and North America', *Journal of Colonialism and Colonial History*, 2, 1–27.

McGrath, A. (2007) 'Being Annie Oakley: Modern girls, New World woman', *Frontiers: A Journal of Women Studies*, 28(1/2), 203–231.

Macionis, N. and Sparks, B. (2009) 'Film-induced tourism: An incidental experience', *Tourism Review International*, 13(2), 93–101.

McVeigh, S. (2007) *The American Western*, Edinburgh: Edinburgh University Press.

Månsson, M. (2011) 'Mediatized tourism', *Annals of Tourism Research*, 38(4), 1634–1652.

Matthiessen, P. (1989) *North American Indians*, ed. G. Catlin, New York: Penguin.

Mercille, J. (2005) 'Media effect on image: The case of Tibet', *Annals of Tourism Research*, 32(4), 1039–1059.

Mesce, B. Jr. (2001) *Peckinpah's Women: Reappraisal of the Portrayal of Women in the Period Westerns of Sam Peckinpah*, Lanham and London; The Scarecrow Press.

Miller, G. (1983) 'Shane Redux', *Journal of Popular Film and Television*, 11(2), 66–77.

Morganstern, D. and Greenberg, J. (1988) 'The influence of a multi-theme park on cultural beliefs as a function of schema salience: Promoting and undermining the myth of the Old West', *Journal of Applied Social Psychology*, 18, 584–596.

Munro, E. (2014) 'Street seen', *The Sunday Age*, 11 May, 8.

Murdoch, D.H. (2001) *The American West: The Invention of a Myth*, Reno and Las Vegas: University of Nevada Press.

Nash, R. (1967) *Wilderness and the American Mind*, 3rd edition, 1982, New Haven and London: Yale University Press.

Nash Smith, H. (1950) *Virgin Land: The American West as Symbol and Myth*, New York: Vintage Books.

National Parks Service (NPS) (2013) 'Voluntary climbing ban in June', *Devils Tower*, 24 May, www.nps.gov/deto/parknews/voluntary-climbing-ban-at-devils-tower-in-june.htm (accessed 16 November 2014).

National Parks Service (NPS) (2014) *Grand Canyon: Park Profile 2014*, www.nps.gov/grca/parkmgmt/upload/2014-grca-park-profile.pdf (accessed 16 November 2014).

Neale, S. (1995) 'The story of Custer in everything but name? Colonel Thursday and *Fort Apache*', *Journal of Film and Video*, 47(1–3), 26–32.

Nicholson, V. (2002) *Among the Bohemians: Experiments in Living 1900–1939*, 2003 edition, London and New York: Penguin.

Nott, R. (2004) *The Films of Randolph Scott*, Jefferson: McFarland.

Ogburn, M. (2009) 'Twenty Years of Film Festivals', in E. Hulse (ed.), *Lone Pine in the Movies: Daredevils of the West* (pp. 14–19), Burbank: Riverwood.

Olsen, R.A. (2011) *Route 66 Lost & Found: Mother Road Ruins and Relics – the Ultimate Collection*, Minneapolis: Voyageur Press.

Palken Rudnick, L. (1984) *Mabel Dodge Luhan: New Woman, New Worlds*, Albuquerque: University of New Mexico Press.

Palken Rudnick, L. (1998) *Utopian Vistas: The Mabel Dodge Luhan House and the American Counterculture*, Albuquerque: University of New Mexico Press.

Paradis, T.W. (2002) 'The political economy of theme development in small urban places: The case of Roswell, New Mexico', *Tourism Geographies*, 4(1), 22–43.

Pearson, R. (1995) 'Custer's still the hero: Textual stability and transformation', *Journal of Film and Video*, 47(1–3), 82–97.

Peary, D. (1982) *Cult Movies*, London: Vermilion.

Peary, D. (1983) *Cult Movies 2*, New York: Delta.

Peary, D. (1989) *Cult Movies 3*, London: Sidgwick & Jackson.

Peñaloza, L. (2000) 'The commodification of the American West: Marketers' production of cultural meanings at the trade show', *Journal of Marketing*, 64, 82–109.

Peterson, J. (1996) 'The competing tunes of "Johnny Guitar": Liberalism, sexuality, masquerade', *Cinema Journal*, 35(3), 3–18.

Pfitzer, G. (1995) 'The only good alien is a dead alien: Science fiction and the metaphysics of Indian-hating on the high frontier', *Journal of American Culture*, 18(1), 51–67.

Philbrick, N. (2010) *The Last Stand: Custer, Sitting Bull and the Battle of the Little Bighorn*, New York: Viking.

Pilkington, W.T. and Graham, D. (1979) 'Introduction: A fistful of westerns', in W.T. Pilkington and D. Graham (eds), *Western Movies* (pp. 1–13), Albuquerque: University of New Mexico Press.

Pippin, R.B. (2010) *Hollywood Westerns and American Myth: The Importance of Howard Hawks and John Ford for Political Philosophy*, New Haven: Yale University Press.

Pitchford, S. (2008) *Identity Tourism: Imaging and Imagining the Nation*, Bingley: Emerald.

Poling-Kempes, L. (1989) *The Harvey Girls: Women who Opened up the West*, Cambridge, MA: Da Capo Press.

Pomeroy, E. (1957) *In Search of the Golden West: The Tourist in Western America*, New York: Knopf.

Prassel, F.R. (1993) *The Great American Outlaw: A Legacy of Fact and Fiction*, Norman and London: University of Oklahoma Press.

Reijnders, S. (2009) 'Watching the detectives: Inside the guilty landscapes of Inspector Morse, Baantjer and Wallander', *European Journal of Communication*, 24(2), 165–181.

Reijnders, S. (2011) 'Stalking the Count: Dracula, fandom and tourism', *Annals of Tourism Research*, 38(1), 231–248.

Reisner, M. (1986) *Cadillac Desert: The American West and its Disappearing Water*, New York: Penguin.

Riley, G. (1999) *Women and Nature: Saving the 'Wild' West*, Lincoln and London: University of Nebraska Press.

Riley, R.W., Baker, D. and Van Doren, C. (1998) 'Movie induced tourism', *Annals of Tourism Research*, 25, 919–935.

Robertson, P. (1995) 'Camping under Western stars: Joan Crawford in Johnny Guitar', *Journal of Film and Video*, 47(1/3), 33–49.

Rodríguez, S. (1989) 'Art, tourism, and race relations in Taos: Toward a sociology of the art colony', *Journal of Anthropological Research*, 45(1), 77–99.

Rodríguez, S. (1990) 'Ethnic reconstruction in contemporary Taos', *Journal of the Southwest*, 32(4), 541–555.

Rodríguez, S. (1997) 'The Taos Fiesta: Invented tradition and the infrapolitics of symbolic reclamation', *Journal of the Southwest*, 39(1), 33–57.

Roesch, S. (2009) *The Experiences of Film Location Tourists*, Bristol: Channel View.

Rosenstone, R.A. (1995) *Visions of the Past: The Challenge of Film to Our Idea of History*, Cambridge, MA: Harvard University Press.

Roth, L. (1985) 'Vraisemblance and the Western setting in contemporary science fiction film', *Literature/Film Quarterly*, 13(3), 180–186.

Rothel, D. (1991) *An Ambush of Ghosts: A Guide to Great Western Film Locations*, Los Angeles: Empire.

Rothman, H.K. (1989) *Preserving Different Pasts: The American National Monuments*, Urbana: University of Chicago Press.

Rothman, H.K. (1996) 'Selling the meaning of place: Entrepreneurship, tourism, and community transformation in the twentieth-century American West', *Pacific Historical Review*, 65(4), 525–557.

Rothman, H.K. (1998) *Devil's Bargains: Tourism in the Twentieth Century American West*, Lawrence: University of Kansas Press.

Runte, A. (1979) *National Parks: The American Experience*, Lincoln and London: University of Nebraska Press.

Rydell, R. (1984) *All the World's a Fair: Visions of Empire at International Expositions, 1876–1916*, Chicago: University of Chicago Press.

Sanders, J. (1996) 'A comparative study of the planning and management of Monument Valley Tribal Park and Canyon de Chelly National Monument', *Landscape and Urban Planning*, 36, 171–182.

Schaffer, M.S. (2001) *See America First: Tourism and National Identity, 1880–1940*, Washington, DC: Smithsonian Institution Press.

Schaffer, M.S. (2004) ' "The West plays West": Western tourism and the landscape of leisure', in W. Deverell (ed.), *Companion to the American West* (pp. 375–389), Malden, MA and Oxford: Blackwell.

Schefter, J. (1999) *The Race: The Complete Story of How America Beat Russia to the Moon*, 2000 edition, New York: Anchor Books.

Schwer, R.K., Gazel, R. and Daneshvary, R. (2000) 'Air tour impacts: The Grand Canyon case', *Annals of Tourism Research*, 27(3), 611–623.

Schwer, R.K. and Daneshvary, R. (2011) 'Symbolic product attributes and emulatory consumption: The case of rodeo fan attendance and the wearing of Western clothing', *Journal of Applied Business Research*, 11(3), 74–81.

Scott, W. (1819) *Ivanhoe*, 1965 reprint, London: Dent.

Seal, G. (1996) *The Outlaw Legend: A Cultural tradition in Britain, America and Australia*, Cambridge: Cambridge University Press.

Seelye, J.D. (1963) 'The American tramp: A version of the picaresque', *American Quarterly*, 15(4), 535–553.

Seymour, M. (1992) *Ottoline Morrell: Life on the Grand Scale*, Sevenoaks: Sceptre.

Sharpe, J.A. (2005) *Remember, Remember: A Cultural History of Guy Fawkes Day*, Cambridge, MA: Harvard University Press.

Shefrin, E. (2004) '*Lord of the Rings, Star Wars*, and participatory fandom: Mapping new congruencies between the Internet and media entertainment culture', *Critical Studies*, 21(3), 261–281.

Sherez, S. (2014) 'Cowboys and indolence', *The Weekend Australian*, 19–20 April, 10.

Shumway, D.R. (1999) 'Rock and roll soundtracks and the production of nostalgia', *Cinema Journal*, 38(2), 36–51.

Sickels, R.C. (2006) 'Landscapes of failure in John Ford's *The Grapes of Wrath* (1939)', in D. A. Carmichael (ed.), *The Landscape of Hollywood Westerns: Ecocriticism in an American Film Genre* (pp. 61–80), Salt Lake City: University of Utah Press.

Sides, H. (2006) *Blood and Thunder: The Epic Story of Kit Carson and the Conquest of the American West*, New York: Doubleday.

Simpson, J.W. (1999) *Visions of Paradise: Glimpses of Our Landscape's Legacy*, Berkeley and Los Angeles: University of California Press.

Slocum, J.D. (2007) 'An outlaw-couple-on-the-run film for the 1990s', in B. Cook (ed.), *Thelma & Louise Live! The Cultural Aftermath of an American Film* (pp. 122–145), Austin: University of Texas Press.

Slotkin, R. (1973) *Regeneration Through Violence: The Mythology of the American Frontier 1600–1860*, Middletown: Wesleyan University Press.

Slotkin, R. (1992) *Gunfighter Nation: The Myth of the Frontier in Twentieth Century America*, New York: Athenaeum.

Smith, P. (2009) 'Seven men from now', in E. Hulse (ed.), *Lone Pine in the Movies: Daredevils of the West* (pp. 89–94), Burbank: Riverwood.

Spaceport America (2013) *Preview Bus Tours*, http://spaceportamerica.com/plan-a-visit/preview-tours/ (accessed 25 May 2013).

Spaceport America (2014a) *Spaceport America is Just Getting Started*, 23 November, http://spaceportamerica.com/press-release/november-19th-albuquerque-journal-editorial-spaceport-america-is-just-getting-started/ (accessed 28 November 2014).

Spaceport America (2014b) *New Mexico Spaceport Sets Sights on New Customers*, 22 November, http://spaceportamerica.com/web-articles/new-mexico-spaceport-sets-sights-on-new-customers/ (accessed 28 November 2014).

Spangler, J. (2008) 'We're on a road to nowhere: Steinbeck, Kerouac and the legacy of the Great Depression', *Studies in the Novel*, 40(3), 308–327.

Spoto, D. (2010) *Possessed: The Life of Joan Crawford*, New York: HarperCollins.

Squires, M. and Talbot, L.K. (2002) *Living at the Edge: A Biography of D. H. Lawrence and Frieda von Richthofen*, Madison: University of Wisconsin Press.

Stall-Meadows, C. (2011) *Fashion Now: A Global Perspective*, Upper Saddle River: Prentice Hall.

Stebbins, R.A. (1992) *Amateurs, Professionals, and Serious Leisure*, Montreal and Kingston: McGill-Queen's University Press.

Steinbeck, J. (1939) *The Grapes of Wrath*, 2014 edition, London: Penguin.

Stevens, B. (1996) '*Pat Garrett & Billy the Kid*', in I. Cameron and D. Pye (eds), *The Book of Westerns* (pp. 269–276), New York: Continuum.

Stiles, T.J. (2002) *Jesse James: Last Rebel of the Civil War*, New York: Knopf.

Sturma, M. (2002) 'Aliens and Indians: A comparison of abduction and captivity narratives', *The Journal of Popular Culture*, 36(2), 318–334.

Sturtevant, V. (2007) 'Getting hysterical: *Thelma & Louise* and laughter', in B. Cook (ed.), *Thelma & Louise Live! The Cultural Aftermath of an American Film* (pp. 43–64), Austin: University of Texas Press.

Sullivan, J. (2006) *Jeans: A Cultural History of an American Icon*, 2007 edition, New York: Gotham.

Taos Community Foundation (2014) 'Great news: The D.H. Lawrence Ranch is now open to the public!', *Taos Community Foundation*, www.taoscf.org/dh-lawrence-ranch (accessed 5 November 2014).

Taos.org (2014) *Remarkable Women*, http://taos.org/women (accessed 20 November 2014).

Tarter, J. (2004) 'Life, the universe and SETI in a nutshell', in R.P. Norris and F.H. Stootman (eds), *Bioastronomy 2002: Life Among the Stars*, IAU Symposium, Vol. 213 (pp. 397–407), San Francisco: Astronomical Society of the Pacific.

Tefertiller, C. (1997) *Wyatt Earp: The Life behind the Legend*, New York: Wiley.

Terrie, P.G. (1990) 'Wilderness: Ambiguous symbol of the American past', in R.B. Browne, M.W. Fishwick and K.O. Browne (eds), *Dominant Symbols in Popular Culture*, Bowling Green: Bowling Green State University Popular Press.

Tiffin, J. (1999) 'Digitally remythicised: *Star Wars*, modern popular mythology, and *Madam and Eve*', *Journal of Literary Studies*, 15(1–2), 66–80.

Tilden, F. (1957) *Interpreting our Heritage*, 2007 reprint, Chapel Hill: University of North Carolina Press.

Tompkins, J. (1992) *West of Everything: The Inner Life of Westerns*, New York and Oxford: Oxford University Press.

Turner, F.J. (1962 [1893]) 'The significance of the frontier in American history', in *The Frontier in American History* (pp. 1–38), New York: Holt, Rinehart, and Winston.

Turner, F. W. (2004) 'On her conquest of space', in B. Buhler Lynes, L. Poling-Kempes and F.W. Turner (eds), *Georgia O'Keeffe and New Mexico: A Sense of Place* (pp. 109–122), Princeton and Oxford: Princeton University Press and Santa Fe: Georgia O'Keeffe Museum.

Tzanelli, R. (2004) 'Constructing the "cinematic tourist": The "Sign Industry" of *The Lord of the Rings*', *Tourist Studies*, 4(1), 21–42.

Urry, J. (2002) *The Tourist Gaze*, 2nd edition, London: Sage.

Utley, R. (1991) 'Foreword', in E.T. Linenthal (ed.), *Sacred Ground: Americans and their Battlefields* (pp. ix–xi), Urbana and Chicago: University of Chicago Press.

Van Allsburg, C. (1985) *The Polar Express*, Boston: Houghton Mifflin.

Verne, J. (1873) *Around the World in Eighty Days*, 1994 reprint, Ware: Wordsworth.

Walle, A.H. (2000) *The Cowboy Hero and its Audience: Popular Culture as Market Derived Art*, Bowling Green: Bowling Green State University Popular Press.

Wallmann, J. (1999) *The Western: Parables of the American Dream*, Lubbock: Texas Tech University Press.

Watts, S. (2003) *Rough Rider in the White House: Theodore Roosevelt and the Politics of Desire*, Chicago: University of Chicago Press.

Weddle, D. (1996) *Sam Peckinpah: 'If they move … kill 'em!'*, London: Faber.

Weigle, M. (1989) 'From desert to Disney World: The Santa Fe Railway and the Fred Harvey Company display the Indian Southwest', *Journal of Anthropological Research*, 45(1), 115–137.

Weigle, M. (1992) 'Exposition and mediation: Mary Colter, Erna Fergusson, and the Santa Fe/Harvey popularization of the Native Southwest, 1902–1940', *Frontiers: A Journal of Women Studies*, 12(3), 116–150.

Weigle, M. (1997) 'Canyon, caverns and coordinates: From nature tourism to nuclear tourism in the Southwest', *Journal of the Southwest*, 39(2), 165–182.

West, L. and Chure, D. (2001) *Dinosaur: The Dinosaur National Monument Quarry*, Vernal: Dinosaur Nature Association.

Wheeler, F., Laing, J., Frost, L., Reeves, K. and Frost, W. (2011) 'Outlaw nations: Tourism, the frontier and national identities', in E. Frew and L. White (eds), *Tourism and National Identities: An International Perspective* (pp. 151–163), London and New York: Routledge.

White, R. (1991) *'It's Your Misfortune and None of My Own': A New History of the American West*, Norman: University of Oklahoma Press.

Wills, G. (1997) *John Wayne's America: The Politics of Celebrity*, New York: Simon & Schuster.

Wilson, L. (1991) '"I was a pretty proud kid": An interpretation of differences in posed and unposed photographs of Montana cowboys', *Clothing and Textiles Research Journal*, 9(3), 49–58.

Wilson, L. (1996) 'The cowboy: Real and imagined', *Dress*, 23(1), 3–15.

Wilson, L. (2001) 'American cowboy dress: Function to fashion', *Dress*, 28(1), 40–52.

Wister, O. (1902) *The Virginian*, P. Durham (ed.), 1968 edition, Boston: Houghton Mifflin.

Wolfe, T. (1979) *The Right Stuff*, New York: Farrar, Straus & Giroux.

Wright, W. (1974) *Six Guns and Society: A Structural Study of the Western*, Berkeley: University of California Press.

Wrobel, D.M. and Long, P.T. (eds) (2001) *Seeing and Being Seen: Tourism in the American West*, Lawrence: University of Kansas Press.

Youngs, Y. (2011) 'On Grand Canyon postcards', *Environmental History*, 16, 138–147.

Zeppel, H. (2009) 'National Parks as cultural landscapes: Indigenous peoples, conservation and tourism', in W. Frost and C.M. Hall (eds), *Tourism and National Parks: International Perspectives on Development, Histories and Change* (pp. 259–281), London and New York: Routledge.

Filmography

The following are the films we watched for this book. Most of the more recent were viewed as cinema releases. The others were mainly seen on television or DVD, with a small number accessed via YouTube.

The list provides the title, director and year.

The Big Trail	(Raoul Walsh, 1930)
It Happened One Night	(Frank Capra, 1934)
Dodge City	(Michael Curtiz, 1939)
Frontier Marshall	(Alan Dwan, 1939)
Stagecoach	(John Ford, 1939)
Go West	(Edward Buzzell, 1940)
Northwest Passage	(King Vidor, 1940)
Santa Fe Trail	(Michael Curtiz, 1940)
Sullivan's Travels	(Preston Sturges, 1941)
They Died With Their Boots On	(Raoul Walsh, 1941)
The Outlaw	(Howard Hughes, 1943)
Detour	(Edgar G. Ulmer, 1945)
Abilene Town	(Edwin Marin, 1946)
The Harvey Girls	(George Sidney, 1946)
My Darling Clementine	(John Ford, 1946)
The Angel and the Badman	(James Edward Grant, 1947)
Fort Apache	(John Ford, 1948)
Red River	(Howard Hawks, 1948)
3 Godfathers	(John Ford, 1948)
She Wore a Yellow Ribbon	(John Ford, 1949)
Annie Get Your Gun	(George Sidney, 1950)
Colt .45	(Edwin Marin, 1950)
The Gunfighter	(Henry King, 1950)
Montana	(Ray Enright, 1950)
Rio Grande	(John Ford, 1950)
Winchester '73	(Anthony Mann, 1950)
The Slaughter Trail	(Irwin Allen, 1951)
Bend of the River	(Anthony Mann, 1952)

High Noon	(Fred Zinnemann, 1952)
Montana Belle	(Alan Dwan, 1952)
Springfield Rifle	(Andre De Toth, 1952)
Calamity Jane	(David Butler, 1953)
Hondo	(John Farrow, 1953)
Shane	(George Stevens, 1953)
War Paint	(Leslie Selander, 1953)
Johnny Guitar	(Nicholas Ray, 1954)
Vera Cruz	(Robert Aldrich, 1954)
The Man From Laramie	(Anthony Mann, 1955)
The Searchers	(John Ford, 1956)
Forty Guns	(Samuel Fuller, 1957)
Gunfight at the OK Corral	(John Sturges, 1957)
Revolt at Fort Laramie	(Leslie Selander, 1957)
The Tall T	(Bud Boetticher, 1957)
3:10 to Yuma	(Delmer Daves, 1957)
The Big Country	(William Wyler, 1958)
The Bravados	(Henry King, 1958)
Buchanan Rides Alone	(Bud Boetticher, 1958)
The Left-Handed Gun	(Arthur Penn, 1958)
Man of the West	(Anthony Mann, 1958)
Touch of Evil	(Orson Welles, 1958)
The Horse Soldiers	(John Ford, 1959)
Ride Lonesome	(Bud Boetticher, 1959)
Rio Bravo	(Howard Hawks, 1959)
Warlock	(Edward Dmytryk, 1959)
Yellowstone Kelly	(Gordon Douglas, 1959)
The Alamo	(John Wayne, 1960)
Comanche Station	(Bud Boetticher, 1960)
The Magnificent Seven	(John Sturges, 1960)
The Commancheros	(Michael Curtiz, 1961)
Two Rode Together	(John Ford, 1961)
Geronimo	(Arnold Laven, 1962)
How the West was Won	(John Ford, Henry Hathaway, George Marshall, 1962)
The Man Who Shot Liberty Valance	(John Ford, 1962)
Ride the High Country	(Sam Peckinpah, 1962)
A Fistful of Dollars	(Sergio Leone, 1964)
Cat Ballou	(Elliot Silverstein, 1965)
For a Few Dollars More	(Sergio Leone, 1965)
Major Dundee	(Sam Peckinpah, 1965)*
The Sons of Katie Elder	(Henry Hathaway, 1965)
The Professionals	(Richard Brooks, 1966)
Ride in the Whirlwind	(Monte Hellman, 1966)
The Good, the Bad and the Ugly	(Sergio Leone, 1967)*

Bandolero!	(Andrew McLaglen, 1968)
Custer of the West	(Robert Siodmak, 1968)
Will Penny	(Tom Gries, 1968)
Butch Cassidy and the Sundance Kid	(George Roy Hill, 1969)
Easy Rider	(Dennis Hopper, 1969)
Mackenna's Gold	(Lee Thompson, 1969)
Midnight Cowboy	(John Schlesinger, 1969)
Moon Two Zero	(Roy Ward Baker, 1969)
Once Upon a Time in the West	(Sergio Leone, 1969)
100 Rifles	(Tom Gries, 1969)
True Grit	(Henry Hathaway, 1969)
Valley of the Gwangi	(James Connolly, 1969)
Chisum	(Andrew McLaglen, 1970)
Little Big Man	(Arthur Penn, 1970)
Duel	(Steven Spielberg, 1971)
Two Lane Blacktop	(Monte Hellman, 1971)
Cahill US Marshal	(Andrew McLaglen, 1973)
Pat Garrett and Billy the Kid	(Sam Peckinpah, 1973)*
The Train Robbers	(Burt Kennedy, 1973)
Westworld	(Michael Crichton, 1973)
From Noon Till Three	(Frank D. Gilroy, 1976)
Missouri Breaks	(Arthur Penn, 1976)
Star Wars	(George Lucas, 1977)
Apocalypse Now	(Francis Ford Coppola, 1979)*
Urban Cowboy	(James Bridges, 1980)
Priest of Love	(Christopher Miles, 1981)
National Lampoon's Vacation	(Harold Ramis, 1983)
Footloose	(Herbert Ross, 1984)
Silverado	(Lawrence Kasden, 1985)
Young Guns	(Christopher Cain, 1988)
Dances with Wolves	(Kevin Costner, 1990)
Back to the Future Part III	(Robert Zemeckis, 1990)
Young Guns II	(Geoff Murphy, 1990)
Son of the Morning Star	(Mike Robe, 1991)
Thelma & Louise	(Ridley Scott, 1991)
Unforgiven	(Clint Eastwood, 1992)
Tombstone	(George Cosmatos, 1993)
Maverick	(Richard Donner, 1994)
Dead Man	(Jim Jarmusch, 1995)
Contact	(Robert Zemeckis, 1997)
Wild Wild West	(Barry Sonnenfield, 1999)
Open Range	(Kevin Costner, 2003)
Renegade	(Jan Kounen, 2004)
Brokeback Mountain	(Ang Lee, 2005)
Cars	(John Lasseter and Joe Ranft, 2006)

No Country for Old Men	(Ethan and Joel Coen, 2007)
3:10 to Yuma	(James Mangold, 2007)
Georgia O'Keeffe	(Bob Balaban, 2009)
My One and Only	(Richard Loncraine, 2009)
Meek's Cutoff	(Kelly Reichardt, 2010)
True Grit	(Ethan and Joel Coen, 2010)
Cowboys and Aliens	(Jon Favreau, 2011)
Paul	(Greg Mottola, 2011)
Django Unchained	(Quentin Tarantino, 2012)
The Guilt Trip	(Anne Fletcher, 2012)
The Lone Ranger	(Gore Verbinski, 2013)
The Homesman	(Tommy Lee Jones, 2014)

* Restored versions

Index

For Product Safety Concerns and Information please contact our
EU representative GPSR@taylorandfrancis.com Taylor & Francis
Verlag GmbH, Kaufingerstraße 24, 80331 München, Germany